Rare Birds
of the British Isles

Rare Birds of the British Isles

A personal survey of over 300 unusual visitors

David Saunders

Patrick Stephens Limited

For Shirley, who shared the ultimate, a new bird for the Western Palearctic, a blackburnian warbler, Skomer Island, 5 October 1961.

© 1991 David Saunders

First published in 1991

British Library Cataloguing in Publication Data

Saunders, David *1937–*
Rare birds of the British Isles.
1. Great Britain. Rare birds
I. Title
598. 0420941

ISBN 1-85260-287-2

Patrick Stephens Limited, a member of the Haynes Publishing Group, has published authoritative, quality books for enthusiasts for more than 20 years. During that time the company has established a reputation as one of the world's leading publishers of books on aviation, maritime, military, model-making, motor cycling, motoring, motor racing, railway and railway modelling subjects. Readers or authors with suggestions for books they would like to see published are invited to write to: The Editorial Director, Patrick Stephens Limited, Sparkford, Nr. Yeovil, Somerset BA22 7JJ.

Printed in Great Britain

1 3 5 7 9 10 8 6 4 2

Contents

The exceptional appearance of stray birds far outside the normal range of their species is a well-known phenomenon.

Sir Landsborough Thomson

Preface

As a youth I thought that I had made history when I saw my first really rare bird. While returning along the sea-wall at Frampton-on-Severn on 9 April 1955, there to my unbounded joy, feeding in a flooded reen, was a splendid little egret. Full field notes were taken, and hurriedly posted to the journal *British Birds*. I then anxiously scanned each issue with expectancy, hoping to see my name enshrined with then only the twenty-fifth little egret to be seen in the British Isles. To my chagrin others had discovered it the previous day, and the published note was above the name of Peter Scott.

My first long-tailed duck provided as much excitement. I have my diary open at the page, the date 7 January 1956. It was a female which had arrived at Frampton Gravel Pits. Imagine my further joy when seven weeks later one — was it the same bird? — was located during my lunch hour at Longfords Lake close to home. It does not have to be just rare birds that arouse interest and excitement. More regular species in a new location, the expansion of a list of those seen in some particular, well-visited spot, the list of opportunities seems endless.

We all have disappointments where rare birds are concerned. A record not accepted, even though one is absolutely sure, the distant view, the all too brief view, the words 'It was here 15 minutes ago, but we haven't seen it since'. Mine, I think, concerns a first hoopoe. As a boy I pored over bird books both at home and in the local library, and that of all species was my goal. My first, on a troop ship in the Red Sea in July 1958, was a very worn individual, not at all the bird I expected, though subsequently others have more than made amends.

Now, over 30 years later, it seems appropriate to put pen to paper to summarize briefly the history and the status of over 300 species of rare bird seen in the British Isles. By the time the book is published several more will have been added to the list, some anticipated, others not. Many others will have added to their totals; indeed as I write this shortly after dawn I anticipate seeing later in the day only the second white-throated robin for the British Isles. One has been on Skokholm in the past 24 hours. Will it still be there, I ask myself?

This book is not meant to be either field guide or statistical account, but rather to give the flavour of those rare birds which have by accident or design reached the British Isles. In this I am particularly conscious of the debt to all those who provided illustrations. I am only sorry that more could not have been used. My grateful thanks are due to Dave Beadle, Andrew

Birch, Tony Broome, D. W. Burns, David Cottridge, Dennis Coutts, Jack Donovan (with whom I shared both the white-throated robin and northern oriole), E. A. Fisher, Jeffrey Hazell, Tim Loseby, Chris McCarty, Anthony McGeehan, Bill Morton, Alan Roberts, Richard Smith, Barry Wright and Steve Young. Special thanks are also due to Peter Fullagar, who in 1961, having missed the Skomer Blackburnian warbler by one day, later presented my wife and I with the fine illustration it is my pleasure to use on the rear of the dust wrapper. Hopefully readers will agree that these small fragments of the wealth of photographic and artistic material available help convey the magic and the lure of rare birds.

No book is possible without the commitment and understanding of the publishers, and I am conscious of the debt I owe to Patrick Stephens Ltd, and in particular Darryl Reach and his staff, both for their patience with a tardy author and for seeing the book through all its stages.

★   ★   ★

28 May 1990

PS I did manage to see the white-throated robin. There can be few more appropriate ways for an author of such a book to conclude his writing.

Introduction

I s it the thrill of the chase? Is it the latent thrill of the collector? Is it the thrill of seeing something for the first time? Whatever the reason few fail to be moved by the sight of a new bird, a bird not previously encountered, sometimes a bird well-known from one's reading of the bird books, but on those extra special occasions one whose occurrence in the British Isles is a complete surprise. As a novice birdwatcher it may be the discovery of a lesser spotted woodpecker searching for food on the highest tree, and previously overlooked during walks through the nearby woodlands. Or that magic moment when in a flash of blue a kingfisher speeds under a bridge, and just as promptly on to one's life list. Even those whose birdwatching is very much a garden activity will from time to time have cause for great excitement. A wintering siskin that appears for the first time and finds the peanut-holder a welcome source of food, or the passage black redstart seeking shelter for a few days around the outbuildings.

It is not long before, as one's experience develops, new places are visited, the marshlands of East Anglia, the Pembrokeshire islands possibly, the Highlands of Scotland, and then further afield to the continent and sometimes beyond. On each occasion new birds will be encountered, the life list expanded, mostly with the expected, but from time to time with the unexpected, the rare bird. These visitors have always been much sought after. In days gone by most were shot, according to the adage 'What's hit is history, what's missed is mystery'. A glance at any early avifauna will reveal a melancholy catalogue of those birds, which, far from their normal range, fell to the gunner, or the bird-snarer, and by way of the local taxidermist's bench into the hands of some wealthy landowner, collector, or the local museum.

Times have changed but the seeking of rare birds in the British Isles is as keen as ever. Now there is a large army of birdwatchers, equipped with field guides and detailed identification papers, with increasingly sophisticated optical aids, and supported by an information grapevine. Many will travel long distances, the length and breadth of the country if need be, to see a rare bird. They have developed words and phrases of their own, of which I will include but one, the word *twitcher* being used to describe those who seek rare birds. I deprecate such a word, and will not use it further here, nor any of those others now alas to my mind commonly in use.

Great lengths will be taken to see rare birds, and on occasions this has caused problems both for the bird, and sometimes the local community. If you are seeking rare birds, please ensure you do not cause any unnecessary disturbance to the bird, or to local residents. Sometimes quite extraordinary

numbers of birdwatchers will gather, like the 3,000 estimated for the golden-winged warbler in Kent. Most are of a generous nature, only too willing
to make a donation to the funds of the local wildlife trust — in
Worcestershire nearly £500 in a single day at the Upton Warren reserve, or
the £1,020 to the Dyfed Wildlife Trust when a northern oriole frequented
a member's garden for several months. Tremendous efforts will be made to
reach a location where a rare bird has just been seen. On occasions planes
will be chartered to reach remote Scottish islands, boats will venture forth
into the Western Approaches, and lengthy journeys will be made by road,
sometimes even on foot.

Rare birds are news, rare birds are still very collectable, but now in the
form of lists, reports, photographs, and above all treasured memories. As
Norman Elkins writes in his classic *Weather and Bird Behaviour* :

> 'Arguably one of the more exciting events of a birdwatcher's career is
> the discovery of an individual bird which is clearly thousands of kilo-
> metres from the edge of its range or migration route.'

What actually constitutes a rare bird? Those species, currently some 300*
in number recorded in Great Britain and Ireland normally no more than 15
times annually, many considerably less frequently than this. Such birds have
come from all parts of the world; from the high Arctic, species like the gyrfalcon and Brunnich's guillemot; from the North Pacific the Aleutian tern;
from the southern oceans Wilson's storm-petrel, claimed by some to be the
most numerous bird in the world; of North American wildfowl and waders,
of landbirds blown across the Atlantic, like the gray catbird, scarlet tanager,
ovenbird, and yellow-rumped warbler, in a list which increases almost
annually. From nearer home, but just as unexpected, are the trumpeter
finch from south-east Spain, Marmora's warbler from the islands in the
western Mediterranean, the rose-coloured starling, a voracious eater of
locusts, from south-east Europe, and the great reed warbler, a clamorous
denizen of marshlands as close to us as the Netherlands. A whole range of
species make their way from the east, some in journeys which despite being
overland are just as remarkable, just as unexpected, as those which cross the
Atlantic. Birds like the red-breasted goose and pechora pipit, the eye-
browed thrush and pine bunting to mention but a few.

The first official List of British birds was published in 1883 by the British
Ornithologists' Union (BOU), the senior ornithological body in the British
Isles. Several subsequent Lists have appeared, the most recent being that of
1971 and now alas somewhat out of date, though additions are published
from time to time in the journal *The Ibis*. The British Ornithologists Union
Records Committee (BOURC) is the accepted body for the assessment of
all records of new birds to the British Isles. The Committee investigates
every aspect of each previously unrecorded bird, takes advice as required,
and eventually a decision is reached on whether the bird be accepted to the
British List. Most that occur are reasonably straightforward acceptances,
but for some the path is tortuous to say the least, and a few, where the
nature of the record is one of complexity, may remain in the pending tray

* *The figure of 300 includes a number not yet currently accepted to the British and Irish
Lists.*

for years. Currently this includes species like yellow-nosed albatross, falcated duck, marbled duck, south polar skua, northern mockingbird, and yellow-headed backbird.

Once accepted to the British List, a bird may be placed in one of five categories:

A Species which have been recorded in an apparently wild state in Britain or Ireland at least once within the last 50 years. Transatlantic visitors, for which the possibility of assisted passage cannot be ruled out, are included in this category.

B Species which have been recorded in an apparently wild state in Britain or Ireland at least once, but not within the last 50 years.

C Species which, although originally introduced by man, have now established a regular feral breeding stock which apparently maintains itself without necessary recourse to further introduction.

D Species which have been recorded within the last 50 years and would otherwise appear in Category A except that:
   i   there is a reasonable doubt that they ever occurred in a wild state;
   ii   they have certainly arrived with ship-assistance;
   iii they have only ever been found dead on the tide-line. Also species which would otherwise appear in Category C, except that their feral breeding populations may or may not be self-supporting.

E Species which would otherwise appear in Category A or B but have only ever been recorded in British and Irish waters between 3 and 200 miles from land.

Most of the birds described in the main part of this book are in Category A, with a small number of Category B and D species, and one in E. In addition, a small number of species are included in the book which have not yet been admitted to the British List yet whose inclusion is warranted by the available evidence, and their occurrence here urgently requires reappraisal. Additionally several which have been deleted but whose claim to have occurred should not be forgotten, are also included, because after all they will be recorded here again.

So much for first occurrence, but what of subsequent sightings? Although in the past many records were submitted to the premier journal *British Birds* published monthly since June 1907, others were dealt with by the county bird recorders, and those who compiled county avifaunas, often working in isolation, and with little opportunity of seeing the wider picture and thus ensuring a proper assessment of the record. Concern had been increasing during the 1950s that some records were being accepted on rather flimsy evidence and unless proper procedures were quickly instituted a quite chaotic situation could develop. This view was shared by most recorders who were single-minded in their determination to institute a reliable system with acceptable criteria.

Thus the Rarities Committee was formed during the late 1950s. It has naturally become known as the British Birds Rarities Committee, BBRC for short, and covers England, Scotland and Wales. The main purpose of the Committee is to adjudicate on records of rare birds, and to publish annually in *British Birds* a report on their occurrence. In their introduction to the first report, the Committee makes the point that:

'Each individual record of a rare bird has comparatively little value on its own, but when all are taken together they act as pointers to the origins of drift and other migratory movements, while at the same time illustrating trends in range-expansion and such aspects of behaviour as the differences between the wanderings of adults and first-year birds.'

Records are submitted by observers, preferably on the standard record form, a copy of which is reproduced on pages 14 and 15. These are then circulated round a Committee of some 10 experts, who during the course of a year expect to receive some 100 batches of reports, each batch containing about 15 records for consideration. Currently the acceptance rate is about 85 per cent, and while many of the records submitted are processed in a straightforward manner a proportion take much detailed consideration, and often consultation with additional experts. A report is published annually in *British Birds*, usually in the November issue, and reports, which extend back to 1958, are a treasure trove of information on the occurrence of rare birds in the British Isles. In Ireland records of rare birds are adjudicated by the Irish Rare Birds Committee and appear in the annual Irish Bird Report published by the Irish Wildbird Conservancy. A summary of these is included in the reports in *British Birds*.

For some rare birds occurrence in the British Isles is now an annual event, perhaps an indication of a change in status. There are increasing populations, like those of the little egret and black kite; could we ever see these species remaining to breed? For others the story is one of decline, the crakes and bustards due most probably to habitat declines, the alpine accentor perhaps as a result of climatic change. Observations of rare birds are thus something more than just a pleasurable activity, though some would say disparagingly a sport, since they do provide scientific evidence as to the well-being of bird populations throughout the northern hemisphere and indeed further afield.

The list of birds considered by the Rare Birds Committees is not a static one. As status changes, in particular genuine increases, or possibly where improved observer coverage and expertise means many more birds are noted, so species may be removed from the list. Both the icterine and melodious warblers were included in the 1958 report, as were the Richard's and tawny pipits. All have subsequently proved to be more frequent here than previously realized, and are now no longer considered by the Committee. The crane is another with a great upsurge in records, no fewer than 1,171 during the period 1958 to 1985. As I write this the news has been revealed that cranes have indeed been breeding 'somewhere in the British Isles' for several years, a further example of changing status of the most exciting kind.

The most classic case of a change of status must be that of the ring-billed gull, a North American species rather similar to the common gull. The first record, an adult at Blackpill on 14 March 1973, was rapidly followed by others. Was it a change of status, or having made the first discovery were birdwatchers able to improve their techniques and locate examples from among resident gulls? Whatever the reason, by the time it was removed from the list of rare birds to be considered in 1987, no fewer than 611 had been accepted, with many others still to be adjudicated on. Will it eventually remain to breed? Perhaps it already does so somewhere in north-west Europe.

Rare avian visitors from North America have always excited special attention among birdwatchers. A wader, a duck, from North America, has long been accepted without question as a genuine migrant, but small landbirds for many years were all dismissed as escapes, or the result of deliberate introductions. The chances of a warbler or wood thrush, a hawk owl or junco making an Atlantic crossing were not considered possible by some authorities.

In 1955, in *British Birds*, a classic paper though probably now alas largely forgotten, 'American Landbirds in Europe' by W. B. Alexander and R. S. R. Fitter re-opened the case for American landbirds occurring in western Europe, with a summary of the old and largely disregarded records. The authors, while recognizing the possibility of escapes and introductions, nevertheless clearly demonstrated peaks of occurrence which coincide with spring and autumn passage. Their conclusions have been amply confirmed by more recent events when not a year now goes by without one or more North American landbirds reaching our islands. Alas the old records are by and large still neglected and in urgent need of careful investigation.

Ship-borne passage may well play a part, and there are some well-documented examples of American passerines, sometimes in numbers alighting on ships crossing the Atlantic. Most stay but a short while, some die, some are blown out to sea, even taken by predators, and few make the complete crossing. Their arrival on our shores seems much more likely to be a displacement eastwards associated with strong west to south-west winds. Birds caught in these will be rapidly carried across the Atlantic, and indeed a rapid passage is essential for survival. To tarry on a ship for even a short while probably means death.

Few birdwatchers at one time or another have not, with quickening pulses and a reach for the field notebook, encountered what on reflection and careful consideration turned out to be an escaped cage-bird. They could well benefit from occasionally visiting the large aviary bird shows as a means of seeing the quite astounding range of birds kept in captivity in this country, and to obtain hints as to their identification.

Equally astounding is the number of cage birds that do escape, or are possibly from time to time deliberately released. Although rather extreme cases, several have become established in the British Isles as breeding species; birds like the mandarin duck now breeding in many counties in southern England, or the ruddy duck which has extended over a much larger area since the first escaped from the Wildfowl Trust at Slimbridge, in the late 1950s. Both the golden pheasant, and Lady Amherst's pheasant have become permanent residents in several areas as the result of deliberate releases. The ring-necked parakeet, sometimes known as rose-ringed parakeet, was released in southern England in the late 1960s and has subsequently established small populations in a number of areas, so that it too now lays claim to being part of our avifauna.

Such species are fairly obvious escapes or deliberate releases, but for

BRITISH BIRDS RARITIES COMMITTEE - RECORD FORM

SPECIES

Number of birds: Sex: Age:

PLACE   County (new):
                                                       (old):

DATE(S) of your observations:
                        Times:
                Total duration:

Earlier/later dates by others, if known:

First and last dates, if known:

OBSERVER (BLOCK CAPITALS):
        Address: Telephone:

Other observers (BLOCK CAPITALS):

Who found it?:   Who first identified it?:

Who is also reporting it, if known?:

Was it trapped for ringing?:   Date, if known:
                                        Ringer, if known:

If dead, is it preserved?:   Where?:

Was it photographed?:   Photographer (and address, if known):

Optical aids used: Distance from bird:

Previous experience of the species:

Experience of similar species:

Weather conditions:

Details of trapped bird to be completed by ringer
Date trapped: Ring number:
Note: If you were the ringer, this report should be submitted via BTO Ringing Office.

                                                       P.T.O.

DESCRIPTION: Include account of the relevant circumstances of the observation
and a detailed description of the bird(s), preferably based on notes taken at
the time of the observation before reference to books. Attach original field
notes if available. Attach extra sheets if required.

And finally, is this record 100% certain?:

Any who disagree?:

PACK PHOTOGRAPHS AND SLIDES CAREFULLY - keep copies if possible.

British Birds Rarities Committee Record Form

many small passerines the case is not so clear. Take the rose-coloured starling, certainly a rare visitor to the British Isles, but also a bird found in captivity. The red-headed bunting is another classic species, a common bird in captivity, so much so that all records in the British Isles are open to suspicion as to their origin.

There are several points to bear in mind when assessing whether a bird is an escape or a genuine migrant. First of all its normal range and status, which on its own will rule out many species without further consideration. Do not be misled by the fact that you meet some exotic species on a remote Scottish or Irish island, or some other spot far from most habitations. Escaped cage birds are just as likely to greet you there as at the edge of towns. Take the case of a barbary dove which within two weeks of its disappearance from Virginia Water was found at the Tuskar Rock Lighthouse off Wexford, Ireland. A recent report for Spurn Bird Observatory listed cockatiel, budgerigar, African grey parrot, Chinese bulbul and red-eared waxbill as having occurred there within a single year. Proof, if any were needed, that cage birds do range widely once free.

Escaped cage-birds sometimes beg for food and are usually unafraid of man. However, if neither of these criteria is met it may indicate that it has been at large for some time and regained its normal habits. Worn plumage, especially on the wings and tail are to be expected in cage birds, though once again their absence does not rule out a captive origin.

There is one other possibility when it comes to considering records of rare birds, though fortunately it is rather unlikely today. This is deception, which was undoubtedly practised in the past when exotic species were sold to unsuspecting collectors as have been obtained in this country, when in fact they had been obtained abroad. The classic case surrounds the so-called Hastings Rarities, some 542 specimens, with a further 55 sight records, of rare birds seen within a 20 miles radius of Hastings between the years 1892 and 1930. Some 134 species with many sub-species were involved including a number which at the time of their occurrence were the first for the British Isles. E. M. Nicholson and I. J. Ferguson-Lees, the authors of a report not surprisingly titled 'The Hastings Rarities' which appeared in the journal *British Birds*, August 1962, bring together much detail about the records and state that many inherent probabilities call for explanation. Particular to the thrust of their arguments is the fact that the number of birds reported is so high, far higher than one would expect for such a small area, or indeed any similar area in the British Isles, as is the proportion of new species and sub-species. As a result they proposed that the records be deleted from the British List, and this was subsequently done.

Not all agreed with their sweeping conclusions, most notably David Bannerman in his classic *The Birds of the British Isles* and Dr James Harrison author of *Birds of Kent*, who mounted a spirited defence of the records, and in particular the taxidermist George Bristow in a book *Bristow and the Hasting Rarities* published in 1968. Both strongly support those who collected or received many of the birds now alas summarily deleted from the British List. Even the authors of the report themselves admit that probably half the records are likely to be genuine, and if this is the case then it seems clear that each should have been taken on its merits, rather than the sweeping away of the good with the bad.

Clearly this was a remarkable episode in British ornithological history, one that certainly does not deserve to be forgotten for whatever reason, because it is very much a part of the great saga of rare birds in these islands. It is an indication of their lure, then for different reasons than now, but a remarkable lure none the less, and one which goes from strength to strength as knowledge and experience increase.

What can watchers in the final decade of the twentieth century expect, and, even more intriguing, what will the twenty-first century bring? Who would have dreamt in 1890 of the ornithological riches which were to be unfolded over the following 100 years? Two authors have attempted to predict some of the species yet to be seen in the British Isles.

Firstly D. I. M. Wallace for Palearctic passerines in *British Birds* September 1980, predicted a list which contained several, including the crag martin, white-throated robin and Pallas's rosefinch, which have confirmed his forecast and subsequently reached us. The remainder provide a challenge for observers, and are, from their geographical areas as follows:

North-east Europe

Siberian Tit	Azure Tit	Siberian Jay

Southern Europe

Olive-tree Warbler	Semi-collared	Cinereous Bunting
Spotless Starling	Flycatcher	

South-west Asia

Long-billed Pipit	Menetrie's Warbler	Grey-necked Bunting

Central Asia and Siberia

Siberian Accentor	Eastern Crowned	Narcissus Flycatcher
Whistling Nightingale	Leaf Warbler	Daurian Jackdaw
Siberian Blue Robin	Dark-sided	Oriental Greenfinch
Eversmann's Redstart	Flycatcher	Long-tailed
Grey-backed Thrush	Grey-streaked	Rosefinch
Pale Thrush	Flycatcher	Black-faced Bunting
Gray's Grasshopper	Mugimaki Flycatcher	Meadow Bunting
Warbler		

In the following month in the same journal Chandler S. Robbins made similar predictions in respect of North American landbird vagrants to Europe, placing them in order of likelihood of occurrence on the western seaboard of the North Atlantic, a further exciting list. Twenty years later no fewer than 11 had arrived, while reviews of early records of a further four were outstanding, so leaving some 23 possibilities as given below. It will not be easy even in this day and age, bearing in mind the identification difficulties of several in autumn plumage, to add these to the British List.

Connecticut Warbler	Dickcissel	Black-throated Blue
Eastern Kingbird	Alder Flycatcher	Warbler
Common Grackle	Blue Jay	Canada Warbler

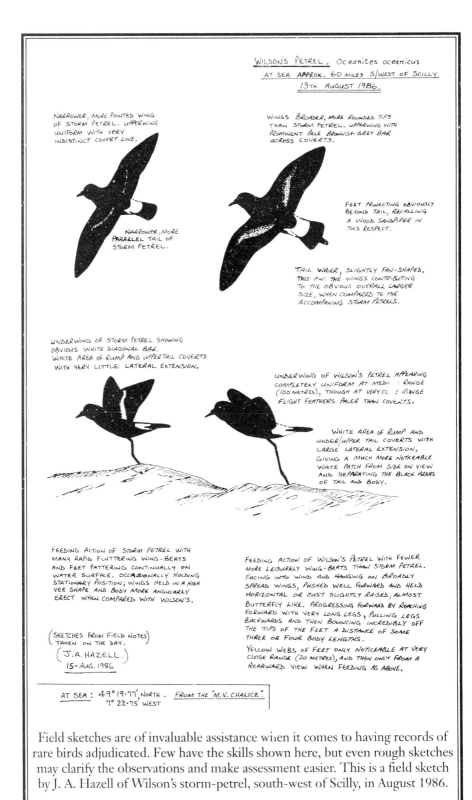

WILSON'S PETREL. Oceanites oceanicus
AT SEA APPROX. 60 MILES S/WEST OF SCILLY.
13TH. AUGUST 1986.

NARROWER, MORE POINTED WING
OF STORM PETREL. UPPERWING
UNIFORM WITH VERY
INDISTINCT COVERT LINE.

WINGS BROADER, MORE ROUNDED TIPS
THAN STORM PETREL. UPPERWING WITH
PROMINENT PALE BROWNISH-GREY BAR
ACROSS COVERTS.

NARROWER, MORE
PARALLEL TAIL OF
STORM PETREL.

FEET PROJECTING OBVIOUSLY
BEYOND TAIL, RECALLING
A WOOD SANDPIPER IN
THIS RESPECT.

TAIL WIDER, SLIGHTLY FAN-SHAPED.
THIS AND. THE WINGS CONTRIBUTING
TO THE OBVIOUS OVERALL LARGER
SIZE, WHEN COMPARED TO THE
ACCOMPANING STORM PETRELS.

UNDERWING OF STORM PETREL SHOWING
OBVIOUS WHITE DIAGONAL BAR.
WHITE AREA OF RUMP AND UPPERTAIL COVERTS
WITH VERY LITTLE LATERAL EXTENSION.

UNDERWING OF WILSON'S PETREL APPEARING
COMPLETELY UNIFORM AT MEDIUM RANGE
(100 METRES), THOUGH AT VERY CLOSE RANGE
FLIGHT FEATHERS PALER THAN COVERTS.

WHITE AREA OF RUMP AND
UNDER/UPPER TAIL COVERTS WITH
LARGE LATERAL EXTENSION,
GIVING A MUCH MORE NOTICEABLE
WHITE PATCH FROM SIDE ON VIEW
AND SEPARATING THE BLACK AREAS
OF TAIL AND BODY.

FEEDING ACTION OF STORM PETREL WITH
MANY RAPID FLUTTERING WING-BEATS
AND FEET PATTERING CONTINUALLY ON
WATER SURFACE. OCCASIONALLY HOLDING
STATIONARY POSITION; WINGS HELD IN A HIGH
VEE SHAPE AND BODY MORE ANGULARLY
ERECT WHEN COMPARED WITH WILSON'S.

(SKETCHES FROM FIELD NOTES)
TAKEN ON THE DAY.

(J.A. HAZELL.)
15-AUG. 1986

FEEDING ACTION OF WILSON'S PETREL WITH FEWER
MORE LEISURELY WING-BEATS THAN STORM PETREL.
FACING INTO WIND AND HANGING ON BROADLY
SPREAD WINGS, PUSHED WELL FORWARD AND HELD
HORIZONTAL OR JUST SLIGHTLY RAISED, ALMOST
BUTTERFLY LIKE. PROGRESSING FORWARD BY REACHING
FORWARD WITH VERY LONG LEGS, PULLING LEGS
BACKWARDS AND THEN BOUNCING INCREDIBLY OFF
THE TIPS OF THE FEET A DISTANCE OF SOME
THREE OR FOUR BODY LENGTHS.
YELLOW WEBS OF FEET ONLY NOTICEABLE AT VERY
CLOSE RANGE (20 METRES), AND THEN ONLY FROM A
REARWARD VIEW WHEN FEEDING AS ABOVE.

AT SEA : 49° 19·77' NORTH .   FROM THE "M.V. CHALICE".
                 7° 22·75' WEST

Field sketches are of invaluable assistance when it comes to having records of
rare birds adjudicated. Few have the skills shown here, but even rough sketches
may clarify the observations and make assessment easier. This is a field sketch
by J. A. Hazell of Wilson's storm-petrel, south-west of Scilly, in August 1986.

Orange-crowned
  Warbler
Black-capped
  Chickadee
Yellow-bellied
  Flycatcher
Whip-poor-will

Mourning Warbler
Yellow-breasted Chat
Great Crested
  Flycatcher
Eastern Pewee
Black-throated
  Green Warbler

Least Flycatcher
Blue-winged Warbler
Prairie Warbler
Bay-breasted Warbler
Northern
  Mockingbird

In the same paper there is a further list of North American landbirds of which, despite the low probability of making a crossing, seven have subsequently been recorded in the British Isles, while another, the American goldfinch, is worthy of re-examination. The remaining 27 are given here in specific order. When and where will others be added to the British and Irish Lists?

Downy Woodpecker
Hairy Woodpecker
Acadian Flycatcher
Long-billed Marsh
  Wren
Carolina Wren
House Wren
Blue-grey Gnat-
  catcher
Carolina Chickadee

Boreal Chickadee
Tufted Titmouse
White-breasted
  Nuthatch
White-eyed Vireo
Solitary Vireo
Warbling Vireo
Purple Finch
House Finch
Nashville Warbler

Pine Warbler
Worm-eating Warbler
American Tree
  Sparrow
Chipping Sparrow
Field Sparrow
Grasshopper Sparrow
Seaside Sparrow
Lincoln's Sparrow
Northern Cardinal

Ocean Nomads

Black-browed Albatross	Wilson's Storm-Petrel	Royal Tern
Soft-plumaged Petrel	White-faced Storm-Petrel	Elegant Tern
Capped Petrel	Madeiran Storm-Petrel	Lesser Crested Tern
Bulwer's Petrel	Magnificent Frigatebird	Bridled Tern
Little Shearwater		Sooty Tern
Audubon's Shearwater		

Of all the rare birds to visit the British Isles the ocean nomads have a special attraction. Some pass our shores annually on movements which have brought them from the far extremes of the South Atlantic, birds like the sooty shearwater from the Falklands, and the desolate islands about Cape Horn, and the great shearwater from lonely Tristan da Cunha. Then there is Cory's shearwater from islands in the Mediterranean and off north-west Africa. Such birds largely move past western Britain during the late summer with on occasions major passages of many hundreds, in some years thousands, so affording a glimpse of seabirds on their ocean journeys.

Among the regular visitors will be vagrants, true ocean nomads, lured away from their normal haunts by as yet unknown forces, perhaps unusual weather patterns or simply a bird becoming lost. A number are accepted to the British and Irish Lists, others, where the antecedents are unclear or even now largely forgotten, or where, even among recent sightings with modern optical aids, the detailed features sufficient for certain identification could not be obtained. These include birds like the Cape pigeon, Kermadec petrel, collared petrel, red-tailed tropic bird and south polar skua.

Can anyone fail to be moved, to feel that extra excitement, at the thought of birds making their way, sometimes thousands of miles across previously unvisited North Atlantic seas to reach our shores? Even when they arrive, some are only seen by those most dedicated to the art of seawatching, those who spend hours, even days, watching seabird movement from remote headlands, or by those, perhaps more intrepid than most, who set out to sea. Enthralled as the watchers on the headland are by the regular movements of seabirds, there is always the dream of seeing an albatross, deep ocean shearwater or storm-petrel, frigatebird or tropical tern.

Above all, they dream of the albatross, for as Robert Cushman Murphy, North American pioneer seabird biologist wrote, 'it is a special moment when one sees the first albatross.' The black-browed albatross breeds no closer than the Falklands, Staten Island and South Georgia, and normally disperses no further north than the Tropic of Capricorn, so its occurrence in the North Atlantic is exceptional. Actually there has been one resident in British waters since 1967. In May that year, Professor W. H. Thorpe, one of few ornithologists to be elected a Fellow of the Royal Society, was photographing gannets on the Bass Rock where, much to his amazement, he saw an albatross. Was it the same bird which a year before had soared with the gannets around their colony on the Westmann Islands, Iceland?

It remained on the Bass Rock until 28 September, returned the following summer and then vanished, some would suggest due to disturbance by birdwatchers. In 1972 what was probably the same bird was re-discovered in the gannet colony at Hermaness, to which it has returned annually ever since. It has built a nest, but hopes that it might attract a mate have alas not been realized. Perhaps this is not surprising when there have been so few sightings — 24 in all — in British and Irish waters. Records have been in all months except for March and June, though most have occurred in late summer and autumn.

Even with improved optical aids and observer expertise, the black-browed albatross remains one of the greatest prizes in all senses of the word for seawatchers. Yet strangely the first two records were both inland, one found exhausted at Linton on 9 July 1897 and sent to London for inspection, the second at Stavely in August 1952. This bird was found caught in telegraph wires, released and taken to Skegness for return to the sea.

In addition to the long-staying Hermaness bird, the black-browed albatross has been recorded from Orkney (two), Yorkshire (five), Kent, Sussex, Dorset, Devon, Cornwall, Scilly, Wexford, Cork (five), Kerry and Mayo. There are also 47 sightings of unidentified albatrosses in British and Irish waters with much the same distribution of occurrences, with the addition of Northumberland, Norfolk and Caernarvon. Most were probably the black-browed albatross, though several other species can be expected, the most likely being the wandering albatross, yellow-nosed albatross and sooty albatross. Do not neglect the possibility of confusion with the giant petrel, a southern giant petrel having reached Ushant in France in November 1967.

The soft-plumaged petrel, a small to medium shearwater, grey above and white below, with a grey breast band and underwings, breeds at Madeira, the Desertas and Cape Verde Islands in the northern hemisphere, and at Tristan da Cunha, Kerguelen, that remarkable archipelago of over 300 windswept islands and islets, and St Paul Island in the south. Its status as a species is currently the subject of debate. Is it one species or indeed three? That which breeds on Madeira and is known as the freira must be one of the world's most endangered seabirds, for the population is probably no more than 30 pairs and much threatened by rats. If it becomes extinct it will be the first European species lost since the Great Auk in 1844. The larger gongon of Bugio in the Desertas and on the Cape Verdes has a population of several hundred pairs. It too faces threats, even from man, for the bird's fat is thought to have medicinal properties.

A single soft-plumaged petrel off Cape Clear on 5 September 1974 was the first for the British Isles. In view of the small North Atlantic population the chance of seeing another in our waters was considered small so that the sightings in August 1989 of single birds on three consecutive days at Porthgwarra, Prawle Point and at the Old Head of Kinsale were remarkable by any standards.

A bird of mystery, the capped petrel, also known as the diablotin, a medium-sized shearwater which is probably restricted to a few colonies on heavily forested limestone ridges up to 6,000 ft (2,000 m) above sea level in Haiti, and the Dominican Republic where the population may number no more than 4,000 birds. There are only two records from the British Isles. The first, killed by a boy on Swaffham Heath after it bit his hand as he retrieved it from a furze bush, was described by Alfred Newton in his first major scientific paper. Equally remarkable was the discovery of a long dead juvenile found at Barmston on 16 December 1984.

The small, but long-winged, sooty-brown Bulwer's petrel breeds on Atlantic islands from the Azores to the Cape Verde Islands, and on several island groups in the North Pacific. So far there are just four records from British waters: a bird near Tanfield on the River Ure on 8 May 1837, one at Beachy Head in February 1903, followed by one washed ashore at Scalby Mills at the end of February 1908, and one recent record off Cape Clear on 3 August 1975.

Of all the ocean wanderers recorded in British and Irish waters only two can lay claim to being more or less annual in their occurrence. These are the little shearwater and Wilson's storm-petrel.

The little shearwater, about two-thirds the size of the Manx shearwater which it closely resembles, occurs in no fewer than nine races of which two are in the northern hemisphere, both in the Atlantic. One is in the Cape Verde Islands where it was discovered in 1887 by Boyd Alexander, the same Boyd Alexander who made the first crossing from the Niger to the Nile, and was later murdered at Wadai, central Africa. This race is appropriately known as *boydi*; the other in the Azores, Madeira, Desertas, Canaries and Selvegans is *baroli*. Elsewhere it breeds at Tristan da Cunha, Gough Island, and in Australasian and New Zealand waters.

The report 'Rare birds in Great Britain in 1988' published in the journal *British Birds* 82: 505-563 has a salutary comment which applies to all seabirds:

'Seawatchers know that a seabird rarely gives a second chance: it flies by and any characters not noted then probably never will be. It is essential therefore, that observers of a possible little shearwater should concentrate on the right features in the time available: flight action, preferably in comparison with Manx Shearwaters (hopefully nearby), structure and head pattern should have priority, with the underwing-tip pattern something else to get if there is time.'

Some 74 have occurred in British waters since the first, a bird that came on board a sloop off the Bull Rock in May 1883 and is now preserved in the National Museum of Ireland; so much for naval hospitality! Such an end to a rare visitor is not unknown even today — a little shearwater shot at Cleveleys on the Fylde coast in 1975 now resides in the Liverpool Museum.

Most little shearwaters are seen in British waters during August and September, the majority off western coasts, particularly south-west Ireland. Seawatch enthusiasts at places like Flamborough and Hartlepool have also been fortunate; but why so few in the English Channel, where the only birds so far are two from Dorset and one from Kent?

Of all the records, those from Skomer in 1981 and 1982 are the most surprising. A little shearwater, later identified as a male, was heard calling from a burrow among large boulders near the Mew Stone on the south side of the island from 26 June through July, flying in from the sea each night with the resident Manx shearwaters. It returned to the same area on 21 June the following year and again remained until July. A female was heard one night in May 1983, but never again. Such visits raise the exciting possibility that other shearwater colonies may be visited by this, and indeed other rare petrels from time to time, certainly something to look and to listen for.

Audubon's shearwater is a small, stocky shearwater which occurs as a number of races throughout tropical seas. That which breeds on islands in the West Indies disperses into the Gulf of Mexico, and north-east in the Gulf Stream as far as New England. It was while becalmed off Florida in June 1826 that the great American naturalist and illustrator was given four specimens taken in a single shot by the ship's mate, and from one of these the bird was first described.

There is one record from the Western Palearctic, though not accepted on to the British List. A bird seen being harried by gulls on the beach at Bexhill-on-Sea on 7 January 1936 was rescued, but died shortly afterwards and the skin preserved.

Wilson's storm-petrel breeds in immense colonies both on the Antarctic continent and on many islands in Antarctic seas. Its northward migration into the Atlantic and Pacific Oceans is one of the most remarkable of any bird. In a straight line the return journey must encompass 14,000 miles (22,400 km). What can the true distance flown be?

That Wilson's storm-petrels regularly come in some numbers as close to the British Isles as the Bay of Biscay and the Western Approaches has been well documented. The paucity of records from land is therefore surprising, even on the coasts of France and Iberia. In the British Isles the first was a bird found dead near Polperro in November 1838, followed by at least six others during the nineteenth century. There were no further sightings until keen seawatchers at St Ives observed a single bird on 29 October 1967. Of the 10 subsequent records no fewer than six have been from St Ives, but be prepared for a long wait, as these have been spread over 20 years.

Don't despair. If you wish to see Wilson's storm-petrel in British waters there are now opportunities to travel west towards the edge of the continental shelf in large, well-appointed launches and motor yachts. From one that has made numerous voyages some 60 miles (100 km) south-west from Scilly to the so-called Wilson's triangle, no fewer than 101 of these dainty petrels were seen during August 1988. The petrels, together with other seabirds, can be attracted to the vicinity of the vessel by pouring minced fish, commonly known as 'chum' on the water. This oily mixture lures the birds close, at times so close that the yellow feet webs of Wilson's storm-petrel can be observed. On the Grand Banks fishing grounds, Newfoundland, fishermen once attracted seabirds close with similar oily wastes and then caught them on baited hooks for use as bait. Wilson's storm-petrels were frequently taken by this method, though their small size meant they were less attractive. It is good to see an old practice now being put to good effect, so enabling scarce birds to be seen at close range at sea.

In August 1988 observers at sea on board the MV *Chalice* observed a large dark-rumped storm-petrel, most probably Matsudaire's storm-petrel. This is a bird of the western Pacific which only breeds on the Volcano Islands south of Japan, dispersing through the China Sea with a few into the Indian Ocean. Other dark-rumped storm-petrels have recently been caught in the Salvage Islands and identified as Swinhoe's storm-petrel, a species previously only thought to breed on islands off China, Japan and Korea. Add to this several sightings of storm-petrels with dark rumps on the north-east coast of England, with two birds caught and ringed at Tynemouth, at present identified as Swinhoe's. Clearly another chapter of seabird history and distribution is about to be written, though alas not all the facts are yet fully available.

With its dancing flight and striking plumage the white-faced storm-petrel, sometimes known as the frigate petrel, is one of the more easily identified. Its white face and underparts and grey rump are distinctive, while the long legs project well beyond the tail. The white-faced storm-petrel in the Atlantic only breeds in the Selvegens and the Cape Verde Islands, where these colonies may hold up to 300,000 pairs, but they are small compared to populations in Australasian waters. Movements away from the colonies in the North Atlantic are largely a mystery. The only records from British waters are of a bird captured alive on the coast of Colonsay in the Inner Hebrides in January 1897 which now resides in the Royal Scottish Museum, and one off Cornwall in August 1963. For some reason one washed ashore on Walney Island during a severe gale in November 1890 has never been accepted.

The Madeiran storm-petrel is small and sooty-black, and can easily be confused with Leach's storm-petrel, though it has a more prominent white rump and a less forked tail. In the North Atlantic it breeds in the Azores, Madeira, Desertas, Porto Santo, Selvegens, and Cape Verde Islands, away from which its range is largely unknown. Elsewhere it breeds at Ascension, St Helena, Galapagos, Hawaii, and off Japan. The first record was of one found dead at Milford on 19 November 1911. The only other was one at Blackrock Lighthouse in October 1931.

The magnificent frigatebird, a large, mainly black seabird with slender pointed wings and deeply pointed tail, is easy to recognize as a frigatebird but very difficult to separate from the other four members of the family. It is a complete master of the air, claimed by some to be the most marvellous and most perfect flying machine that has ever been produced. Possibly a few pairs of the magnificent frigatebird still nest in the Cape Verde Islands, otherwise in the North Atlantic it breeds in numerous colonies throughout the Caribbean, and in the Pacific on the coast from Baja California to Equador, and in the Galapagos Islands.

The only definite record of the magnificent frigatebird in the British Isles is of an immature female found exhausted on a small freshwater loch on Tiree in the Inner Hebrides. Caught in a landing net it unfortunately died the next day. Its occurrence was subsequently reported in *The Times*. There have been several sightings of unidentified frigate birds, one about 150 miles south-west of Ireland in late May 1953. Was this the bird which succumbed on Tiree seven weeks later? The others were off Forvie in

August 1960, off Cape Clear in August 1960, and more recently off Fairview in June 1988 and at Dalkey a year later.

Six of the species of rare tern which have occurred in the British Isles come into the category of ocean nomad. All are coastal or oceanic birds, and all are among the rarest of visitors to north-west Europe.

There is much danger of confusion between the royal tern and other large terns. Indeed some records previously accepted have been deleted as more criteria are recognized. It is the second largest tern and easily confused with the largest, the Caspian tern, but has narrower wings, and an unmarked orange-red bill, whiter forehead, more prominent crest, underwing pattern, and a deeper forked tail. The royal tern is a coastal species breeding on both the Atlantic and Pacific coasts of the southern United States and in the West Indies, also in north-west Africa from Mauretania to Gambia, dispersing south from its breeding colonies in winter.

The first royal tern in Europe was one found long dead on 24 March 1954 on the shore of North Bull, that most excellent of birdwatching localities on the coast of Ireland close to Dublin. Detailed examination of the remains excluded the possibility that the corpse had drifted any distance before reaching the shore. However, David Bannerman writing in his classic *The Birds of the British Isles* Volume XI (1962) felt disposed to question the validity of the record:

'I fear I shall run counter to my friends in Ireland when I refuse to recognise the royal tern as a proven Irish record. To add a species to the already overloaded British List on the evidence of a corpse half buried in the sand without knowing *for certain* how it reached its destination seems to the writer the height of indiscretion.'

Strong words indeed. Fortunately there have been subsequent records so that the place of the royal tern on the British List is secure, one at Sandwich Bay in July 1965 was followed by another at St Ives in September 1971. The only other was quite remarkable, an immature bird seen briefly in late November 1979 at Kenfig Pool and initially thought to be a lesser crested tern. However, the observer, Steve Moon, warden of the reserve, managed to get within 10 ft (3 m) of the bird by wading in up to his thighs as it perched on a post, and was able to read part of a ring which revealed it had been ringed in 1978 or 1979 on the eastern seaboard of the United States.

The elegant tern is another large tern easily confused with the royal tern, though more especially with the lesser crested tern, but it has a larger and much finer slightly 'drooping' bill, and a white rather than grey rump and tail. It breeds only on the Pacific coast of America from southern California to Mexico, moving south in winter to Peru and Chile.

Just one is on record, a bird seen with Sandwich terns at Greencastle Point from 22 June to 3 July 1982 and on 1 August at Ballymaconda. One which was present in a colony of Sandwich terns at the Banc d'Arguin on the Gironde Estuary, France, for 10 summers from June 1974 was originally identified as a lesser crested tern, so beware of the problems should you encounter any of the large terns.

A graceful bird, the lesser crested tern is slightly larger than the Sandwich tern, with a bright orange dagger-shaped bill. It breeds off Libya, in the Red Sea and Persian Gulf, Australia, and New Guinea. A regular migration route along the southern side of the Mediterranean takes the lesser crested tern through the Straits of Gibraltar and south to Senegal and Gambia. In recent years there have been an increasing number of sightings, both of single birds, and of breeding pairs, in tern colonies on the northern shores of the Mediterranean, so clearly this is a bird currently attempting to extend its range.

The first record of a lesser crested tern in the British Isles was one at Cymyran Bay on the south-west coast of Anglesey in July 1982. Since then it has been an annual visitor to several coastal counties from East Lothian to Devon, though how many individuals there have been is difficult to quantify. Almost certainly in some cases it is the same bird returning for several years. Since 1985 a female has summered on the Farne Islands, in 1986 was seen associating with a chick in a colony of Sandwich terns, and in 1987 was apparently paired with a Sandwich tern and incubated two eggs, one of which was lost. If the trend continues then more lesser crested terns will be seen in the British Isles. Can we even look forward to its establishment as a British breeding bird?

In flight the bridled tern is surely one of the most buoyant and graceful of all terns, its plumage dark grey above and pale grey-white beneath. It breeds on islands and coast in tropical seas through the West Indies, at several points in Africa and Madagascar, the Red Sea, and Persian Gulf, islands in the Indian Ocean, and through the East Indies to Australia.

The first five records of the bridled tern in the British Isles were of birds found dead, at Dungeness on 19 November 1931, North Bull in 1953, Three Cliffs, Gower in 1954, at Sand Bay in 1958, while the fifth, identified only from a wing, was on Lundy in 1977. Two years later an immature at Stromness in August 1979 was the first live bridled tern to be found here. Since then a further six have occurred, all coastal sightings save for one at Rutland Water in June 1984, the others being at the Calf of Man in September 1980, St Ives in October 1982, Lodmoor in July 1984, and in 1988, only the second year in which there have been two sightings of birds at Cemlyn for much of July, while at Coquet Island another was present through much of July and August.

The sooty tern, about the size of the Sandwich tern, is distinctly larger and more strongly built than the bridled tern with which it might be confused, but is mainly black above, white below. It occurs on islands in all tropical and sub-tropical seas from where the birds disperse widely out of the breeding season.

The first sooty tern for the British Isles was one killed at Tutbury near Burton-on-Trent in October 1852. A further 15 were recorded up to 1957, then another 10, all single records between May and mid-August, but none since 1984. All have been coastal between Northumberland and Devon save two, an immature at Staines Reservoir in August 1971, and the sad case of a sick bird at Ditchford Gravel Pits at the end of May 1980. Rescued from the attentions of a crow and nursed back to health, all efforts to arrange for its return to a breeding colony failed, and it succumbed the following November.

Arctic Birds

White-billed Diver	Steller's Eider	Ivory Gull
Lesser White-fronted Goose	Gyrfalcon	Brunnich's Guillemot
	Thayer's Gull	Snowy Owl
Red-breasted Goose	Ross's Gull	Arctic Redpoll
King Eider		

Although slightly larger and more heavily built, the white-billed diver may easily be confused with the great northern diver. Most which occur in the British Isles are wintering or immature birds and identification of these has always been a problem. This resulted in a major review in 1974 in the journal *British Birds* 67: 257-296, but even with this to hand the difficulties must not be underestimated, and the white-billed diver is probably under-recorded. It breeds mostly within the Arctic Circle from Varanger Fjord in Norway, across Siberia, Alaska, and north-west Canada to the shores of Hudson Bay. Wintering quarters are at sea south of the breeding areas.

Some 118 white-billed divers have been recorded in the British Isles since the first, an adult shot at Embleton in December 1829 and now in the Newcastle Museum. Thirty years were to elapse before the white-billed diver was described as a full species, from specimens collected by James Ross when his expedition was trapped in the ice on the Boothia Peninsula in 1830. Until 1958 only 17 others had been recorded, of which eight were found dead or dying, a characteristic of this species in British waters where casualties have been from several causes, including oiling in most recent years. Although the records span every month save July, the majority have been from January to June, with a slight peak in May suggesting a northward return movement to the breeding grounds. Such spring birds are often in breeding plumage which considerably alleviates identification problems.

Nearly half the white-billed diver records since 1958 have been in Shetland, where one individual has returned to Whalsay each winter since 1979. There are records from most northern Scotland and east coast counties to Kent, with three from Cornwall, in 1967, 1985, and 1988, when Devon had its first record. There are single records in Ireland from counties Down, Wexford, Cork and Sligo. An adult at Audenshaw Reservoirs on the eastern edge of Manchester in December 1987 was a remarkable record, the only one inland so far in the British Isles.

Equally remarkable was the white-billed diver located by the redoubtable Bobby Tulloch of Shetland, using his boat's radar. Having been alerted to the presence of the bird in Uyeasound at the south end of Unst in May 1983, he set off by boat. His account published in *British Birds* 77:168 must surely record the first time such an event has taken place.

'. . . By the time we reached the harbour at Uyeasound visibility was down to less than 100 m — in fact we entered the harbour without seeing either side of the entrance. Once inside, the radar screen showed up various features — large blips were moored boats and smaller ones mooring buoys. Three smaller blips were also constant on the radar screen and when these were checked out the first two proved to be Great Northern Divers; we moved carefully up towards the third mark and, when it loomed up out of the fog, it was indeed the White-billed Diver.'

Watchers at Hartlepool in February 1981 required no such aids. One bird swam within a few feet of the quayside as it searched for fish discarded by the fishing fleet.

A trim, dusky-brown goose, the lesser white-fronted goose has a small rounded head, small bill, and short neck. The extensive white forehead is immediately apparent, but this is not a key identification feature when one comes to separating this bird from the usually larger white-fronted goose. It breeds from northern Scandinavia eastwards on the tundra lands where it nests among polar willow and dwarf birch close to the melting snows. Most winter in south-east Europe, around the Caspian, in Iran, Iraq, and east to the great river valleys of China.

The lesser white-fronted goose was probably overlooked in the past and not recorded in the British Isles until 1886, when one was shot at Fenham Flats on the unusually early date of 16 September. Six years later one was shot on the Nith Estuary, but the remains were eaten by a dog. The next joined a pinioned pair in Lincolnshire in 1943. Since then a further 109 have been recorded, and it is now almost annual in occurrence. Most consort with white-fronted geese, but careful searching of all goose flocks can bring rewards like the one with pink-footed geese at Ainsdale in 1983, while they have also joined bean geese in Norfolk and Kircudbright. Usually single birds are recorded, so the five at the New Grounds at Slimbridge in February 1966 is exceptional. Birds occur between late November and the end of March, most between December and mid-February. The majority of lesser white-fronted geese are seen on grazing meadows beside the Severn estuary in Gloucestershire, and from the Yare Valley, but there are scattered records from Argyll to Kent, with one from Wales, a bird at Dryslywn in March 1971, and one from Ireland, with a party of European white-fronted geese on the North Slob in late March 1969.

The red-breasted goose is unmistakable, a strikingly patterned black and white, with rich chestnut, it has a tiny bill and a short neck. Don't be lulled, however; it can easily be overlooked among other geese. It breeds from the Gulf of Ob east to the Taymyr Peninsula, often choosing to nest close to predators like the peregrine and rough-legged buzzard from which it derives protection. The total population probably does not exceed 25,000 birds, of which 15,000 are breeding adults, with much evidence of a continual decline. Most winter around the Caspian, in Iraq, and with a small number in south-east Europe.

First winter Lesser White Fronted Goose

white blaze on forehead from gape to within level of eye. Distinctive in the field.

Small rounded head with steep forehead

Prominent yellow eye-ring visible from 250 yds

Upper-parts
uniform brown-grey, slightly darker than Pink-footed Goose and neatly marked with pale grey-brown fringes

Short stubby bill uniform bright pink

HEAD
whole of head and neck rather dark brown, though not quite as contrasting with upper and under parts as on accompanying Pink-feet.

Underparts lightly barred
Pale tan brown with no black belly barring, though dark brown smudge down rear of flanks more prominent than Pink-foot

General Jizz
About the same size or slightly smaller than Pink footed Goose. Short lumpy neck with rounded head, short bill, bright swollen yellow eye-ring white blaze around bill similar to that of White-fronted Goose (Russian form) but rather ragged at top.

L W F G on the move

While Pink footed Geese usually spent some time feeding in one general area the L W F. Goose moved continually through the flock, sometimes quite rapidly while feeding with a mowing side to side motion.

W. S. MORTON

Lesser White-fronted Goose, Southport, January 1985 *(Field sketch by W. S. Morton)*

The first red-breasted goose in the British Isles was one near London in 1776 during hard weather, while another early record is of one taken alive about the same time near Wycliffe, and kept in captivity until 1785, Even now the number of records is just 39 of which 24 have been since 1957. Most occur in mid-winter, though the span is from early October until March. Records are from coastal counties between Yorkshire and Hampshire, and in Devon, but above all at Slimbridge where they mingle with the white-fronted geese, while in Norfolk it seems equally at home with brent geese. There is just one record from Scotland, on the Beauly Firth in the winter of 1956/7, and one from Wales, a bird at Milford Haven in January 1935, but as yet none has reached Ireland. Birds occasionally escape from waterfowl collections, and the five in Berwickshire in March 1966 were probably in this category. Presumably an aviculturalist shed many tears of anguish over such a loss.

Perhaps the most abundant of all ducks is the king eider, and the male is also one of the most striking. Its front is a creamy white, the rear black, save for a white patch either side of the rump. Look at the head: a marvellous pattern of grey and green, with an orange-red bill and orange facial shield. Despite such markings even a king eider can be overlooked amongst other seaduck pirouetting on a North Sea swell, or when the eyes run and the fingers are numb in an east wind hurtling up a Shetland voe. King eiders breed throughout the high Arctic, the nearest locations to the British Isles being Spitzbergen, the Kanin Peninsula east of the White Sea, and in east Greenland north from about Scoresby Sound. Most only move a short distance from their breeding grounds to ice-free waters for the winter months.

The first record for the British Isles was one obtained in Orkney, and exhibited by Gould on 27 November 1832 at the Zoological Society. Now some 192 have been recorded, two-thirds of these since 1957, with records in every month though with a predominance in March and April. Shetland is the place to go, since king eiders are seen there annually, usually several birds being located in the voes and sounds. Elsewhere in Scotland most are seen on north-western coasts, though surprisingly only four from Orkney. There are just five records from England, including one which reached Portsatho, where it remained from January to March 1986. Five were shot in Ireland in the last century, then none until a male at Baltimore in February 1959, to be followed by a remarkable series of records commencing in 1971, of a male at several locations in Donegal and Londonderry, each spring and summer until August 1982. Such annual returns are not unusual, and there have been several similar occurrences for shorter periods in Scotland. The possibility of visiting king eiders pairing with female eiders should not be ignored. This probably occurred at Loch Ranza on the north coast of Arran in the late 1970s.

Steller's eider is a compact sea-duck about the size of a goldeneye, the male having a unique plumage pattern of a white head with black eye-patch, and green on the rear of the crown, buff flanks and underparts. The steep angle of the nape, and the longish pointed tail carried clear of the water are specially important features when it comes to the female, which otherwise is a uniform dark brown. The Arctic coasts of Siberia east of the Taymyr Peninsula and the coasts of Alaska are its breeding areas, though occasionally birds may nest in Novaya Zemlya and elsewhere. Most winter in the southern Bering Sea, the sea named after the Dane Vitus Bering who during his expeditions employed the German naturalist Georg Wilhelm Steller, who collected the first specimens of this duck before he died of fever in western Siberia in 1746, aged just 37 years. The naming of Steller's eider was left to Pallas in 1859.

There are only 13 records of Steller's eider in the British Isles, all save the first two being in Scotland, a male at Caister on 10 February 1830, and another at Filey on 15 August 1845. Over a hundred years were to elapse before the next, two males seen near Gairsay in January 1947 by George Arthur, pioneer of bird protection in Orkney, where single-handed he ensured the continuation of the hen-harrier as a breeding species. Four of the others have also been from Orkney, including a male on Papa Westray from October 1974 to July 1982. There have been single records from Shetland and Sutherland, while in the Outer Hebrides there was another long-staying male, present from May 1972 to August 1984 at Vorran Island, an island only at low tide, on the west coast of South Uist. Two females joined it briefly in April 1974. An increase in the number of wintering birds in the Baltic which commenced in the late 1970s has so far not been reflected in the British Isles.

Most northerly of falcons, the gyrfalcon is also the largest and most powerful. Heavier built than the peregrine, the gyrfalcon normally flies with slower wingbeats, but dramatically increases speed when in full chase after its prey, which includes seabirds, duck, and gamebirds. The plumage varies from almost pure white through darker phases of grey and brown. The gyrfalcon breeds throughout the Arctic, only rarely below 60° north. The nearest to the British Isles are those in Iceland where about 200 pairs nest, and in Norway where the population has declined and now numbers no more than 30 pairs. Gyrfalcons move slightly south from the breeding areas in winter.

The gyrfalcon always seems to have been a regular, almost annual visitor to the British Isles, mostly between September and March, some 87 having been recorded since 1957 of which nearly a quarter have been in Shetland. Scotland has received the majority of the remaining records, though birds occasionally wander much further south, even to the Isles of Scilly. There are a scattering of records from Ireland, 14 since 1965, though the total is a little vague due to the possibility of one bird having returned to Londonderry on several occasions between 1981 and 1984. Gyrfalcons are occasionally reported from ships and offshore installations. One on Marathon Brae A platform, some 140 miles (224 km) east of Aberdeen in November 1983, caused great excitement when it killed a long-eared owl which it then devoured in full view of numerous, almost incredulous onlookers among the oil men.

Gulls in many plumages present identification problems for the observer and it seems new criteria are always being propounded and old ones discarded. Added to this is the confusing status of some; are they full species or are they races or sub-species? The well-known herring gull is very much in this category with at least ten sub-species which may be separated in the field, at least in some plumages. To add to the possible confusion will be hybridization where sub-species overlap, and if that is not enough add hybridization by the herring gull with closely related species like the glaucous gull, glaucous winged gull, great black-backed gull, Iceland gull, and lesser black-backed gull. This then is the challenge for those who search gull flocks; the rewards are there for careful and astute observers.

On 11 March 1989 an unusual gull in first-winter plumage was located at a rubbish tip on the edge of Galway City in the west of Ireland, and first identified as Kumlien's gull, currently considered a race of the Iceland gull. Later, after further observation and consultation, its identity was confirmed as Thayer's gull, a bird intermediate between the herring and Iceland gull. The dark eye is characteristic of this species, while the smaller bill and white underside to the outer primaries are other distinguishing features. It breeds on sea cliffs in Arctic Canada, most migrate south to winter on the coast from British Columbia to California, with some around the Great Lakes, and on the east coast south to Florida.

The first Thayer's gull in Europe was the one at Galway which remained there until the end of March 1989, with one further record, an adult at Dungeness in mid-March 1990. Now that birdwatchers are becoming familiar with this species, and the necessary identification features, we can surely anticipate many more records.

A Polar explorer is commemorated by a gull. Ross's gull belongs to James Clark Ross who shot the first specimen, during Edward Parry's second expedition, at Iglookik on the Melville Peninsula in the Canadian Arctic in 1823. The description of the incident in the expedition journal succinctly describes the key features:

> ' . . . which latter [Arctic tern] it somewhat resembles in size as well as in its red legs; but on closer inspection easily distinguished by its beak and tail as well as by a beautiful tint of most delicate rose-colour on its breast.'

Fifty years were to elapse before Ross's gull was found in any numbers, this time by the ill-fated *Jeanette* expedition while trapped in the ice near Wrangel Island, off north-east Siberia, one of the survivors returning with three precious skins under his shirt. The first nest was not discovered until 1905, when a colony of Ross's gulls was located in the Kolyma River delta in eastern Siberia from where it breeds westwards to the Khatanga river, with small colonies in the Canadian Arctic, Greenland, and Spitzbergen. It winters at sea, most probably at no great distance from the icepack edge.

Ross's gull was first recorded in the British Isles a quarter of a century after its discovery by Ross, when a bird was shot near Tadcaster in the winter of 1846/7. This remains the only inland record. There is another accepted early record, one caught at a fishing boat between Whalsay and the Out Skerries in April 1936. However, those indefatigable chroniclers of Shetland wildlife, L. S. V. and U. Venables list four others there between 1934 and 1948, and it seems churlish to disregard these. Of the 49 since 1957 most occurred between November and February, though there are records for nearly every month, including one which summered in Christchurch Harbour in 1974. They have become an annual visitor since that time, the majority being from the north-east where nearly a quarter of the records are from Shetland, just eight for Ireland, all since 1981, and just one from Wales, at Fishguard Harbour in February 1981.

The adult ivory gull is a plump all-white gull about the size of a common gull, with short legs and wings, a rather long tail and a stubby bill. It breeds in the high Arctic and winters along the edge of the pack ice where it fishes for Arctic cod and scavenges at polar bear kills or on walrus faeces.

The first ivory gull in the British Isles was shot in Balta Sound in December 1822, a further 75 being accepted up to 1957. Unlike most other scarce gulls the number recorded has declined in recent decades and despite vastly increased observer coverage and expertise there have been only 30 more since, the majority between November and early January. Although occasionally seen in south coast counties, and in Ireland where there have been five records since 1965, the majority are from Scotland, especially Shetland, with none in Wales since 1957.

Brunnich's guillemot was named after the founder of Danish zoology, of whom Linnaeus once wrote 'would that we had more Brunnich's; natural history would then soon be perfect'. His guillemot does, however, present a problem. Slightly larger and more thick set than the guillemot with which it is easily confused, Brunnich's guillemot has black-brown upperparts and a shorter, thicker bill with a white line on the edge of the upper mandible. It has a circumpolar distribution, mainly at high latitudes, the nearest colonies to the British Isles being those in Iceland and in northern Norway.

There seems much confusion over early records of Brunnich's guillemot and only that from East Lothian in December 1906 is now accepted. This is a most difficult species to identify, indeed its occurrence here is largely dependent on the vigilance of those birdwatchers who scour our strand lines. Since 1957 there have been a further 24 records in 15 years, and all but five of these have been found dead. The exceptions to this sad tale were birds at the Farne Islands in July 1977, Fair Isle in October 1980, Hamnavoe, Burra in February 1987, and remarkably one in a guillemot colony at Sumburgh Head in June 1989, and the only record from Ireland, also the furthest south so far, one in Ballyteigue Bay in December the same year. Most records are from north-east Scotland, and despite the casualties it probably means that Brunnich's guillemot winters at not too great a distance from our northern shores.

The snowy owl, a largely diurnal owl is an almost unmistakable huge white owl, up to half the size again of a barn owl with which it might be confused. It has broad, rather rounded wings and a cat-like expression. In Shetland it is known as the *catogle* or cat owl. The snowy owl has a circumpolar distribution in the high Arctic, choosing dry raised areas to nest amongst the surrounding wet tundra. Nomadic movements are made south in winter, and some years, when its main food supply of brown lemmings fails, major eruptions take birds much further to the south. Stragglers on such occasions have even reached Bermuda, the Azores, Yugoslavia, Albania, and Peshawar in Pakistan.

Shetland has always been the place to see the snowy owl in the British Isles. The first recorded occurrence was in 1808 when one was seen on Unst by Dr Edmonston of the family of famous Shetland naturalists and historians. The snowy owl was certainly a common visitor to Shetland in the early decades of the last century, with suggestions of nesting having taken place on at least two occasions. Collectors prized the bird, and crofters sold them, perhaps none more profitably than Robert Nicolson who is said to have slaughtered no fewer than 30 on Unst. The adjective 'many' is used to describe the number seen in the British Isles up to 1958, though most of these were in the nineteenth century and the early years of this century. Since 1957 a further 92 records are accepted though the situation is possibly more confused than with any other rare bird, but in the nicest possible way, by formerly the successful breeding, and the presence still of a small resident population in Shetland.

In 1963 a single male snowy owl was seen in Shetland in mid-summer, and the following year it remained until November. Several birds were noted throughout 1965 and 1966, being seen from Unst to Fair Isle. Then in 1967 a nest of seven eggs was found on the 400 ft (122 m) hill of Stakkaberg on the north side of Fetlar, from which five young successfully fledged. Snowy owls nested in the same locality annually to 1975 with some 20 young being reared. Some have remained in Shetland ever since, indeed the remains of one ringed as a nestling in 1969 was found at Ronas Hill on North Mainland in 1984. Alas since 1980 these residents have all been female, and fervent hopes for the reappearance of a male have not been realized.

Probably some of the Shetland snowy owls have wandered further afield, but as far as can be ascertained new immigrants have occurred in seven years since breeding ceased. In addition to the Shetland birds and others in Orkney and the Outer Hebrides, snowy owls have been reported at one time or another since 1957 in most east coast counties of Scotland and England, in Hampshire, Devon, Scilly, Gwent, Glamorgan and Anglesey, and in Rosscommon in Ireland. When the last Shetland female dies it seems as if the occurrences of this most Arctic of owls will be of as extreme a rarity as at any time in the last 200 years.

The largest of the redpolls, the Arctic redpoll can only be distinguished with great care from the mealy redpoll, a northern race of the redpoll. Look for the clear white rump, whiter underparts, and the bolder wing-bars. It has a circumpolar breeding distribution in the high Arctic where it nests in dwarf willow and birch, or amongst rocks. There is some southward movement in autumn.

The true historical picture of the Arctic redpoll in the British Isles is uncertain due to problems of identification, but some 30 records are accepted up to 1957 and 126 subsequently. Since the mid-1970s it has occurred annually except for 1983. Most are from late September to March, with records in every month save June and August with the majority in October and November. The July records were both of birds trapped and ringed, on Foula in 1965 and the Isle of May in 1982. Annual totals vary, usually only a handful a year, but there were 33 in 1984, of which no fewer than 25 were on Fair Isle, and 19 in 1985. The majority occur on the east coast south to Kent, the only records elsewhere being an April bird in 1962 from Lewis, and autumn records from South Uist, Calf of Man, Bardsey, and Scilly.

Eurasian Waterbirds

White Pelican
Dalmatian Pelican
Little Bittern
Night Heron
Squacco Heron
Cattle Egret
Little Egret
Great White Egret

Black Stork
Glossy Ibis
Ruddy Shelduck
Baikal Teal
Harlequin Duck
Little Crake
Baillon's Crake

Great Black-headed
  Gull
Slender-billed Gull
Gull-billed Tern
Caspian Tern
Whiskered Tern
White-winged Black
  Tern

W ho can mistake a pelican? The white pelican can, however, be confused with the Dalmatian pelican, from which it may be separated in all plumages by the black underwing pattern. It breeds on lakes and marshes from south-east Europe into Central Asia, India, and in Africa, mainly from the Rift Valley southwards. In Europe there has been a major reduction of range and numbers during the present century, largely due to the drainage of wetlands.

Pelicans have long been kept in captivity in large gardens and parks, and this casts a shadow over the occasional sighting of one in the British Isles so much that the handful of records are all placed in Category D. One at Great Yarmouth from 9 July 1964 to 20 February the following year seems to be the first. Three were at Breydon Water in the same county at the end of August 1971 with two at Dungeness in November 1972. No fewer than four were on Islay between 1 and 10 May 1973 at the same time that there was one, possibly two, on Gadloch, and one at Barn Elms Reservoir. This was followed by five sightings in the summer of 1975. Was the same bird involved at Minsmere, Hanningfield Reservoir, Fordwich, on the River Humber on the York/Lincoln border, and at Portland? Finally a bird was recorded at Appledore in September 1977. Whilst carrying out a seabird survey with friends on Caldey Island on 16 May 1970, a superb sunny day, I was suddenly surprised when the herring gulls erupted in a huge commotion to mob two pelicans, the first for Wales, which appeared out of the haze to the east and flew directly over the island. Where had they come from? Where were they going? It seems amazing that such large and conspicuous birds should have escaped notice elsewhere on their journey.

The Dalmatian pelican is the largest and most powerful of the pelicans. According to Pliny it once nested in the coastal marshes of north-west Europe, but in recent times its range has been restricted to the extreme south-east where high numbers were present until the end of the last century. Since then the population has declined, largely due to a loss of habitat, so that it now only occurs at a handful of sites, and then east to Iran, and the Aral Sea, Lake Balkash, and into Mongolia. Winter quarters are in the eastern Mediterranean, the Caspian and on the great rivers of India.

There is just one record; a Dalmatian pelican first seen near Colchester on 29 October 1967 remained there until 8 November, then wandered south and west through Kent, Sussex, Hampshire, Dorset and Cornwall during the remainder of November and into December, being finally seen in the Isles of Scilly in January 1968. Like the previous species it is placed in Category D, as an escape from captivity cannot be ruled out.

By contrast there is no doubt that the little bittern is a genuine vagrant to the British Isles. It is also small and of a skulking disposition. The male is especially well marked with black upperparts, pale creamy-buff underparts and large creamy-white wing patches visible in flight. Females are less striking and have buff wing-patches. Neither is likely to be confused with others in the family on account of their size and the plumage markings. Little bitterns breed throughout much of southern Europe, parts of Asia, Africa, and Australia. European birds are migratory, and those which occur in the British Isles probably overshoot as they move north in spring. Indeed stragglers have even reached Iceland on occasions.

Some 310 little bitterns have been recorded from the British Isles, just over half since 1957. Indeed its occurrence here is now almost annual, and in recent years only 1974 and 1982 were without a sighting. Most are seen during spring and early summer. Are those discovered later in the year ones that have remained unnoticed in a reed or osier bed? In some years there seems to have been a mini-invasion like the 13 in 1964, 20 in 1970, and 13 in 1976, though such numbers have not been repeated more recently. In spring the majority of records are from coastal counties between Norfolk and Cornwall, with occasional sightings north to Inverness and in Ireland. The autumn records are almost wholly restricted to counties south of Yorkshire with none in the west save for a single bird in Cornwall. One most extraordinary record was an adult female little bittern which came on board the MV *City of London* off Suez in April 1980 and was released, appropriately, at Egypt Bay 10 days later.

Little bitterns were strongly suspected of breeding in East Anglia during the nineteenth century, and this may have occurred in Kent in 1947 and Surrey in 1956, while pairs have summered on several occasions elsewhere. The first definite record was in 1984 at Potteric Carr, a fine wetland reserve of the Yorkshire Wildlife Trust set in an industrial area near to Doncaster. At least three young fledged and were observed being fed on a number of occasions before dispersal in mid-August. A pair returned in 1985 but did not breed, the cold and wet conditions that year probably the cause of failure.

The night heron or black-crowned heron, is a stocky grey and white bird with glossy green-black upperparts and long white head plumes. It spends the day in thick cover, being mainly crepuscular in habit, feeding at the edge of reedbeds and along ditches. It is extremely widespread, occurring in southern Europe, Asia, Africa, North and South America. The European population winters largely in tropical Africa with many birds crossing the Sahara by means of the oases rather than through the Nile Valley, or along western coasts.

A night heron shot near London in May 1782 was the first of some 392 in the British Isles, 228 since 1957. In spring most are found in southern and central England, while later in the year the emphasis is largely the eastern counties. Most years the number reported is small, usually less than five, though there were 19 in 1983 and an unprecedented invasion by 42 in 1987, and possibly even larger numbers in 1990 when there were at least seven in Pembrokeshire in March. Rather few normally reach the west coast, except in Cornwall and Scilly, and there have been only 11 in Ireland since 1965. Night herons have been expanding their range north in Europe so that an increase in sightings can be anticipated. Can we also look forward to it coming to breed in our reedbeds? An interesting record was of an immature night heron found dead at Skegness on 1 January 1980, which had been ringed as a nestling the previous June near Belyayevka, in the Black Sea region of the USSR.

Doubts are expressed on occasions as to whether all night herons seen in the British Isles are genuine wild birds. The reason is the free-flying colony at Edinburgh Zoo. Established since 1936, some wander away from time to time, though fortunately most do not stray more than a few miles, but occasionally they reach further afield like that seen in Wiltshire in late 1987.

The squacco heron is a small, short-legged heron with a bittern-like shape and posture, being brownish-buff above, paler beneath. More skulking than the other herons, its breeding range extends from southern Spain to the Caspian and the Persian Gulf and throughout much of Africa to which the European birds largely move in winter.

David Bannerman in *The Birds of the British Isles* Volume 6 says:

'There have been far too many records of the squacco arriving on our shores for there to be more than a general statement of the fact.'

This generous statement may have been true from when the first was taken, a bird in Wiltshire in 1775, up until 1957, a period during which 95 squacco herons were recorded in the British Isles, the majority in the nineteenth century. There have been but 25 since, so the trend is exactly opposite to that for the little egret (see pages 39–40) and the purple heron. These were the great prizes 70 or more years ago, but now both are seen annually, sometimes in numbers, so much so that the purple heron has been taken off the list of rare birds and classed as a scarce visitor.

In many years only single squacco herons are recorded, the four in 1979 being exceptional. The majority of those since 1957 have been between April and October with most in May and June, and virtually all in southwest counties. One reached Seaton Burn in June 1979, while the only recent Irish record is of one found dying in the grounds of Trinity College in October 1967, the first since 1919.

A small, stocky, predominantly white heron, the cattle egret has a short bill and legs and brown-buff plumes on the head and mantle (hence the alternative name buff-backed heron), though much of this colour and the plumes are lost during the winter. Cattle egrets habitually associate with grazing animals, obtaining much food — grasshoppers, crickets, and spiders — as a result of disturbance by the trampling herds.

One of the most remarkable extensions of range of any bird is that undergone by the cattle egret, probably to some extent aided as forests have been cleared in tropical regions to make way for large grazing pastures among other uses. Birds reached South America from Africa in 1880 and have gradually colonized several countries, one ornithologist sadly commenting about the lack of information surrounding this dramatic extension.

'The unhappy feeling remains that a wonderful event has occurred about which we know very little.'

A northward movement has continued ever since, first through the Caribbean, then into the United States in the 1950s and eventually to Canada — British Columbia and the North-west Territories in the west and Newfoundland in the east. In Europe the cattle egret is still restricted to Iberia and southern France, while elsewhere it breeds in a few localities in Central Asia, in India, south-east Asia, Indonesia east to New Guinea, and in Australia and New Zealand.

The first cattle egret in the British Isles was shot towards the end of 1805 at Kingsbridge, though over 100 years were to elapse before the next, a male on Breydon Marshes on 23 October 1917. Then there was a further gap until 1962 when four, possibly five, birds were seen at Pagham. Subsequent records have on occasions been suspected of including escapes. However, there seems no reason to suspect the majority of being anything other than genuine vagrants with a total of 50 accepted since the first. In most years the number seen is small, but 14 in 1986 was an exception so far not repeated. Most have occurred in southern and eastern counties with just one from Scotland, a bird at the Loch of Kinnordy in May 1979, with records from four counties in Wales and four in Ireland, where a total of five birds have been noted. One possible source of these western birds might well be the colonies along the east coast of North America between Newfoundland and Florida, for transatlantic vagrancy cannot be ruled out.

The little egret, a medium size slender white heron, in summer sports two long crest feathers, while the legs are black and the feet yellow. It breeds in a discontinuous range from southern Europe, through much of Africa, southern Asia to Japan and through Indonesia and parts of Australia.

The first little egret in the British Isles was obtained at Paull on the Humber Estuary in March 1826, to be followed by several others during the nineteenth century. For some reason scepticism was expressed over most records, the question of escapes being referred to, despite the fact that the squacco heron was a regular visitor at the time, even the American bittern, so that vagrancy by herons was accepted. None was recorded from 1879 until 1930 when one frequented the River Axe, while another on the Gann Estuary seen by H. Lloyd-Philipps, owner of Skokholm, in May 1938 was still thought likely to be an escape. By 1952 a total of 12 had been accepted, this number doubled between 1953 and 1955, while since 1957 447 little egrets have been recorded, a quite extraordinary change in fortune. This may well be the result of an expansion of range in Europe during the past 40 years or so, as it now nests in Holland and in northern France. Indeed one shot at Moulton Marsh in 1979 had been ringed earlier as a nestling from the first Dutch breeding record.

Little egrets are most widespread in spring, particularly in coastal counties from Norfolk to Cornwall, but with smaller numbers elsewhere, even as far north as Shetland, Outer Hebrides, and in Ireland. Fewer are seen in autumn, though even then birds are likely to occur anywhere. A helpful feature of the little egret is that of remaining at a site for long periods, even overwintering on some estuaries. Is this a bird which will breed in the British Isles in the not too distant future?

The snowy egret of America is almost impossible to separate in the field, even in breeding plumage, from the little egret. It is not unreasonable to suggest that it too might occasionally be recorded here, but identified as a little egret. Certainly little egrets have made transatlantic flights, birds having reached both Nantucket and Newfoundland, while others ringed in Spain have wandered to Martinique and Trinidad. Beware also of the western reef heron, a bird of the West African coast which has occurred several times in Europe, and the problems of identification of this species, or subspecies, as there is still controversy as to its true status.

The great white egret is a large, entirely white heron, which lacks the head plumes but has a longer neck and a slimmer build than the previous species with which it might be confused. The legs and feet are black, while at close quarters look for the dark line which extends behind the eye. Most cosmopolitan of any heron, the great white egret occurs in all continents save for Antarctica.

The first great white egret in the British Isles was shot at Hornsea Mere in the winter of 1821. There were just nine other records until the arrival of two birds in May/June 1974 which were seen at several localities from Poole Harbour to Scaling Dam Reservoir. Since then the great white egret has been almost annual in its appearance though never more than five in any one year. This change of status, as with the little egret, must be linked to an expansion of range in Europe, and in particular the colonization of the Netherlands, where a pair nested for the first time in 1978.

The widest distribution occurs in spring, with birds predominantly in eastern counties north to Shetland. Late summer/autumn records are largely restricted to counties from Yorkshire to Suffolk. In western Britain there are single records from Mull and Islay, Caerlaverock, Gronant, Minfford, Penmaenpool, St David's, and in Ireland at Moneygold. This then is one vagrant which has yet to make its mark in the far south-west of England.

The possibility that great white egrets cross the Atlantic to occur in the British Isles cannot lightly be dismissed. Autumn records must always be suspect, especially those in the west, but none more so than the bird which shared a drainage ditch with a green heron at Stone Creek in November 1982 (see page 48).

A handsome, largely all black bird with white underparts, the black stork is unlikely to be confused with any other species in the British Isles. A small outpost in Iberia with about 150 pairs is separated by some 1,500 miles (2,400 km) from a scattering of colonies in eastern Europe from where it extends across central Asia to the Sakhalin Peninsula and Korea. Another population resides in southern Africa.

The first black stork in the British Isles was a wounded bird captured on West Sedgemoor and which lived for over a year in the possession of George Montagu, a colourful army officer who compiled the first dictionary of birds. Just 25 more black storks were seen up to 1957, some 40 since, and almost annually since 1969, but only in small numbers, the eight in 1985 being the highest. Most occur between April and June with smaller numbers in late summer to October, the majority in eastern and southern counties though birds have reached both Orkney and Shetland. There are no records from Wales and just one from Ireland, a bird at Blackrock in August 1987.

Care must be taken to exclude from the record the occasional escape from wildlife collections. It is probable that the incidence of black storks in the British Isles will increase, as their numbers are rising in eastern Europe and it now breeds as close as Belgium.

A curlew-like bird in every sense other than the colour, the glossy ibis as befits its name has glossy chestnut upperparts, glossy green wings and tail. It has a stately walk, while in flight the wing-beats are more rapid than any heron of a similar size. It occupies a discontinuous range from south-east Europe to south-east Asia, also Australia, parts of Africa and the south-eastern United States.

The glossy ibis was a much more frequent visitor to the British Isles in the last century and the early part of this; indeed large parties were noted on several occasions, like the 20 or so at Sandwick in September 1907. Alas 10 were shot by wildfowlers, and a similar number at Cahore Point in October 1934. There has been a dramatic decline in the European population of the glossy ibis due to drainage of its breeding and feeding areas, and since 1957 only 51 have been recorded in the British Isles. Have some of these made transatlantic passages rather than coming from the south-east?

Most glossy ibis seen have been in coastal counties from Cornwall to Yorkshire, though single birds have reached north to Orkney, and west to Flint, and to Pembroke in Wales, and Cork and Galway in Ireland. No fewer than 17 of the total were during an 'invasion' in the autumn of 1986 when birds were seen in 10 counties. Several have made long stays, in particular those at Stodmarsh and nearby areas where individuals which arrived in 1975 and 1979 were reported until 1985, with one still present in 1988. Were these possibly escapes?

A favourite and well-known resident in waterfowl collections since at least the mid-nineteenth century, the ruddy shelduck is a large orange-chestnut bird with handsome black and white wing-patches visible in flight. Despite such features it can be confused with both the cape and the paradise shelduck, also frequent residents of waterfowl collections. It is now an extremely rare breeding bird in the far south-east of Europe, but numerous in Asia where its range extends east to western China and Mongolia. In addition there are small discrete populations in north-west Africa and Ethiopia, birds from the former wintering in southern Iberia.

Does the ruddy shelduck occur in the British Isles as a genuine vagrant? This is a question which only the recovery of a marked bird will throw light upon. The balance of probability is heavily weighted towards escapes, though some of those seen in the last century were almost certainly vagrants. The first in the British Isles was one killed near Blandford during the severe winter of 1776, and this together with some other early sightings was probably genuine. Likewise the parties of ruddy shelduck which have occurred, especially those in 1892 when severe droughts in south-east Europe made birds move westwards. Some were seen in many localities from Sule Skerry, one of the remotest of islands off northern Scotland, southwards, including a flock of no less than 30 at Durness in June that year, and also in Ireland. It must have been a massive emigration, for other birds reached Iceland and West Greenland. During the present century the only ones accepted as genuine are those which may have numbered as many as seven, at localities in Wexford and Dublin during the winter of 1945-6, when a remarkable number of glossy ibis were also recorded in Ireland.

One of the most handsome of ducks, the male Baikal teal has a superb head pattern of yellow, buff, black, and green, and a pink breast. Females can be confused with the females of several other species, though the head pattern is diagnostic. It breeds on rivers and lakes among the forests of north and east Siberia, moving to Japan, and eastern China for the winter.

In September 1954 a strange female teal was seen for several days at Hestigeo on Fair Isle. It was subsequently identified as a Baikal teal, but despite its extreme wildness, and the presence of other Siberian birds including the first citrine wagtail, lesser whitethroats of the Siberian race, an Arctic warbler, and scarlet rosefinches, while within a few days the Isle of May was to have the first Siberian thrush, some 26 years were to elapse before it was accepted to the British List. 'No duck has struggled harder to become accepted,' wrote one of the observers, D. I. M. Wallace, while another, Kenneth Williamson, then warden of Fair Isle, thought it doubtful if it 'will ever present better credentials to British ornithology'. The belated acceptance of this bird as a genuine vagrant, and as a result other early records from Essex in January 1906, Hampshire about 1915, Sussex in 1927, Norfolk in 1929, and Suffolk in 1951, finally placed this delightful duck firmly on the British List. The other more recent occurrences of the Baikal teal have been a female shot at Loch Spynie in 1958, one at Crom in 1967, one at Abberton Reservoir in November 1970, and finally the male which delighted birdwatchers at Caerlaverock from 19 February to 17 April 1973. When will we see another?

The scientific name of the harlequin duck *Histrionicus histrionicus* is a reference to the high-pitched squealing and whistling voice at its breeding grounds. It is a small stocky seaduck with a distinctive pointed tail, the male having white marks on the head and body, hence the English name. About 3,000 pairs nest as close to the British Isles as the fast-flowing rivers of Iceland. Elsewhere they breed in southern Greenland, eastern Canada from the Gulf of St Lawrence northwards and on the west side of the continent from Colorado to Alaska. They are widespread in eastern Siberia where those which occur in western Europe probably originate.

The first record of a harlequin duck in the British Isles was a male found dead on the shore at Filey in the autumn of 1862. There have been just 10 further sightings, all in Scotland, the most recent a female at Claggain Bay, Islay in October 1987, discovered by members of the Young Ornithologists Club from Edinburgh. What a delight for these junior birdwatchers, for unless there is some dramatic change in fortune the harlequin duck will remain one of our rarest waterfowl. What a memory to treasure.

The little crake is a small slender crake with a long neck, wings and tail, the upperparts being a pale olive-brown, the underparts of the male a blue-slate grey, in the female pale brown, while the bill is green with a reddish base. It breeds in freshwater wetlands from Poland eastwards into Central Asia, and also locally if somewhat sporadically in western Europe. It is known to be migratory, with probably most wintering in the Mediterranean basin and into Africa.

Such a small and skulking species may well be frequently overlooked. Some 67 were recorded from the first one in Sussex in 1791 up to 1957, the vast majority in England. The subsequent distribution of records has been much the same, 25 of the 31 since 1957 being in England, all but one south-east of the Humber–Severn line, mostly on spring and autumn passage. There are just two recent records from Scotland, one dead at Uyeasound, Unst in April 1959, and one killed by a cat on Fair Isle in May 1970. All four records from Ireland since 1957 have been at Cape Clear, while one at Llangennith Moors on the Gower Peninsula in January 1967 is the only recent record from Wales. Not all are skulking, a female little crake at Cuckmere Haven in March 1985 was confident enough to walk between the observers.

Despite the name of the previous species, Baillon's crake is even smaller, though with a much rounder build, almost like a ball, even in flight. The upperparts are a rich red-brown, the underparts blue-grey with black and white bars, the legs olive-brown, the bill green. Baillon's crake breeds locally in small numbers over much of Europe south of the Low Countries, though only becomes regular from the Dniester basin from where its range extends to China and Japan. It also breeds in southern Africa, Madagascar, parts of Australia, and throughout New Zealand.

Baillon's crake once nested in the British Isles, eggs being taken from two nests in Cambridgeshire in 1858, at Hickling in 1866, and Sutton Broad, both Norfolk in 1889. It might have been more frequent than these records suggest, for this is one of the most skulking of birds. Despite this many were collected in the British Isles, mainly from southern counties, though several reached Scotland and Ireland, during the nineteenth century. There have been far fewer records since, indeed since 1957 just five. Birds were seen at Guisborough in May 1965 and Fairburn Ings in June 1970, the same year one was caught by a cat at Fleckney but released unharmed. The next one was at Thatcham Marsh new Newbury in February 1972, and then one at Llantwit Major in February 1976. When and where would the next Baillon's crake be seen? Unless there was some upturn in its fortunes it hardly seemed likely this dainty marshland bird would again grace our bird reports. Yet in the spring of 1989, one was discovered in the most unlikely setting of a town park in Sunderland where it foraged along the stone surrounds of a pool quite unconcerned by the numerous onlookers. Such an event only confirms that where rare birds are concerned anything is possible.

The great black-headed gull is unmistakable in breeding plumage, though immatures can easily be confused with other large gulls, especially the great black-backed gull and herring gull. Note, however, the long head, bill and the long wings. The lakes and rivers from south-east Russia and across Central Asia to Mongolia are the breeding haunt of the great black-headed gull which winters largely on coasts from the Red Sea to the Bay of Bengal.

The five records of the great black-headed gull for the British Isles are all from southern England. The first was shot off Exmouth at the end of May or early June 1859, and was followed by birds at Telscombe in January 1910, Bournemouth in November 1924, Cromer in March 1932, and Hove in December the same year. By coincidence the two Sussex birds were both seen by H. Walpole-Bond, historian of the birds of that county, and once described as 'a magical field-finder of every inconspicuous little passerine that ever squeaked a confusing call-note, or hid its nest where none could come across it'.

The slender-billed gull is slightly larger than the familiar black-headed gull, with a bill up to a third longer, a feature which together with the flat-tened forehead, long neck and tail, gives a particularly striking profile, while in flight it adopts an almost hump-backed appearance. Its breeding range is a curious discontinuous one from Mauretania on the west coast of Africa, through the Mediterranean, Black, and Caspian Seas, the lower basin of the Euphrates and Tigris and so into Central Asia. There is some movement south in winter with birds reaching into the Persian Gulf and Red Sea.

A slender-billed gull was discovered in mid-June 1960 at a sewage outfall at Langley Point, where it remained for almost a month. Just four subse-quent records have been added, an immature at Rye Harbour in April 1963, and adults at Dungeness and Minsmere in the summer of 1971. Then per-haps most remarkable of all, two birds, probably a pair, at Cley and Blakeney in May 1987. This must have sent a few hearts fluttering with thoughts as to whether they might breed. Is this a portent of things to come?

The gull-billed tern is a little smaller than the Sandwich tern with which it is often confused, but with a stockier build and having a gull-like bill. It does not plunge-dive so frequently as other terns, preferring to take surface food from shallow water or coastal flats. One at Titchwell in July 1980 rather outstayed its welcome, for over a three-week residence it robbed both little and common terns of eggs and chicks. The gull-billed tern is a cosmopolitan species, breeding in North and Central America, Europe, southern Asia, Africa and Australia.

Some 53 gull-billed terns were recorded in the British Isles up to 1957 since the first were obtained in Sussex at the beginning of the nineteenth century. The most remarkable of this series was the pair which nested at Abberton Reservoir in 1949 and 1950 when water-levels were such as to attract several species of duck and wader, black-headed gulls, common, and also little terns to nest. Since 1957 some 183 records of gull-billed terns have been accepted, all between March and November and in every year since 1970. Annual totals vary, usually less than eight, but there were 12 in 1967 and 1974, 11 in 1982 including no fewer than seven off Beachy Head on 13 May, and nine in 1987. Most are seen in south-eastern counties, espe-cially in spring, with a wider distribution in late summer when there are more records further afield including the only three from Ireland, birds at Ballyconneely in 1969, the Roe Estuary 1982 and the Bridges of Ross, one of Ireland's premier seawatching points, in 1984.

The largest tern, a massive tern in every sense, the Caspian tern is strongly built and almost the size of a herring gull. The bill, a bright vermil-ion is tipped black in non-breeding and immature plumages. Despite its size the Caspian tern has a graceful, almost gull-like flight with slow, deliberate wing-beats on broad rather blunt wings while the tail is only forked for about a quarter of its length. The Caspian tern breeds in increasing num-bers around the Baltic, and this may explain the greater frequency of records for the British Isles in recent years. Elsewhere there are scattered colonies in North America, across Central Asia to the coast of China, in Africa, and Madagascar, Australia, and New Zealand. Birds from Europe mostly winter in central and west Africa.

Up to 1958 some 30 records of the Caspian tern had been accepted for the British Isles, including one found dead at Whitby in August 1939 which had been ringed 12 years previously at Shoe Island on Lake Michigan, United States. There have indeed been two other interesting recoveries. The remains of one at a fox earth at Haddon in July 1972 were of a bird ringed at Li Oulu, Finland, in 1970, while one dead on the shore of Yell in 1976 had been ringed the previous year near Stockholm.

Since 1957 163 Caspian terns have been reported, of annual occurrence save for 1963 and 1983. Records extend from mid-April to October, though most are in mid to late summer, presumably birds wandering at the end of the breeding season. In most years up to eight birds are seen, but in 1988 the number was 19. There could have been more, but there were several instances of birds possibly moving from one inland water to another, causing much joy for watchers but despair for bird report editors and statisticians. English Channel counties and the east coast to Yorkshire are the favoured areas, though there are many inland records when birds have frequented large gravel pits, lakes and reservoirs. There are 15 records from Scotland, four from Wales and just two from Ireland.

The whiskered tern, largest of the marsh terns, is distinctive in breeding plumage with its dark red dagger bill, black cap, white cheeks and slate-grey underparts. In all plumages care must be taken to avoid confusion with species like the Arctic and common terns, when note should be taken especially of the extremely narrow fork to the tail. It breeds in southern Europe and across parts of southern Asia to India, and Australia and also in southern Africa. Most move closer to equatorial regions for the winter.

The first whiskered tern in the British Isles was one at Lyme in August 1836, with a further 19 to 1957. Since then a further 83 have been accepted, with records in 23 out of the past 30 years. Annual totals are generally small, but exceptions were nine in 1970, eight in 1983 and 10 in 1988. The majority are seen from April to June, probably birds which overshot on northward migration. Smaller numbers occur to September with exceptional records of one in Norfolk in late October, and in mid-November at Nimmo's Pier which remained over winter.

Most whiskered terns are reported from the southern counties of England and Wales with six from Ireland, but there are so far no modern sightings from Scotland where the only record is of one in Nithsdale a century ago. The furthest north in recent years have been two in Northumberland and one in Cumberland. Many of the records are of birds inland on reservoirs, gravel pits and lakes, while the coastal records are largely from lagoons and estuaries. The presence of first summer birds in spring in recent years has raised comment, as they should have remained in African winter quarters. Have the drought conditions there caused a change in habits, or are they here prospecting for new breeding areas?

The white-winged black tern is a dumpy bird with a tiny bill, short, rather rounded wings and a short, barely forked tail. In summer plumage it is unmistakable being black save for white wing-panels but not so easy to distinguish out of the breeding season. It breeds from south-east Europe, though occasionally elsewhere in the south, across Central Asia to southern China, with southward movements in winter to central Africa, south-east Asia, and northern Australia.

One of the most numerous of all the rare visitors to the British Isles, the first white-winged black tern was shot in Dublin Bay in October 1841. There have been some 49 subsequent records up to 1957, with the massive total of 508 since, occurrences now being annual. Unless there is some diminution in the number of records its status will shortly change from that of a rare visitor to a scarce migrant. Save for an exceptional record from Carmarthenshire in early March 1958, the records span from late April until early November. By far the majority, two-thirds or so, occur in August and September, so that wandering post-breeding season birds rather than northward-moving spring migrants form the majority of visitors. Numbers do, however, seem to have declined in the 1980s compared with annual totals of up to 30 in several of the previous 15 years. Estuaries, coastal lagoons, reservoirs, lakes, gravel pits, indeed any area of open water is likely to be visited, and there is hardly a county in England without a record, mostly in the south and south-east. Smaller numbers occur in Wales and Ireland and even in Scotland birds have reached Shetland, Orkney and the Outer Hebrides.

North American Waterbirds

Pied-billed Grebe	Lesser Scaup	Sandhill Crane
Double-crested	Surf Scoter	Laughing Gull
Cormorant	Bufflehead	Franklin's Gull
American Bittern	Barrow's Goldeneye	Bonaparte's Gull
Green Heron	Hooded Merganser	Forster's Tern
American Wigeon	Sora Rail	Least Tern
Black Duck	American Purple	
Blue-winged Teal	Gallinule	
Ring-necked Duck	American Coot	

A small stocky grebe, the adult pied-billed grebe is unmistakable, but requires much more care in non-breeding or immature plumages when it can be mistaken for the slightly smaller little grebe. Add to this its often skulking nature and this is a bird easily overlooked. It breeds widely from southern Canada to Argentina and Chile, those from the northern parts of the range moving south in winter.

An old record of a pied-billed grebe killed near Weymouth in January 1881 was not accepted at the time, so improbable seemed the occurrence of such a bird this side of the Atlantic. In December 1963 such doubts were finally quashed when a first winter bird was found swimming with coot and several species of duck in a pool amongst the ice on Blagdon Lake. Some two weeks were to elapse before the fortunate observers, one of whom even managed to film the bird, were able to confirm its identification.

Since then 12 others have been seen, an interesting characteristic being that several stayed for long periods or returned in successive years, like the first which was subsequently seen discontinuously at Blagdon, or nearby Chew Valley, from 1965 to 1968. Another spent from 1983 to 1985 on Loch na Liana Moire, one of the smaller of the numerous lochs along the western seaboard of South Uist. More recently one at Kenfig Pool from January to March 1987 returned in October to overwinter. Other counties where pied-billed grebes have been reported are Aberdeen, Caernarvon, Donegal, Dorset, Dumfries, Kircudbright, Norfolk, Wexford, and York. At least one ship-assisted passage is known; a pied-billed grebe which came on board the Shell tanker *Ondina* three days out from Venezuela in the summer of 1965, died shortly after arriving at Liverpool.

The double-crested cormorant is noticeably smaller than the cormorant with which it may nevertheless be confused in all but adult breeding plumage. It is the most numerous of the North American cormorants, being found inland on many lakes and rivers, and on the coast from the Aleutians and Newfoundland south to Baja California, Florida, and Cuba.

There is just one record of the double-crested cormorant from the Western Palearctic when there was a bird at Charlton's Pool in the midst of industrial Billingham from about 8 December 1988, although it was not positively identified until mid-January. It remained there somewhat intermittently until late April. One remarkable ship-assisted visitor, a double-crested cormorant found in the hold of a cargo-ship, just arrived in Glasgow from Newfoundland in December 1963.

The American bittern is a stocky brown bird, slightly smaller than the bittern, from which it may be told by its chestnut or grey crown, prominent black mark down the side of the neck and black flight feathers. It breeds in freshwater and brackish marshes over much of North America from Hudson's Bay and the Great Salt Lake south to the central United States, Many move to the West Indies and Central America in winter.

The first American bittern in the British Isles was killed at Puddletown in 1804 and distinguished as a new species by Montagu. Most of the subsequent records, indeed nearly 50, were before 1914, since when rather few have been seen, with only eight since 1962, a change in occurrence which cannot be explained. Has it declined in North America, or altered its migration pattern? Two of the more recent sightings have been of birds which delighted many observers by remaining for some weeks. One at the Magor Reserve of the Gwent Wildlife Trust from 29 October 1981 to the following January was seen by numerous birdwatchers and at the same time helped raise funds for the Trust. Another was at Kilmalcolm from 4 November 1981 until early January. Both moved on, or possibly died with the onset of bad weather. Indeed two of the others since 1957 have been found dying, those on Bardsey in September 1962 and at Malahide in October 1970, while one was shot at Loch Corrib in December 1964, and another alas at Tincleton in November 1980. The other records are of birds at Marazion in September 1977 and Malin Beg in October 1973.

The green heron, a small, large-billed heron, with a wide range of plumage variations breeds from the Great Lakes to Panama while about 26 other races — there is some dispute as to the precise number — occur in South America, Africa, India, over much of southern Asia, parts of Australia, and on island archipelagos in the Indian, and Pacific Oceans. That from North America seems the most likely to occur in the British Isles and has a black crown with crest, dark blue-green underparts with deep chestnut cheeks and neck, and a grey-brown underside.

Just three green heron have been recorded. The first was shot in October 1889 by the gamekeeper to Sir Charles Sawle, Bt, at Penrice. Although identified at the time by the Reverend Murray Mathew, chronicler of birds in both Devon and Pembroke, where he retired for the woodcock shooting, seen at the British Museum, and eventually deposited in the County Museum at Truro, the record was never accepted. Not until the occurrence was re-investigated in 1971 was the green heron finally admitted to the British List. Subsequently one was seen at Stone Creek during the latter part of November 1982 where it shared a ditch, much to the delight of birdwatchers, with a great white egret (see page 40). Lastly one was found freshly dead, possibly the victim of a fox, at Tyninghame in October 1987.

The male American wigeon has a distinctive grey head with a glossy green patch and white forehead, a pinkish-brown body, white beneath. Females are rufous and unstreaked. It breeds from Alaska to Nova Scotia and south into California, Nevada, Colorado, and Nebraska. Winter quarters are mainly along the Atlantic coasts of the United States into the Gulf of Mexico, and in central America.

An American wigeon in a London market in 1837 and another at a Leeds game-stall in 1895 are the earliest records for the British Isles, while the first live bird seen also had a similar destination, for it too was shot in January 1907 on Benbecula. There have been a further 19 records to 1957 and 177 since, with occurrences annually since 1970. There is always doubt as to the origin of some birds; they may be escapes, for the American wigeon is regularly kept in waterfowl collections. However, the majority are clearly genuine vagrants, and although recorded in every month there is a definite peak in the autumn. Annual numbers vary, the peak year being 1968 with 18 birds, but mostly less than 10 are seen. Kerry and Cornwall are the two most likely counties to encounter American wigeon in autumn, while in spring the former county and Shetland are the places, though there are few counties in the British Isles which have not had at least one record. Pairs were seen on Loch Leven in May 1977, and at Uyeasound, Unst, in June 1983.

Most interesting have been the recoveries of ringed American wigeon, birds from New Brunswick, Canada, in 1965, 1968 and 1986, the 1968 one being shot from a party of 13 in Kerry. One near Tuam in October 1977 had been ringed the previous year on Prince Edward Island, Canada.

Although darker and heavier-built, both sexes of the black duck may be confused with the female mallard. The male is especially dark while both have a pale grey-brown head and silvery white underwings. It is a wary and much sought-after sporting duck which breeds in North America from northern Manitoba to North Carolina. Some move south in winter to Florida and the Gulf of Mexico.

An astute observer in Februry 1954 saw in Flanagan's poulterer's in Waterford a duck labelled as a mallard shot near Mullinavat. Recognizing it as something different he endeavoured to purchase the duck but found it was already sold. Fortunately the owner was quite happy to eat mallard instead and what was subsequently found to be a black duck passed to the National Museum of Ireland. The next was seen at one of Europe's great wildfowl sites, the North Slob, in February 1961, to be followed by one at Yantlet Creek in March 1967. There have been 12 further records, birds in Caernarvon, Cornwall, Dublin, East Lothian, Inverness, Renfrew, Scilly, and York.

Records of rare duck are open to confusion. There is as always the chance of escapes from waterfowl collections, while in the case of the black duck some individuals have taken up residence for long periods and even mated successfully with local mallard and produced hybrid offspring. A female on Tresco was most prolific. First seen in 1976 she was at least seven years old when she disappeared in 1984 and had reared no fewer than 22 young. A male black duck at Aber from February 1979 to January 1985 also produced hybrid young and likewise much consternation among bird-watchers.

The blue-winged teal is a garganey-like dabbling duck, males having a purple-grey head with pronounced white face crescent. Females can cause much confusion with both the cinnamon teal, an escape in Europe, the teal and even a dull juvenile garganey. It breeds across much of North America from the Great Slave Lake south to California and North Carolina. It migrates to the Gulf of Mexico, Central America and as far south as Peru and Brazil for the winter.

The first blue-winged teal, a female, was shot near Dumfries in 1858, with a further 19 recorded until 1957. Seen annually since 1966, the total since 1957 now stands at 131, with records in all months save for July. The majority occur from late August until the end of October with a smaller peak from April to June, with birds likely to be encountered throughout the British Isles. Pairs at Lough Funshinagh in May 1984 and Loch Hallan, South Uist, in June the same year raised interesting possibilities, while a female mated with a shoveler on North Uist in 1979. An immature shot on the River Debden in October 1971 had been ringed four months previously at Sackville in New Brunswick, Canada, while one shot in Offaly in January 1984 had been ringed the previous September in Newfoundland.

At a quick glance the ring-necked duck might easily be overlooked among a flock of tufted duck, and perhaps this happened before its occurrence here was appreciated. The triangular head, absence of a crest, the bands on the bill and white peak on the flanks are diagnostic, while the neck ring, despite the bird's name is somewhat inconspicuous. Females which have the bill ring are best identified by the white spectacle and a white patch at the base of the bill. It breeds from British Columbia to Labrador, and south to Washington, Michigan and southern Maine. Winter quarters are in the southern United States, West Indies, and Central America south to Venezuela.

For some reason now unknown, the first ring-necked duck, a male described by Donovan as the type specimen, was never accepted. Taken in 1801 in Lincolnshire and found on a stall in Leadenhall Market, London, these seem quite impeccable references. What other gems were eaten over the years and failed to make history? Not until March 1955 was another seen, a male which caused great excitement among staff at the Wildfowl Trust, Slimbridge, though it only remained two days. Those who were privileged to witness this event little guessed that 20 years later the ring-necked duck would be an annual visitor to the British Isles with a total of 237 birds seen by 1988. Most have occurred between October and May with up to 20 in several years, particularly in the late 1970s, and there are few counties in the British Isles without at least one record, though there is a preponderance in south-west Britain and southern Ireland. Some have returned again and again to chosen waters, one at Lurgan being recorded in no fewer than nine consecutive years. The majority of those seen are males, but females and also males in eclipse plumage are now located more frequently, while a pair was present at Soulseat in late February 1980.

Another interesting occurrence was a bird which had been ringed at Slimbridge in March 1979 and recovered in Greenland the same year. Was it returning to its summer haunts? The exasperation for those who keep track of records and those who write about them was aptly summarized in the *Rare Birds in Great Britain Report* for 1986 with the reference to 'an extremely complicated web of apparently returning and moving individuals'. Clearly the ring-necked duck is established as a regular visitor to the British Isles. Will it one day remain to breed?

The lesser scaup, one of the most difficult of all waterfowl to identify, closely resembles the slightly larger scaup, or as some would prefer, the great scaup. The head shape is, however, distinctive, a high rather than a rounded crown. Also look for the smaller bill. An abundant breeding bird from Alaska and the North West Territories to the northern United States, most winter on the coast south to Central America and the Caribbean as far as northern Columbia.

Difficulties of identification, together with the possibility of confusion with tufted duck–pochard hybrids, means the lesser scaup may well have been overlooked, unless it is really as scarce as the two solitary records suggest. A first-winter male was recorded at Chasewater from 8 March to 26 April 1987, and a male at Corbet Lough and Hillsborough Park Lake in February and March 1988.

The largest of the scoters, the male surf scoter has an all-black plumage broken only by white head patches and a massive, brightly coloured bill. The female also has the massive bill, but largely a black-brown plumage. It breeds on lakes and ponds across northern Canada and in Alaska close to the tree limit, wintering on coasts south to Baja California and North Carolina.

The first surf scoter in the British Isles was obtained in 1838 with no fewer than 74 others recorded up to 1957 and 243 subsequently. Thus it always seems to have been a regular visitor, more observers and superb optical aids confirming the observations and specimens collected previously. Most occur in shallow coastal waters, often where flocks of common scoter and other seaduck gather. There are records from every month with most from October to April. The annual totals have increased to over 20 in each year since 1983, with 35 in 1984 being the highest so far. Some birds are thought to return in subsequent years.

Most coastal counties in the British Isles now have at least one record of a surf scoter, though the majority are seen in Scotland and Ireland. There are three inland records, single birds at Loch Insh on 14 October 1978, at Hemingford Gray on 5 June 1983, and at Draycote Water on 26 October 1986. Although most occur singly there are increasing instances of small parties, like those of seven and nine in Spey Bay in 1978 and 1979 respectively, and the five males and two females at Ballinester early in 1984.

One of the smallest ducks to occur in the British Isles, the bufflehead, is so named, because the shape of the largely white head of the male resembles that of a bull bison. It breeds across much of central and north-west North America from Alaska to Ontario, moving to coastal areas in winter south to Mexico and Florida.

The first bufflehead in the British Isles was shot near Yarmouth during the winter of 1830, followed by a male caught at Bridlington in 1864, one on South Uist in 1870, a female at Tresco in 1920, at Hunstanton in February 1932, and the only inland record one which remained on Foxcote Reservoir for several days from the end of February 1961. Finally there was a second record from South Uist, where there was a male on West Loch Bee in mid-March 1980.

Barrow's goldeneye was named after John Barrow, Second Secretary to the Admiralty for over 40 years, who devoted so much of his energies to promoting Arctic exploration. This is another duck where the head shape is significant, being best described as a flat-crowned, bulbous oval, black-glossed purple in colour, and with a crescent–shaped white face-patch. It breeds in four widely separated areas; in north-east Iceland where there are probably no more than 800 pairs, south-west Greenland, eastern Labrador, and from southern Alaska to California and Wyoming. Most winter on coasts immediately south of the breeding areas, though the Icelandic population seems largely resident.

Barrow's goldeneye in the British Isles presents a problem, and so far just one record is accepted, and that only into Category D where the possibility of origin as an escape cannot be ruled out. The bird in question was a male seen off Irvine on the Clyde coast of Ayrshire in November and December 1982. Two males were shot at Scalloway on 18 March 1913, but for some reason seem to have escaped inclusion even in Category D.

The hooded merganser is much smaller than either the goosander or the red-breasted merganser. The head pattern of the male resembles that of the bufflehead, but note the white breast with two black lines, and the orange flanks. Females are a dull grey-brown and sport a considerable bushy crest. The bill is slender, while the tail, another conspicuous feature, is cocked above the water as the bird swims. It breeds from Alaska to Montana and Oregon and over much of south-east Canada and the eastern United States. Most winter on the coast, usually south of the breeding areas with some reaching the Gulf of California and Mexico.

The first hooded merganser in the British Isles was a first-winter male obtained on the Menai Straits in the winter of 1830-31. This was followed by three from Ireland, a pair which frequented a creek in Cobh Harbour in severe weather, December 1872, and a female, also during hard weather, on the Shannon estuary in January 1881. A male shot in Whale Firth, Yell, in July 1884 has never been accepted, and certainly the date seems out of place. Nearly 80 years elapsed before the next, also in Ireland, a female or immature male at Acton Lake. Just one further record, a female at Willen Lake at the end of December 1983.

The Sora rail resembles the slightly larger spotted crake, and although the differences sound distinctive in print great caution must be exercised in the field, especially when encountering immature birds. The Sora rail lacks the white spotting on the head, neck, throat, and breast, while the black facial mask, especially in adults, is noticeable. The broad-based almost triangular bill is yellow and lacks any red markings. Sora rails breed from southern Canada to the central United States, moving south to winter in Central America, the Caribbean, and northern South America. During autumn migration they are frequently blown eastwards and on occasions arrive in large numbers in Bermuda.

The first Sora rail in the British Isles was shot near Newbury in October 1864 and exhibited at the Zoological Society the following February. There are a further 10 records, the first of which was a bird caught alive at Cardiff in the spring of 1888, to be followed by birds at Tiree, Inner Hebrides in October 1901, at Ness, Lewis, in November 1913, and the only other spring record, one killed when it struck the lantern of Slyne Head

Lighthouse in April 1920. Rather interesting was one about the same time, 100 miles (160 km) west of Ireland and not included in the British List, captured on board HMS *Dragon*, a cruiser, fourteenth and last to bear this name, in a line extending back to the reign of Henry VIII. The next was at St Agnes in late September 1973, then there were birds at Bardsey in August 1981, which trapped itself, St Mary's in September, and Foula in October 1982, Tresco in October 1983, and a particularly long-staying individual at Pagham Lagoon from 26 October to 24 December 1985.

About the size of the moorhen, the American gallinule in adult plumage is a brilliant purple with an irridescent green back and wings and with a white undertail. The bill is red with a broad yellow tip and a white frontal shield. Juveniles lack these bright colours save for the white undertail. It breeds from the southern United States south to Bolivia and Argentina. Although largely resident in the tropics, birds from the extremes of the range are highly migratory despite their weak-winged appearance. There are regular records of vagrants in the southern hemisphere from Tristan da Cunha with some even reaching southern Africa.

A single occurrence of the American purple gallinule in the British Isles was a juvenile on 7 November 1958 found in an emaciated condition in a gutter in Hugh Town, St Mary's. It later died and the skin is now in the British Museum. There are only two other European records, birds in Norway in 1883 and Switzerland in 1967.

The American coot is smaller than the coot, but rather similar, with a slate-black plumage, slightly paler beneath, and with white under-tail coverts. The white bill has a bar near the tip and there is only a small white facial shield. Beware of hybrids between coot and moorhen, though bill and shield colour and a lack of white in the wings should be noted and confusion avoided. It breeds on freshwater from Canada south to the central Andes, and also in Hawaii, and winters mainly on the coast, birds from northern areas reaching the Caribbean and Panama.

There are just four records of the American coot from the Western Palearctic. Birds in Iceland in 1969 and 1971 and in the Azores in October of the latter year, this one ringed in Ontario at the end of August. A single record for the British Isles is a first-winter male discovered at Ballycotton on 7 February 1981, which remained until 3 April. Large numbers of bird-watchers were attracted to Ireland once word of its residence spread, though to call any rare vagrant 'boring', as one journal did, is quite outrageous!

Almost as large as the common crane, the sandhill crane has a slimmer build and narrower wings. The plumage is mainly pale brownish grey with a whitish throat and cheeks, and red on the crown which extends to the bill. It breeds on wet tundras, marshes and deltas and on the edge of lakes in north-east Siberia and from Alaska and Arctic Canada south to Florida and Cuba. Northern birds are highly migratory, many fly at great heights, with parties seen over Mount McKinley at 18,000 ft (6,000 m). These would be travelling to winter quarters in the southern United States and in Mexico.

There are just two records of the sandhill crane for the British Isles. One spent several days in September 1905 near Castlefreke until shot. The second briefly visited Fair Isle for two days in late April 1981. It arrived during a snowstorm on 26 April and was so nervous it circled the island for some hours before landing, thus allowing the somewhat incredulous residents of the Bird Observatory good views. Frightened by the island plane the following morning it quickly departed northwards. There is only one other European record, a bird at Akrabergi in the Faroe Islands in October 1980 subsequently found dead.

Although gulls in many plumages can cause problems for the observer, the laughing gull should only be confused with Franklin's gull. In size the laughing gull is between the black-headed and common gull with long wings with a white trailing edge, and a long, almost drooping bill. The call, as the name suggests is a laughing but strident 'ha-ha-ha-ha'. A largely coastal species breeding from Nova Scotia and southern California to Venezuela, some overwinter in the north but most move south to Peru and Brazil.

The first record of the laughing gull in the British Isles was an adult on a pool near the Crumbles in early June 1923. It was seen and described by Robert Morris, an assiduous diarist for nearly 60 years from 1880. Only after his death did the record come to light, but so excellent was his description, supported by sketches, that there was no hesitation in accepting the record in 1967. This was a double disappointment, however, for two observers who previously had thought their record of a laughing gull at Dungeness in May 1966 to have been the first, for this was also superseded by a belated acceptance of an earlier record, one at Abberton Reservoir in December 1957. Since 1966 a further 50 laughing gulls have been seen, with birds in every month save for March, though with no real pattern having emerged as to their arrival on this side of the Atlantic. Laughing gulls have now been recorded from 26 counties from Shetland to Scilly, Clare to Suffolk. Like other gulls a number have stayed for long periods, or like one which arrived in first-winter plumage at South Shields in January 1984, returned in subsequent years.

It is good to see that the Arctic explorer Sir John Franklin, during whose expeditions so many scientific discoveries were made, has been commemorated by a bird's name. Franklin's gull was shot on the Saskatchewan River in 1827. It is slightly smaller than a black-headed gull, with a short bill and legs, this combined with the rounded head and body gives an almost pigeon–like appearance. The distinct wing-pattern and grey tail centre of the adult are other key features, while as always immature plumages are less distinctive. It breeds on freshwater lakes across central North America, moving south in winter to the shores of Peru and Chile. Few seem to occur on the east coast of North America.

The first Franklin's gull in the British Isles, an adult, was discovered at Farlington Marshes on 21 February 1970, where it remained until 16 May. Six weeks later another adult — or was it the same one? — was located some 55 miles (88 km) to the east at Arlington Reservoir. A further 13 have subsequently been seen, too few for any pattern to be discernible and all widely dispersed from South Uist to Plymouth, but so far none from Wales or from Ireland.

Bonaparte's gull is rather like a small black-headed gull, but in all plumages shows a white underside to the wings, while the legs are orange, and the slender bill is black. It has a rapid, almost tern-like flight, and indeed its repertoire of calls includes a tern-like 'tee-r'. It breeds in scrub and on the stumps and low branches of trees in swamps and beside lakes from Alaska to Hudson Bay, moving south to the coasts of Central America and the West Indies for the winter.

The first Bonaparte's gull in the British Isles was shot on the River Lagan near Belfast on 1 February 1848, with another on Loch Lomond two years later. A further nine were seen up to 1957 though the total does not include one seen at Newtown in August 1948 by David Bannerman and his wife, for in his own words 'In those days I had little use for records where the bird had not been handled'. Since 1958 51 Bonaparte's gulls have been seen in the British Isles and it is now almost annual in these islands and likely to be discovered at almost any time of year, and with records from 22 counties, almost anywhere around the coast or on reservoirs. Cornwall seems the most promising place to look for this delightful gull.

Forster's tern is a little larger than the common tern, and although having shorter wings it has a distinctly larger bill, longer legs, and a tail grey with white sides. In winter and in immature plumage there is a striking black mask through the eye. A marshland species during the breeding season when its range extends south from the prairie provinces of Canada to California and Texas, most winter in Central America and the West Indies.

The first Forster's tern in the British Isles was a bird discovered at Falmouth in late January 1980 and which remained there for nearly two months. Since 1982 it has occurred annually save for 1988, with records in every month except April to June, with three the most in any one year. The situation is a little confusing as in addition to long-staying birds there have undoubtedly been movements between localities and also returning birds, but suffice to say the total of individuals accepted is now 16. Save for records from East Lothian and Kent all the sightings have been from west coast counties, Cornwall, Somerset, Anglesey, Caernarvon, Flint, and Lancashire. In Ireland four, possibly as many as seven, individuals have been recorded from Louth, Dublin, Wicklow, Wexford, Waterford, Londonderry, and Down.

Depending upon which authority you consult, the least tern may be classed as a separate species, or one of several races of the little tern, from which it differs in having a grey rump and tail, and a distinctive call. It breeds on the coasts of the United States and in the Caribbean, wintering south to Brazil.

In the summer of 1983 a least tern was discovered amongst little terns at the Rye Harbour Nature Reserve. Its voice among the shrill grating calls of the little terns meant it was easily located during its sporadic visits which have continued each summer up to 1990. Where does it go when not in Rye Harbour? So far this is the only record for the Western Palearctic, and again emphasizes the value of patient observation. How many other such occurrences remain unnoticed?

Birds of Prey

Black Kite	Red-tailed Hawk	Eleonora's Falcon
Swallow-tailed Kite	Red-shouldered	Saker Falcon
White-tailed Eagle	Hawk	Scops Owl
Bald Eagle	Spotted Eagle	Eagle Owl
Egyptian Vulture	Lesser Kestrel	Hawk Owl
Griffon Vulture	American Kestrel	Tengmalm's Owl
Pallid Harrier	Red-footed Falcon	

The black kite although shorter in length than the red kite is more heavily built with a broader tail, notched rather than forked. Its plumage is a dingy, rather dark brown, slightly greyish on the head. A pale bar is visible on the upperwing in flight. Care, however, must be taken to avoid confusion with the red kite, and both female and immature marsh harriers. An extremely widespread species throughout the Old World, the black kite occurs over much of Europe south of Scandinavia, east across central and southern Asia, in Australia, and over Africa, largely south of the Sahara. It is a bird which will be known to many travellers in ports and cities for it often feeds in close proximity to man, foraging on rubbish tips and along waterways. Birds from much of Europe move into Africa south of the Sahara for the winter.

The first black kite in the British Isles was a male trapped in the deer park at Alnwick in the spring of 1866, the next, also a male, was shot in Aberdeen on 16 April 1901, and was followed by two in Scilly, in September 1938 and May 1942, and then another in Northumberland, in May 1947. The next was one at Tresco on 23 April 1966 in a spring in which birds also occurred in Shetland, Orkney and Norfolk. From that year the fortunes of the black kite have changed in the British Isles, for unlike some other rare raptors in Europe its population is expanding. This is at least partly the result of more food being available, though alas this sometimes takes the form of fish killed during pollution incidents.

Since 1966 a further 108 black kites have been seen in the British Isles, the only blank years since then being 1967, 1969 and 1973. Annual totals have tended to increase with the highest being 13 in 1986, 10 in 1987 and 11 in 1988. Most occur between April and June with smaller numbers in the autumn. The majority are from eastern counties from Norfolk to Sussex, but in spring especially the black kite is likely to be seen anywhere in southern England. Records from further afield include birds in Merioneth, Isle of Man, the Outer Hebrides, where one reached North Rona at the end of

June 1976, and Wicklow and Armagh in Ireland.

Does the increasing number of black kites now recorded in the British Isles hint that birds may one day remain to nest? It would be nice to have an additional raptor in our breeding avifauna, but a word of caution: most seem to pass quickly on, few stay in a locality for more than a day. If you want to see a black kite discover it yourself, or move very quickly if you hear that one has arrived.

The swallow-tailed kite is one of the most graceful of all raptors, a striking black and white bird with a conspicuous 'swallow' tail. It is a bird of swamps and marshes, river banks and lakes in the south-east United States, though it was formerly widespread much further to the north. Although not accepted on the British List we should not lose sight of several early records. Indeed the first, a bird caught alive in Shaw Gill, Wensleydale during a thunderstorm on 6 September 1805, the year of Trafalgar, was at one time considered acceptable. Certainly the date seems suitable for an Atlantic crossing. The others were birds on the River Mersey in June 1843, Eskdale in April 1853, Helmsley on 25 May 1859 and at Glaisdale the same year. Old records they may be, but certainly worthy of more than passing note.

A large, almost vulture-like eagle, the white-tailed eagle has huge broad wings, a short wedge-shaped tail and a large generally pale head, the rest of the plumage being a warm brown. It breeds in parts of Greenland and Iceland, and from there across much of northern Europe and Asia with some movement south from these areas in winter.

At one time it was a widespread bird breeding in both Scotland and Ireland, but persecution meant its demise in Ireland about 1900 and in Scotland, where the last pair nested in Skye, in 1916. A reintroduction programme commenced on Fair Isle in 1968 proved unsuccessful and was followed by one on Rhum, Inner Hebrides by the Nature Conservancy Council since 1975. By 1987 no fewer than six pairs had become established in the west of Scotland and two successfully reared three young. Learning from the experience in Scotland, an attempt may shortly be made to re-establish the white-tailed eagle in Ireland, most probably in Kerry.

The possibility of wandering white-tailed eagles from the west of Scotland casts doubt on some of the records. Are they really genuine migrants, or descendants of the introduced stock, and if these wander why exclude them from the totals? However, 16 have been accepted since 1957, with birds being seen annually since 1982 save for 1987. Eastern England from Durham to Sussex is where most have been reported. A first-year bird found shot near Wells in May 1984 had been ringed the previous year in Schleswig-Holstein, West Germany. One which spent about nine days in the vicinity of the Sizewell power station in January 1982 attracted large numbers of birdwatchers, causing comments to be made that the gathering looked more like an anti-nuclear demonstration than a birdwatching expedition. Just two elsewhere in England, at Nare Head during the last two weeks of December 1973, and, the only inland record, one at Brill which remained from 22 November 1983 until the following February. There were also three in Ireland, one being shot at Garrison in 1973, another in Wicklow at the end of July 1978, a somewhat surprising date, while the third remained in various localities in west Kerry from December 1978 to April 1980. As the Scottish breeding stock increases so will the incidence of birds further south, as they make their way to and from winter quarters in southern Europe.

One of the greatest surprises among the rare visitors to the British Isles must be the bald eagle, national bird of the United States of America. It is best distinguished from the white–tailed eagle by the white head and neck (hence the name) in the adult, but juveniles are much more difficult to separate. The bald eagle breeds over much of North America, wintering along the Pacific coast and in the central and eastern United States where it seeks much of its fish food on the larger rivers and lakes. Northern birds move south in winter with some reaching Mexico.

An adult bald eagle seen at Llyn Coron by two observers on 17 October 1978 was the first on the eastern side of the Atlantic. The observers were incredulous, but almost as incredible is the way such a bird can disappear, never to be located again. Where did it vanish to? The second record was of a juvenile on Castle Island in November 1987. After about a week it was captured and returned to the United States. There is an early record of one, probably trapped near Scarborough in January 1865, and thought to be a white-tailed eagle for many years of its stay in the Scarborough Museum. Although not currently accepted it does seem to merit reconsideration.

Smallest of the vultures to occur in Europe, the Egyptian vulture is a primarily off-white bird with black flight feathers and a yellow face. The bill is long and slender and there is a distinct neck-ruff on an otherwise small head, while the tail is wedge-shaped. Juveniles are generally dark brown. The nearest breeding area to the British Isles is the extreme south of France where probably about 50 pairs still nest. From there it is widespread through much of Spain and in parts of Portugal. Small numbers breed eastwards across southern Europe, then through the Middle East and so to India, also in parts of North Africa and across a large part of central Africa.

Immature Egyptian vultures often wander well away from their natal areas, though it is well over a century since any reached the British Isles. There are but two records, both of immature birds. Two were seen feeding on a carcass of a sheep at Kilve, hard under the Quantock Hills on the southern shore of Bridgwater Bay in October 1825, one of which was shot. The other was killed on 28 September 1868 in a farmyard at Peldon where it had been feeding on the remains of slaughtered geese.

The griffon vulture is a huge, unmistakable vulture with a wing-span of 9 ft (3 m) accentuated by the contrasting pattern of ginger-buff with black-brown. The head, neck and ruff are of soft, white down. It breeds in the Iberian Peninsula, Sardinia and the extreme south-east of Europe, then east to northern India, as well as at a few locations in North Africa and in Egypt.

An immature griffon vulture caught alive near Cork in the spring of 1843 is preserved in the National Museum of Ireland. The only other record for the British Isles is of two at Ashbourne on 4 June 1927.

The pallid harrier is a small harrier very similar to the Montagu's harrier, and indeed the females are almost inseparable except at close range. The male is a pale greyish white, almost wholly white on the undersides and with a black panel in the primaries. It is a bird of dry grasslands, breeding eastwards from the Dienster steppe across central Asia, and wintering in Africa south of the Sahara and in India.

Only four have been recorded. The first, a male on Fair Isle in late 1931, remained until it was shot on 8 May 1932 for dispatch to the Royal Scottish Museum. The indefatigable George Stout saw another there on 6 May 1942, though this was never accepted. The others were at Studland on 11 April 1938, and an immature male shot at Hutton Cranswick in October 1952. This is a significant record, for in that year there was a mini-invasion westwards of pallid harriers with several pairs breeding in Germany and Sweden.

One of the most widespread of the North American buzzards, the red-tailed hawk is a heavily built bird, with, as its name suggests, a reddish tail. It occurs from Alaska south to the Gulf of Mexico, the northern birds being migratory. Just one old record, one in the autumn of 1863 in Nottinghamshire, should not be lost sight of, even if this species is not accepted on the British List. As recently as 1968 one imported from America for falconry escaped in Midlothian and paired with a buzzard. Perhaps fortunately the eggs were stolen, probably by crows, so that possible hybrids did not cause confusion among birdwatchers.

The red-shouldered hawk is one of the most common birds of prey in eastern North America, the red shoulder patches being visible at rest as well as in flight, while the narrow white bars on the tail are also distinctive. A widespread bird in North America from Quebec and Ontario to the Gulf of Mexico, those from the northern parts of the range move south in winter.

Although the red-shouldered hawk is currently not accepted to the British List, consideration should perhaps be given to the old record of one which came into the hands of a dealer at Kingussie in February 1863. There are two other interesting records which should be mentioned, both from transatlantic liners. On 20 October 1961 an immature red-shouldered hawk came on board the RMS *Queen Elizabeth* when midway between New York and Southampton, where it remained for three days, feeding on Leach's storm-petrels, and was last seen near Scilly. In early September 1964 another immature spent time on board the RMS *Mauretania* and also fed on Leach's storm-petrels before disappearing.

The spotted eagle is midway in size between the buzzard and the larger eagles. Adults are a uniform dark brown with a small whitish uppertail-covert patch. The spots belong to the immature which is even darker, with white spots which form almost bars on the wing-coverts, and which gradually disappear over several years as the bird matures. Broad wings make the head and tail seem short, while the widely outstretched primaries in flight, as one authority suggests, makes the bird resemble 'a ragged mat in the sky'. Spotted eagles have vanished from many former haunts in Europe and it now only breeds from Poland and the Baltic states eastwards across Russia, and central Asia to China. Many move southwards for the winter.

The 12 records of the spotted eagle in the British Isles are all between September and January, the first being the only record for Ireland, two shot near Youghal in January 1845. There is just one from Scotland, a bird shot in Aberdeenshire in September 1861 by F. E. Denison, then Speaker of the House of Commons. The others were in Northumberland, Suffolk, Essex, Hampshire, and Cornwall, the most recent being that shot at Brinsop Court on 15 November 1915.

Slightly smaller than the kestrel, the lesser kestrel has a narrower tail and wings, and an even more graceful flight action. The male lacks spots on the upperparts and is paler beneath, but most diagnostic of all is the blue-grey inner wing. Females on the other hand are almost impossible to separate from the female kestrel. A sociable bird, the lesser kestrel breeds widely in Iberia, at scattered locations elsewhere in southern Europe, then widely from Greece and Turkey, and from southern Russia eastwards to the Aral Sea, and in north-east China. It is highly migratory to winter quarters over much of Africa south of the Sahara.

The first lesser kestrel in the British Isles was shot near York in November 1867, with nine others up to 1909 including the only one so far recorded from Ireland, a male resident near Shankhill for nearly three months from November 1890 until it was shot. Between 1909 and 1967 there was but a single record, one in Scilly in February 1926. The 10 since 1967 have been between May and November, single records from Shetland, Essex, Sussex, Glamorgan, and Scilly, and two in Yorkshire and Cornwall.

The distinctive head pattern of three black stripes and a rufous centre to the blue-grey crown means that the American kestrel is easily recognizable in all plumages, while the male in addition has blue-grey wings. It is more the size of a merlin than our own resident kestrel. The American kestrel breeds widely throughout North America, with some moving into Central and South America for the winter.

The first record of the American kestrel in the British Isles was a male on Fair Isle from 25 to 27 May 1976. Surprisingly it was followed little more than two weeks later by a female at the other end of the country, at Bearah Tor on the eastern edge of Bodmin Moor. This bird remained until late June, giving delight to a large number of birdwatchers. Presumably both had arrived during the same Atlantic weather system. There is just one earlier record from Western Europe, one in Kalunborg at the end of 1901.

The red-footed falcon is a small falcon with a most distinctive dark-grey plumage in the male, which contrasts with rich chestnut thighs and lower belly, while the legs and feet are, as the name suggests, a bright red. Females are grey above with an orange-red head and nape and orange-buff underparts with again red legs and feet though these are not so bright as in the male. It has an extensive breeding range from eastern Europe across Asia to central Siberia, with winter quarters in south-west Africa.

The most frequent of the rare raptors to visit the British Isles, the majority of red-footed falcons are seen in May and June, presumably birds overshooting during northward migration. The first record was one near Doncaster in April 1830 with about 100 up to 1957. Since then the red-footed falcon has been recorded annually and the total of accepted records has risen by a further 313. In most years about 10 are seen, the majority quickly moving on, though in 1973 there was a much larger influx with no fewer than 42 records. Southern England, especially south-eastern counties, is the source of most records, though there are now few counties without at least one sighting in recent years. Some extend north to Shetland, mainly single birds in eastern counties, but no fewer than 18 have occurred in Shetland, where one was even caught and ringed on Fair Isle in 1955. In Wales the only records are from Glamorgan and Pembroke, while there are four from Ireland, one in 1832 and three since 1966, from Down, Dublin, and Galway.

Named after a beautiful Sardinian princess from the fourteenth century,

Eleonora's falcon is a medium size falcon with a slim build like a large hobby, and with long narrow wings, and a distinctly long tail. It occurs in two striking plumage types. About one in four individuals are an all dark sooty-grey, a colour only offset by bright yellow feet. The pale variety has dark brown or blue-black upperparts contrasting with rufous undersides, and a creamy throat.

Eleonora's falcon is a colonial species with up to 200 pairs having been recorded as breeding in close proximity, though in most cases the numbers are much smaller. The world population of probably no more than 4,500 breeding pairs is restricted to about 100 colonies on sea cliffs and islets around the Mediterranean, at several sites on the Atlantic coast of north-west Africa, and in the north-east of the Canaries. It once probably even nested at Gibraltar, where the Reverend John White recorded 'hobbies' breeding in the eighteenth century. Perhaps his identification was not sur prising, as it was 1839 before Eleonora's falcon was discovered and described, one of the last European birds to be so. It was not photographed successfully until 1959. Its breeding season is timed to coincide with the autumn passage south of small passerines, on which the young are largely fed. Most then move south about November to winter in East Africa and Madagascar.

A bird seen hawking for insects over a pool in the Formby sand dunes on two days in early August 1977 was the first Eleonora's falcon in the British Isles. There were three records in southern France at the same time, so it seems possible there was a displacement north of this splendid falcon. Our only other record is an unusual one, and also a reminder of the chance and good fortune when it comes to seeing rare birds. The Greenside family of Elm Tree Farm, Patrington, while picking sprouts in late October 1981, found a dead 'hawk'. The significance of their discovery was realized when a local taxidermist saw the bird, and promptly had its identity confirmed by Barry Spence, warden of the nearby Spurn Bird Observatory.

The chances of seeing Eleonora's falcon in northern Europe seem to have slightly improved as the population expands. In addition to the British records there have been two sightings in Poland and one from Sweden since 1982.

The saker falcon is a large and impressive dark brown falcon with a pale head and rather weak facial pattern, while the tail shows oval white spots rather than bars. Identification can be difficult, and there is always confusion with both the gyrfalcon and lanner. It breeds from south-east Europe across central Asia to China. Some winter westwards across southern Europe to Sardinia, but many more move into north-east Africa as far south as Ethiopia.

There are only two records of the saker from the British Isles and both from Shetland. The first was a bird on the Out Skerries in early October 1976, followed by one on Fetlar in late May 1978, at a time when other eastern species reached the British Isles. Neither has been fully accepted to the British List and the saker remains in Category D because of the risk of birds of captive origin.

Scops owl is the smallest owl recorded from the British Isles, being smaller and slimmer bodied than the little owl though with longer wings. Its head is large and there are two ear-tufts, though these are often laid back and not always easily visible. Central France is as close to the British Isles as the breeding range of the scops owl extended, though here it has retreated south during the present century. Elsewhere it marches eastwards into central Asia, and south to the northern edge of the Sahara. Only the northern populations it seems are migratory.

Some 63 scops owls had been recorded up to 1957 since the first was obtained in the spring of 1805 at Wetherby. The smaller number since 1957, just 16, is thought to be a direct result of the decline of the southern European population, perhaps as the consequence of contamination by pesticides. All but three of these 16 have been recorded between April and June, the others being late autumn records. Half of those recorded since 1957 have been dead, while most of the others remained for only short periods. The exception was a bird at Dummer which took up residence for two months from mid-May 1980. Here its soft monosyllabic whistle first led villagers to complain to the GPO, but the true origin was quickly revealed, much to the delight of large numbers of birdwatchers who assembled to listen, and hopefully to catch a glimpse of the bird itself. Most of the 16 recorded have been from southern England, but since 1957 birds have also reached Orkney, the Isle of Man and Fermanagh.

Largest of Western Palearctic owls, the eagle owl is a massive barrel-shaped bird the size of a buzzard, having heavily marked brown plumage and glowing yellow eyes. It breeds widely across Europe, central and southern Asia, the Middle East and parts of northern Africa.

There is much confusion over the origin of the 20 or so eagle owls recorded in the British Isles, all in the previous two centuries. The first seems to have been one in Yorkshire sometime prior to 1768, though Sibbald in his *Scotia Illustrata* published in 1684 refers to the 'great horned owl' as occurring in Orkney. One was killed in Orkney in 1830 and others subsequently reported from Shetland, Argyll, Lincoln, Sussex, Derby, Shropshire, and Wiltshire. Some may have been escapes from captivity and now the only accepted records are the Orkney bird of 1830, those in Shetland in 1863 and 1871 and Argyll in 1883. Birds originally of captive origin are known to have nested in Scotland on at least one occasion recently.

The hawk owl is a medium size owl with a large head, long tail and strongly patterned plumage. It lives up to its name, having a hawk-like silhouette and this, together with its diurnal behaviour, a dashing flight, and a habit of perching conspicuously, means this is a very special owl, though all owls deserve this consideration. It breeds in the forest lands close to the tundras of northern Europe, Asia and North America. When its largely rodent food supply fails it erupts southwards away from the northern forests.

Just 11 examples of the hawk owl have been recorded from the British Isles, and these include several of the North American race, so that this is another transatlantic vagrant among the birds of prey. The first in an exhausted state off Cornwall in March 1830, and the second one shot while hunting one sunny afternoon near Yatton in August 1847, were both from North America. One in Unst during the winter of 1860–61 was the first of the European race. The other records of the hawk owl are of birds in Lanark 1863, Renfrew 1868, Wiltshire 1876, Aberdeen 1898, Northampton 1903, and just three since 1957, one on the Bleasdale Fells above Chipping in September 1959, at Gurnard's Head in August 1966, and lastly one from Lerwick and from Bressay, the island just opposite, in September 1966. This bird may have been connected with a huge influx of hawk owls into southern Scandinavia, though clearly few chose to move further west by crossing the North Sea.

Tengmalm's owl had actually been discovered and was known to Linnaeus some years before the birth of the Swedish medical officer after whom it later became named. It is similar in size to the little owl but has a longer tail. The large, almost rectangular head has facial markings, which together with the eyes give a surprised appearance. The upperparts are dark brown, the underparts a rather blotched white. It breeds in woodlands from central Europe, across Asia, and through much of northern Canada.

During the last century and the early years of this century, Tengmalm's owl was one of the most regularly occurring of rare visitors with nearly 50 accepted records. The first was obtained at Widdrington in about 1812, and was initially mistaken for a little owl, and as such appears among Bewick's woodcuts. Since 1957 there have been but seven of which no fewer than five have been in Orkney. The exceptions are a bird in 1981 at Fishburn of which only the leg was found, but this carried a ring showing that the owl had been caught the previous year in Hedmark, and the other, the furthest south, was one which took up residence for most of March 1983 at Spurn Head.

Out of Africa

Allen's Gallinule   Mottled Swift   Moussier's Redstart

O f all the rare birds which have visited the British Isles just three occur in Africa and nowhere else. None would have figured largely on anyone's list as vagrants to be encountered north of the Mediterranean, and certainly not far into north-west Europe. Such surprises only add further to the excitement of looking for and carefully identifying birds, with on occasions discoveries of major importance, often when least expected.

Rather like a small moorhen, Allen's gallinule has a blue-black head, upperparts of olive-green, and dark blue underparts, crimson legs, and a red bill. Juveniles are a rich sand-brown, more rufous below. First named from a specimen collected during the ill-fated expedition in 1841 led by Commander William Allen to establish trading links on the upper Niger, it breeds in swamps, and beside lakes and rivers throughout much of Africa south of the Sahara. Allen's gallinule is a rains migrant, with regular movements north and south of the Equator depending on the approach of the dry season. It can at times wander far from its normal range, and there are even records from oceanic islands like Ascension and St Helena in the South Atlantic, and the Comoro Islands and Rodriguez in the Indian Ocean.

Northward movements by Allen's gallinule into Europe are not unknown, the first, and so far only, one to have reached the British Isles being a juvenile caught exhausted on board a fishing boat off the Suffolk village of Hopton on 1 January 1902, and taken to a taxidermist in Great Yarmouth. The present whereabouts of this unique specimen are alas unknown. Although accepted by some authorities, it was not admitted to the British List until Robert Hudson, librarian for the British Trust for Ornithology, marshalled impressive supporting evidence and resubmitted the record in 1974. He showed there were no fewer than 18 other records of Allen's gallinule from the Western Palearctic, which included several close to the British Isles, those from Denmark in 1929, Bavaria in 1936 and Brittany in 1951. Most interesting was that nearly all the records were in the period November to February, and that five, including the Suffolk bird, were in 1902. When will the next one straggle to our shores?

The mottled swift is the only other species so far to have reached the British Isles from tropical Africa. This large, broad-built swift has a distinctive flight of a few slow deep wing-beats interspersed with short glides. It breeds in mountain ranges south of the Sahara, normally only making local movements.

A mottled swift at Spurn Point on 23 October 1988 was the first for the British Isles. It arrived in this country at a time of a major invasion of 'southern moths', some of tropical distribution, together with several African locusts. The swift remained at Spurn during a period of mist and fog until 27 October, when it quickly departed towards the south-east as the weather cleared and the coast of Lincolnshire became visible.

Moussier's redstart is a compact bird, smallest of the West Palearctic redstarts. The male has black upperparts offset by a white band on the crown and large white wing-patches, the underparts are rufous, while the rump and tail are orange-red. Females are grey-brown above, paler orange below and with a pale orange-rufous rump and tail. The bird is named after Jean Moussier, a surgeon in the armies of Napoleon who eventually served with the French Foreign Legion in North Africa, but whose place and date of death, even the degree to which he studied birds, are unknown. His redstart breeds largely in the mountainous regions of north-west Africa, from Morocco to Tunisia, moving to lower ground in winter.

On at least two occasions Moussier's redstart has crossed the Mediterranean to reach Malta and Italy, but there is just one record from further north, a male at Dinas Head on 24 April 1988, a very pleasant surprise for the party of birdwatchers and a particular bonus for their leader Graham Walker.

European and Asian Waders

Black-winged Stilt
Pacific Golden
  Plover
Sociable Plover
White-tailed Plover
Great Knot
Red-necked Stint

Long-toed Stint
Sharp-tailed
  Sandpiper
Broad-billed
  Sandpiper
Great Snipe

Little Whimbrel
Slender-billed
  Curlew
Marsh Sandpiper
Terek Sandpiper
Grey-tailed Tattler

Who can mistake the black-winged stilt? Of all the rare birds to visit the British Isles this is one of the most conspicuous, and also one of the easiest to identify. It is a small-bodied, black and white wading bird with the longest legs proportionally of any bird likely to be seen in the British Isles. These legs are pink, so adding to the bird's flamboyance, and are trailed in flight. The bill is black, long and very slightly upcurved. Black-winged stilts are extremely widespread, occurring on freshwater and brackish lagoons in five continents, with some movement towards the tropics in winter. In Europe it is largely restricted to the Mediterranean regions, though it does occasionally breed further north, including the British Isles. Here three pairs nested at a Nottingham sewage farm in 1945, and raised four young from the nine eggs laid, of which three fledged. A pair on the Nene Washes in 1983 failed when their eggs were stolen by a fox while another pair raised two young at Holme in 1987.

Some 98 black-winged stilts were recorded prior to 1958, the first being one in 1684 from a lake near Dumfries, though as in more recent years the majority of those seen have been in southern England. The number since has risen by a further 138. Birds occasionally stray further north like that on the Ythan Estuary in October 1984 and whose remains were found several weeks later. In Wales there have been records from Anglesey, Caernarvon, and Pembroke, the most recent being one at Penally near Tenby in March 1990, which was first seen from a train, as it fed in a flooded field. Since 1949, there had only been two records from Ireland, both in 1981, until the 'invasion year' of 1987 when no fewer than six were seen, in counties Clare, Cork, Down, Kerry, and Tipperary, out of a total of 39 in the British Isles. Of the other 33, all save a bird at Fforyd Bay were in England. The majority of black-winged stilts occur between April and June, and these are probably birds overshooting on northward migration. Smaller numbers are seen in late summer with occasional winter records, though the one at Marston near Grantham, first seen on Christmas Day 1968 and which remained to February, is unique.

The Pacific golden plover, smallest of three closely related species, the others being the golden plover and American golden plover, is also the most difficult to identify. It has a slim build, a generally brighter plumage and a yellow rather than white supercilium. It breeds on tundras from the Yamal Peninsula eastwards in northern Siberia, and also in western Alaska where its range overlaps with the American golden plover: indeed they may breed alongside one another. One of the great migrants, many Pacific golden plovers make a non-stop crossing of 2,700 miles (4,320 km) from the Pribilof Islands to Hawaii, and then on to a wintering area which extends from the Horn of Africa to New Zealand.

There are eight records of the Pacific golden plover in the British Isles, though others, alas, have not been specifically identified and must remain in the category 'Pacific or American golden plover'. The first was one at Bempton Cliffs on 1 September 1975, followed by one at Aberlady Bay from 10 to 16 July 1976. Was it the same bird which returned to the same locality in the same month a year later? The next, also from Yorkshire, was at Fraisthorpe in January 1985, followed by two in the summer of 1986, at Tetney and North Cotes, and at Tacumshin where another occurred in July 1988. The most recent was one at Uyeasound in early November 1988.

Slightly smaller than the lapwing, the sociable plover is unmistakable in breeding plumage when to the general pinkish brown colour is added a striking chestnut and black belly-patch. In flight on the broad wings, the white secondaries contrast with the black primaries, while the white tail is black towards the tip. The legs are black, an important feature in avoiding confusion with the next species, the white-tailed plover. The sociable plover breeds, sometimes semi-colonially, from east of the Volga to the plains about Lake Balkash. Some winter in Arabia and Iraq, others reach Pakistan and north-east Africa.

The first sociable plover in the British Isles was mistaken for a cream-coloured courser (see page 86), when it was shot from among a flock of lapwings at St Michael's-on-Wyre in the autumn of 1860. There were only four others before 1958 and two of these were in Ireland, at Navan in 1889, and Brownstone Head 20 years later. Next was the first of only three from Scotland, a bird shot in mistake for a golden plover at Evie in November 1926 and not followed until one in Northampton in 1951. Since 1957, 27 have been recorded, in every month of the year save August, most in the late autumn and never more than four in any one year. The majority have been birds in England south of the Wash–Severn with just one in Scotland, at Carrick, on Eday in mid-January 1969. Indeed the two other records from Scotland were also in Orkney, in 1926 and 1949. There was one in Wales, at the mouth of the River Neath in October 1983, and one in Ireland, at Blennerville at the end of 1985.

The white-tailed plover, a slim rather pale lapwing with long yellow legs and a graceful action, is unmistakable in most circumstances. The upperparts are sandy-brown, the underparts brown-grey merging to buff-white. In flight the wing-pattern is much the same as the sociable plover, but note the all-white tail. This is a marshland species, breeding in the valleys of the Tigris and Euphrates and discontinuously from the eastern shore of the

Caspian to Lake Balkash. There have been signs of a westward expansion recently with nesting reported from Azerbaydzhan, Syria, and Turkey. Most winter in north-east Africa, the Middle East, Pakistan, and north-west India.

The first white-tailed plover in the British Isles was one which spent six days from 12 July 1975 on a gravel pit at Packington. This very same year birds were noted in no fewer than seven other European countries — Austria, Finland, the Netherlands, Hungary, Sicily, Poland, and Sweden. Just three subsequent records, all of single birds, at Abbotsbury in July 1979, and two — or was it the same bird? — in May 1984 in Durham and Shropshire.

Largest of its family, the great knot differs from the knot in having a larger and thinner bill and longer wings. In breeding plumage it has a bold, dark breast band, but this is lost in winter. The great knot is a bird of mystery as far as its breeding haunts are concerned. Only two nests have been discovered, both in north-east Siberia. Winter quarters are, however, well known and extend on coasts from India to Australia.

There is just one record of the great knot for the British Isles, a bird seen for but a few hours at Scatness and the Pool of Virkie near the southern tip of Shetland on 15 September 1989. Elsewhere in Europe there are single records from Denmark, Germany, France and Spain.

The red-necked stint is very similar to the little stint. Indeed in all but the breeding plumage they are almost inseparable in the field. However, should you be fortunate to be presented with the opportunity, note the shorter legs, more rounded appearance and longer wings. Adults in summer have a rufous head and upper neck, with an absence of white on the chin and little or no streaking. It breeds in northern Siberia eastwards from the Taymyr Peninsula and occasionally in Alaska. Winter quarters are from southern China, and the Philippines, through south-east Asia to Australia and New Zealand.

Although long anticipated, it needed an alert birdwatcher in the face of some initial scepticism from those who thought 'little stint' to observe and provide information for the acceptance of the first and so far only record of a red-necked stint in the British Isles. This was a bird, eventually seen by some 1,800 birdwatchers, at the Blacktoft Sands reserve of the Royal Society for the Protection of Birds, on the south shore of the upper Humber estuary from 22 to 29 July 1986. There are 10 other European records, all since 1957. When will the next be discovered in the British Isles?

The long-toed stint is slightly smaller than the little stint, and very similar to the least sandpiper, though it is more upright and has a longer neck and legs. The toe length is not an easy character to see in the field, either on the ground, or even in flight when the legs extend beyond the tail. It breeds beside rivers in the Siberian forests eastwards from the River Ob and its tributaries. Winter quarters are in south-east Asia to Australia.

Just one long-toed stint has been recorded in the British Isles, a juvenile described as 'superbly confiding' at Saltholme Pool close to the Tees Estuary from 28 August to 1 September 1982.

The sharp-tailed sandpiper, the tail feathers indeed being sharply pointed, is very similar to and easily confused with the pectoral sandpiper, so that special care must be taken, and on discovering a pectoral sandpiper it is always worth taking a close look at all distinguishing features just to make sure. Note that the sharp-tailed sandpiper is slightly larger, more portly, indeed can look 'pot-bellied', has shorter legs, and a shorter bill. The voice is a dry 'cheep' compared with the harsher 'kriiek' of the pectoral sandpiper. Confusion is also possible with both the purple sandpiper and the ruff, though should not last long with proper observations. The sharp-tailed sandpiper breeds in northern Siberia from the Yana River to Kolyma and winters in New Guinea and islands eastwards, Australia where it is especially numerous, and New Zealand.

The first record of a sharp-tailed sandpiper was one shot near Great Yarmouth in September 1848, though its true identity was only revealed when the specimen was re-examined in 1892, prompted by one at Breydon in the same county in September of that year. The other early records were also from Norfolk, birds at Caister in 1865, and Terrington in 1868. Following these nineteenth-century occurrences, when the bird was known as the Siberian pectoral sandpiper, the next was one at Hamilton in October 1956. Since 1957 a further 15 have been reported, all between late July and mid-October, save for one at Langton Herring in early April 1978. Most have occurred in eastern counties, though one reached Frodsham in 1983, and there were two in Wales, birds at Shotton and Morfa Harlech in October 1973. The former shared a field with a buff-breasted sandpiper. These two waders rarely meet because the buff-breasted breeds in Alaska and in Arctic Canada, and winters on the grasslands of Argentina and Uruguay.

The broad-billed sandpiper in size is like the smallest dunlin, with a long bill, down-curved towards the tip, and broad at its base, a feature not always apparent in the field. The short legs are seemingly set far back, while the double supercilium is a further notable feature. Despite this, confusion with other waders, especially dunlin, can easily occur. The breeding distribution of the broad-billed sandpiper is incompletely known, but certainly it breeds from southern Norway, through parts of Sweden and Finland to northern Russia, beyond which its range, if it does indeed occur, is still a mystery. Winter quarters are largely in India, south-east Asia and Australia.

The first broad-billed sandpiper in the British Isles was one shot at Breydon on 25 May 1836, with a further 22 accepted occurrences up to 1959. Save for the three years 1964-6 it has been recorded annually ever since, the majority of records being from May to early June, with a smaller peak from mid-August until late September. Most are of single birds, though trios were recorded on the Humber estuary in May 1984 and again in May the following year. Eastern counties are the main haunts on both spring and autumn passage, when birds occur from Shetland to Kent, with the majority from Lincoln and East Anglia. Some appear inland at sewage-farms and gravel pits, while several have reached Wales and four Ireland since 1957, spring birds in Londonderry and Antrim, autumn birds in Wicklow and Cork.

The great snipe, despite its name and bulkier build is very difficult to separate in the field from the snipe. The rounded head and a shorter bill carried more horizontally are further features to note. The wing-coverts show distinct white spots and accentuate a dark wing-panel. When flushed the

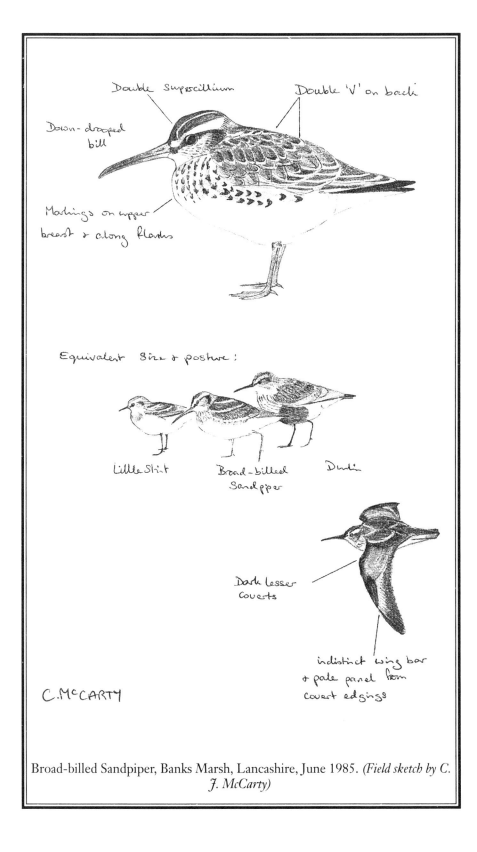

Broad-billed Sandpiper, Banks Marsh, Lancashire, June 1985. *(Field sketch by C. J. McCarty)*

great snipe does not tower, and usually makes only a short, often silent flight with slow wing-beats. Such differences may sound distinctive, but none is easy to assess in a few seconds' field observation, and far more records are rejected than accepted.

The great snipe breeds from southern Norway and the western borders of Russia eastwards to central Asia from where it migrates to winter quarters in Africa south of the Sahara. Although the causes are obscure, the great snipe has decreased markedly in Europe during the present century, the changing status of this bird in the British Isles bears witness to this fact.

Howard Saunders, merchant banker and birdwatcher, known for his skilful editing of Yarrell's *British Birds* and the later *Manual of British Birds*, first published in 1888 with further editions in 1899 and 1927, described the great snipe as 'an annual visitor in small numbers, in most cases singly, to maritime counties from Shetland to the English Channel'. *The Handbook of British Birds* published in 1940 said it was 'a very scarce passage migrant, many of them shot in mistake for snipe'. Some 180 records of great snipe are accepted prior to 1958 with a further 61 subsequently. Late summer and early autumn passage birds still make up the majority of records, with seven in 1976 being the highest annual total. Birds are, however, likely to be seen throughout the winter and from spring to early summer; perhaps some actually overwinter here. So elusive, so retiring, so mysterious is the great snipe that most are seen but once, and then only briefly. There has been one notable recent exception, a bird which frequented the watercress beds at Alderbourne and Rush Green from shortly before Christmas 1962 until the following February. The majority of records since 1957 are from Shetland, the east coast between Northumberland and Sussex, and the Isles of Scilly, with none from Wales and only two in Ireland, at Benderg Bay in 1967 and Dursey Island in 1983.

The little whimbrel is smallest of the curlews, little larger than a male ruff. It is more erect in build than its larger relatives, something accentuated by the long legs. Note particularly the fairly short bill, though this has the typical curlew down-curve. The buffish-brown plumage is paler below while the head is strikingly patterned with a dark crown and eye–stripe, and a pale supercilium. It breeds semi-colonially in river valley clearings among the larch forests of central and north-east Siberia. Winter quarters are in New Guinea and along the Australian coasts.

An adult little whimbrel at Sker Farm near Kenfig on 30 August 1982 was the first for the British Isles. It remained for seven days and those who saw it, or who missed it, hardly believed such a wanderer could return so quickly. But three years later, also on a Bank Holiday, one arrived at Cley and gave excellent viewing opportunities before it disappeared on 3 September. Over 3,000 birdwatchers are thought to have seen this one, indeed so fast did the news spread that it is said over 400 were viewing it within a few hours of the bird being identified. Such is the drawing power which rare birds have. The only other record for Europe is of one at Varanger on 14 July 1969.

A miniature version of the curlew, the slender-billed curlew, shows more white below, especially on the undersides of the wings, and on the upper tail. This is now one of the world's most endangered waders, the population, probably never very large, having declined throughout this century.

Restricted to a small part of central Siberia, where it breeds on bogs among woodlands, its winter quarters are not clearly known, but possibly include Iran and Iraq, and certainly Morocco, where a handful of birds occur each year. Loss of habitat and hunting seem to be the reasons for its demise.

It was hunting that produced the six records of the slender-billed curlew claimed for the British Isles, but alas not now accepted, for they were all taken in the Hastings area. The first two birds on 21 September 1910 and another two days later were followed by single birds in September 1914 and two in May 1919. In the past it occurred in many north European countries so that its arrival here is not too outrageous. Now, alas, it is not a question of where it will occur here again, but will it even survive? The next few years are going to be critical for the slender-billed curlew.

The marsh sandpiper, a strikingly graceful wader, is distinctly the small-est of the 'shanks', and has a plumage most closely resembling the green-shank. In summer the upperparts are a well–marked buff-grey, paler in winter, when the bird is almost white below. A white wedge visible in flight extends up the back from the tail, beyond which the long green legs pro-trude. The bill is long, straight and fine. Marsh sandpipers nest on fresh-water marshes on the steppe lands east from the Dniepner to beyond Lake Baikal, though there are recent reports of nesting in Finland. It winters over an immense area, from Gambia on the west coast of Africa to Australia.

The first marsh sandpiper in the British Isles was one near Tring reser-voirs in October 1887, with a further 11 records up to 1963. In that year three were seen, since when this most delightful of waders has proved to be almost annual in its occurrence. The number seen is usually small, so that the 11 reported in 1984 almost constituted an invasion. Equally remarkable was the fact that no fewer than seven were spring records, for the marsh sandpiper is much more likely to be encountered in late summer or autumn. Some 50 have been recorded since 1963, and the increase in records may be linked to the westward extension of the breeding range. Most occur on the east coast from Norfolk to Kent, though there have been sightings north to Shetland and to Orkney, with just one in Wales, at Maltraeth Pool at the end of June 1977. There are two records of the marsh sandpiper from Ireland, a juvenile at Tacumshin Lake in August 1982, followed by an adult almost two years to the day later. It is not idle to speculate that this might be the same bird returning.

An unmistakable wader, the terek sandpiper with its upturned bill, is unique among small, short-legged waders. About the size of a wood sand-piper, the terek sandpiper has pale brownish-grey upperparts, indeed the description of the first to be recorded in the British Isles refers to the bird looking like a 'ghostly common sandpiper'. The legs are yellow, while in flight the trailing white edge to the wings, and the grey rump and uppertail are important features. On the ground it has the typical sandpiper bobbing action, and it is at its most vigorous when feeding as it rushes about search-ing for invertebrates in shallow water. A tiny population of the terek sand-piper breeds in Finland, while elsewhere it extends east from western Russian across much of Siberia. This is another wader with a winter range extending from the coasts and river estuaries of West Africa to Australia.

The terek sandpiper was first recorded in the British Isles in May 1951 when one was seen by a single observer at the Midrips near Camber. If this had been 50 years before, indeed 21 years before, the record would surely have been deleted from the avifaunas as another of the 'Hastings rarities'. This sadly is the fate of the seven earlier records of the terek sandpiper, all seen in the same area, all in the month of May, between 1912 and 1925. A second — or was it the same bird? — was seen in Suffolk in early June 1951, and the next in September 1952 in Durham. Since 1957 there have been a further 28 records, all between May and mid-August, but mostly in May and June. There has only been one additional late record to that of 1952, one located on the Plym estuary in November 1974, which remained until the following May, a quite unprecedented stay for this species.

Nearly all the records of the terek sandpiper are from England in coastal counties from Durham to Cornwall, a single exception being one at the Royal Portbury Dock and later to the north of the River Avon at Severn Beach in September 1986. The three records for Scotland are all from the far north-east, in Shetland, Orkney and Caithness. As yet none has been reported from either Wales or Ireland.

The grey-tailed tattler (it gets the name from its continual trilling call-notes) looks like no other wader, save the legendary wandering tattler. It has short yellow legs, long wings and a tail with an absence of any white markings. The upperparts are plain grey, the underparts whitish, and in flight, which is fast, the wings have a rather flicking action. The grey-tailed tattler breeds in the mountainous regions of north-east Siberia where the first nest was only discovered in 1959. It winters on mudflats throughout Malaysia, Indonesia and Australia. There is just one record for the British Isles, a bird which frequented the Dyfi Estuary on the borders of Cardigan and Merioneth for just over a month from 13 October 1981. Two shot at Rye Harbour in September 1914 are no longer accepted as being genuine migrants.

North American Waders

Semipalmated Plover	White-rumped	Hudsonian Godwit
Killdeer	Sandpiper	Eskimo Curlew
American Golden	Baird's Sandpiper	Upland Sandpiper
Plover	Stilt Sandpiper	Greater Yellowlegs
Semipalmated	Short-billed	Lesser Yellowlegs
Sandpiper	Dowitcher	Solitary Sandpiper
Western Sandpiper	Long-billed	Spotted Sandpiper
Least Sandpiper	Dowitcher	Wilson's Phalarope

The semipalmated plover is an American version of our own ringed plover, a familiar bird along the shorelines and sandy estuaries of Europe. The two species — or are they, as some authorities suggest, conspecific? — actually overlap in eastern Baffin Island in the Canadian Arctic. They are extremely similar in plumage and behaviour, but note that the semipalmated has a narrower wing-bar, and a lemon-yellow rather than a dark orange orbital ring. The webbing between the toes is slightly more extensive but the most distinctive feature is the call, a high-pitched 'che-wink' rather than the melodious 'too-li' of the ringed plover. It breeds in Alaska and over much of northern Canada, moving south in winter to coasts throughout the Caribbean, and in Central and South America where it reaches as far as Chile and Argentina.

There are just two records of the semipalmated plover from the eastern Atlantic shore. An adult ringed in the Gulf of St Lawrence in July 1972 was recovered two months later in the Azores. In 1978 a juvenile was present on St Agnes where it remained from 9 October until early November.

Largest of the 'ringed plovers', the killdeer is a most handsome bird with a unique combination, as far as plovers likely to be seen in the British Isles are concerned, of having two black chest rings. The rump and uppertail is bright orange-brown, while in flight a broad white wing-bar is immediately apparent. The killdeer is a noisy and vociferous bird, most aptly named, for its main call, both in flight and on the ground, is a shrill 'kill-dee'. It breeds from southern Alaska to Hudson Bay and the St Lawrence, and south to Mexico and the West Indies, with another population in Peru and northern Chile. Northern birds winter mainly in the West Indies and Central America.

The first killdeer in the British Isles was one near Christchurch in April 1859, with a further six during the next 100 years, including one shot near Peterhead in 1867, and misnamed as a ringed plover in a museum drawer for nearly 40 years. Since then 33 more have been recorded, and it was seen annually from 1974 to 1985, but with no records of this superb Nearctic wader since. Five is the most recorded in a single year, when there were four in Scilly during the autumn of 1979 with at least one remaining until the following February, and one at Ballycotton. Birds have occurred in all months from late August until mid-April, with mid-winter records typical. Scilly has been blessed with no fewer than eight of those recorded since 1957, but the remainder are well scattered in four counties in Scotland, 11 in England, three in Wales and four in Ireland, with birds almost as likely inland as on the coast.

Previously named the lesser golden plover before recent separation from the very similar Pacific golden plover, the American golden plover is noticeably smaller than our own resident species, and has narrower wings which usually project well beyond the tail. In breeding plumage it is much darker below, while the upperparts have fine gold spangling. It breeds on the tundra lands of North America from Alaska to Baffin Island. Winter quarters extend from Bolivia and Paraguay south to Patagonia, and are reached by some birds taking a great circle route, non-stop across the western Atlantic, 2,500 miles (4,000 km) from New England to the Lesser Antilles, or even the north coast of South America, a flight which may take up to 37 hours.

With some confusion over the status of the American golden plover, and the difficulties of identification only recently unravelled and brought to wider attention, it is not surprising there are so few early records from the British Isles. The first was found in Leadenhall Market, London, during the autumn of 1882. What a fruitful source of scarce birds, and the not so scarce, this famous old London market proved to be down the years. There were five others prior to 1958, but since the mid-1960s, when birdwatchers grasped the necessary criteria and, armed with information, began to cast a more critical eye at golden plovers, a correct picture of the bird's status in the British Isles has begun to emerge. It is now annual in occurrence and the grand total has risen to 131, the majority being seen from late July until the end of October. This again is possibly a reflection of increased observer awareness and expertise rather than a change in the bird's status, with 12 in 1984 and 13 in 1985 the highest so far. Some 60 per cent of the American golden plovers recorded in the British Isles have occurred in just three counties, Cornwall, Scilly, and Cork. The remainder are well distributed from Shetland southwards, mostly in coastal counties though birds have occurred inland in Cheshire, Nottingham, Offaly, Roscommon, and Tipperary. Look for it in pastures and open areas close to the coast, while airfields in the extreme south-west of England seem to be particularly favoured.

The semipalmated sandpiper is one of a small group of waders which includes the next two species which cause confusion to observers, and to those charged with the assessment of records. It is a rather dull grey stint, slightly larger and more stoutly built than the little stint. It shares with the very similar western sandpiper the distinction of partly webbed toes, though this is a feature not always visible in the field, especially if the bird is in a muddy area. The semipalmated sandpiper breeds on the tundra lands of North America from Alaska to the north-east coast of Labrador. Most winter in the West Indies, Central America and especially on the coasts of northern South America.

The first record of the semipalmated sandpiper was a bird at Cley on 19 July 1953; the next was trapped on Skokholm in July 1964, while the warden Michael Harris was briefly ashore. Since then there have been 53 more, all save two between early July and late October, the exceptions being a spring bird on 31 May 1981 at Ballycotton, and a remarkable individual which overwintered at Felixstowe from 30 October 1982 until mid-April the following year. The annual totals have varied up to a maximum of eight in 1984. Nearly half the semipalmated sandpipers recorded have been in Ireland where to quote from *Birds in Ireland* 'Ballycotton and Tacumshin are the most likely places in Europe to see this rare species'. None has occurred in Scotland, yet, and the bird on Skokholm in 1964 remains the only one from Wales. In England the majority of records are from south-western counties, though there are others on the east coast from Yorkshire to Kent, and one from Cheshire.

The western sandpiper is very similar to the preceding species, but note the longer and more finely tipped, slightly drooping bill. The bird is higher standing, frequently entering the water to feed, rather than probing at its edge. Its voice, a thin, high-pitched 'chirr-rr' is a further distinguishing feature. The western sandpiper breeds in the Chukotskiy peninsula of eastern Siberia and in northern Alaska, moving south in winter to the coasts of the southern United States, the West Indies, Central America, and South America to Peru, and Surinam.

If you had any doubts before about the identification difficulties of this and similar species these will soon be dispelled when you learn that the first record for Europe of the western sandpiper was a bird caught at Fair Isle on 28 May 1956 and first identified as a semipalmated sandpiper. Reconsideration of the record in the light of further information rightly placed the bird as a western sandpiper. There have been just five subsequent records, all late summer birds, at Tresco 1969, Rainham and Axmouth 1973, Sandbach 1975, and at Virkie Pool 1988.

Smallest of the stints, indeed the least sandpiper can perhaps lay claim to being smallest of all the waders. It is a tiny compact bird with short wings, short, flexed legs, and a small rather square head. It is extremely active yet very tame and approachable, although if eventually flushed will rise swiftly. The least sandpiper breeds mainly on bogs and marshes within the northern forests from Alaska to Newfoundland and Nova Scotia, while winter quarters extend from the southern United States to northern South America.

A least sandpiper at Mount's Bay in October 1853 was the first in the British Isles, being followed by three others, all in the south-west, up to 1892. Then there was a gap with none recorded until 1955, followed by another in 1957 since when there have been a further 26, most between July and October with just two early summer records, birds at Marazion in early June 1970, and Farlington Marshes in late May 1977. One discovered at Portscatho in February 1986 and which remained until 20 April may well have overwintered. Most have been in south-west England and in Ireland, with just two in Scotland, birds in Aberdeen and Lanark. There has been a single occurrence in Wales, at Aberthaw in September 1972. A good year on Lundy for least sandpipers was 1966, when two were caught and ringed in September, one at the same time as a semipalmated sandpiper. There have been several inland sightings, the localities including Cannock Chase Reservoir, Brimpson Gravel Pits, and the Upton Warren nature reserve of the Worcestershire Wildlife Trust, that superb area of freshwater and saline ponds, marshes and rough grazing, between Bromsgrove and Droitwich.

The white-rumped sandpiper was originally known as Bonaparte's sandpiper after Charles Bonaparte (1803-57), a nephew of the great Emperor, and perhaps more appropriately, since the white is on the uppertail rather than the rump. Slightly larger than the stints, but smaller than a dunlin, the white-rumped sandpiper has long wings which protrude beyond the tail and give an elongated appearance. In winter the upperparts are greyish brown, the underparts white with greyer markings on the breast. The call-note is unlike that of any other wader, a thin, almost metallic squeak, resembling more a mouse or bat. It breeds on coastal tundras from Alaska to southern Baffin Island and winters southwards from Paraguay.

The first white-rumped sandpiper in the British Isles was in about 1836 when one was obtained at Belfast Lough, to be followed by a further nine up to 1870, then a surprising gap of nearly 80 years before the next, a bird at Musselburgh in October 1948, quickly followed by 13 more. Since 1957, 290 others have occurred in the British Isles, all but a handful — and these were probably overwintering birds — in the late summer and autumn. Occurrences have been from Shetland to Scilly, Norfolk to Kerry, with a strong westerly bias to the records during the later autumn, presumably of storm-driven birds. Indeed the white-rumped sandpiper is an annual visitor to Ireland, mainly on the southern coast from Kerry to Wexford. The number seen annually has risen, reaching a peak of 27 in 1984, though in most years it is less than 15. Hardly a coastal county in eastern Scotland and in England and Wales has not been visited by the white-rumped sandpiper while there are not infrequent inland records from reservoirs and gravel pits. In Ireland most have occurred in the coastal counties from Kerry to Wexford with only a handful elsewhere.

Records of the white-rumped sandpiper from eastern England are of interest as they occur largely in late summer and it has been suggested that these have a different origin from those in the west, even that there may be some small and so far undiscovered breeding population in northern Europe. Or is it perhaps more likely that they are genuine long-distance vagrants which have made a westerly passage across Siberia?

Baird's sandpiper named after the great American naturalist, Spencer Fullerton Baird (1823-87), is very similar to the white-rumped sandpiper. Like that species, its wings when closed extend well beyond the tail, and in flight provide a rather loose action. The legs are short, while the relatively short and straight bill is a useful character in separating Baird's sandpiper from similar species. A bird of upland high Arctic tundra from the extreme east of Siberia across north Alaska and Arctic Canada to north-west Greenland, winter quarters are mainly below the Equator in South America from Ecuador to Tierra del Fuego.

The first Baird's sandpiper in the British Isles was obtained at Hunstanton on 16 September 1903, with four others up to 1961, including one on St Kilda in 1911. The grand total has subsequently risen to 142 with almost annual occurrences, the majority from July to November with September the peak month. Just three records outside this period, two in

May and one in early June, and one which overwintered, a first-year bird which frequented Staines Reservoir from mid-October 1982 until late April the following year. In Scotland, records of Baird's sandpiper are from east coast counties with just one elsewhere, a bird which frequented Village Bay on Hirta, St Kilda for a few days in September 1986. It has occurred in many counties in England and Wales, both coastal and inland, and in Ireland where again the majority of records have been in coastal counties from Kerry to Wexford.

Most appropriately named, the stilt sandpiper is a stately long-necked wader with long, usually dull green legs and a long heavy bill, down-curved towards the tip. The red cheek band of breeding plumage is distinctive, but winter birds are grey above and whitish beneath. In flight the feet extend well beyond the tail which is white on the lower rump and upper coverts. The stilt sandpiper feeds in shallow water with a rapid, almost sewing-machine-like-chopping action. The breeding range extends from north-east Alaska to the western shores of Hudson Bay while the normal wintering grounds are in central South America.

A stilt sandpiper at Kilnsea at the end of August 1954 was the first for the British Isles. A further eight years elapsed before the next arrived, one at Chichester Gravel Pits in early September 1962. Since then 19 have been recorded, of which all but three were in late summer, three in August 1988, and all in Ireland, so doubling the Irish total, being the most in a single year. Despite an impeccable western origin the majority of stilt sandpiper records have been in eastern coastal counties from Yorkshire to Sussex, with just two in Scotland, and none so far for Wales. Most have remained for only short periods, though the only one in western England, a first-summer bird at Frodsham, remained from mid-April to the following October. Indeed one ponders whether it had wintered somewhere in the area previously undetected.

The short-billed dowitcher is another difficult wader to identify. Indeed it was only classified as a separate species in 1950, so similar is it to the long-billed dowitcher. One excellent characteristic, however, is the voice, a mellow 'tu–tu–tu' in flight or when alarmed. It breeds on marshes and ponds in three separate areas of Arctic North America, in southern Alaska, central and north-west Canada, and northern Quebec. Winter quarters extend from the southern United States to Peru and Brazil.

There has been considerable and quite understandable confusion over the status of the short-billed dowitcher in the British Isles. Some previously accepted records are now assigned to the long-billed dowitcher or are now classed as 'dowitcher species', leaving just five, specimens from Stone Bridge in 1862, Christchurch in 1872, and Stanpit Marsh in 1902. The only acceptable sight records are of birds at Cley in October 1957 and at Tacumshin at the end of September 1985.

Separating immature long-billed and short-billed dowitchers in the field is reasonably straightforward, but much more difficult are breeding or winter-plumaged adults, hence the confusion and doubts over many records. Most that are seen in the British Isles are long-billed dowitchers, but that in no way obviates the need for the most careful observations and note-taking before identification is pronounced upon. The long-billed dowitcher breeds in north-east Siberia, in north and west Alaska, and in the delta of the Mackenzie River in Arctic Canada. Winter quarters are from the southern United States to Central America. The occurrence of the long-billed dowitcher in Europe seems strange in view of the distance it needs to travel. Indeed it must pass through the range of the short-billed dowitcher which so infrequently arrives here.

Some 141 long-billed dowitchers have been recorded in the British Isles, the first being one in Devon about 1800, at which time it was known as the brown snipe, later the red-breasted sandpiper. The majority, 132, have occurred since 1959, and only in 1961, 1962 and 1972 were none reported. The maximum number in a single year was 15 in 1987. Most arrive from mid-September to late October, but there are records from every month and birds regularly overwinter, with some staying for long periods. None can yet compete, however, with one first seen at Ballycotton in October 1980 and which remained until the following April, returned in July, and was to remain there until mid-November 1983. Sightings are widely distributed throughout the British Isles, though with a strong southerly bias, both in coastal and inland counties, birds seemingly equally at home on gravel pits and reservoirs as on coastal saltings and estuaries.

The Hudsonian godwit is midway in size between the bar-tailed and black-tailed godwits. Indeed it closely resembles the latter, but black rather than white axillaries and underwing coverts are a key feature providing, of course, that clear views can be obtained. The shorter legs and short neck cause further confusion, as in this respect the Hudsonian godwit more closely resembles the bar-tailed godwit. It breeds in Alaska and parts of Arctic Canada where virtually the whole population gathers in late summer on the shores of Hudson Bay and James Bay. From there migration takes birds non-stop to South America and eventual winter quarters in Uruguay and Argentina.

It seems strange that a bird which apparently takes an easterly migration route in North America, part of which is over the Atlantic, should not have been seen in Europe before 1981. In September that year a Hudsonian godwit was at the Blacktoft Sands nature reserve of the Royal Society for the Protection of Birds on the Humber estuary. Although first noted on 10 September, some two weeks elapsed before its identity was elucidated, though the warden, Andrew Grieve, had been puzzled from the very first. A hint here possibly that others may have been overlooked in the past, and the need to give black-tailed and bar-tailed godwits that extra scrutiny in future. The Blacktoft bird remained until 3 October. Three weeks later another — or was it the same? — was discovered in a riverside meadow on the outskirts of Exeter where it was to remain until mid-January. The only other record is equally intriguing, one at Blacktoft Sands for some 10 days from 26 April 1983. Was it the same bird again? Where had it been in the meantime? Having crossed the Atlantic, was it destined to fly north and south in the wrong hemisphere, seeking solace with the company of black-tailed and bar-tailed godwits?

The Eskimo curlew is about two-thirds the size of a whimbrel and closely resembles the little whimbrel, though it can be identified by the rich cinnamon rather than buff underparts and underwings. The legs are shorter and in flight do not extend beyond the tail. One of the great tragedies of the bird world, the Eskimo curlew was once so numerous that Audubon and other early observers in North America remarked on the vast flocks which crossed the great plains on migration. Pioneer settlers on these same plains saw the birds as a source of easy food, and they shot them by the thousand so that by the end of the century the Eskimo curlew faced extinction. It only narrowly missed the fate of the passenger pigeon, and now just a tiny population still clings on, breeding in the Canadian Arctic, wintering on the pampas–grasslands of central Argentina.

Until the fortunes of the Eskimo curlew improve it seems very unlikely that it will be seen again in the British Isles. We have therefore to be content with just eight records, all in the last century: two at Woodbridge in November 1852, then single birds in Kincardineshire on 6 September 1855, one found in a Dublin market on 21 October 1870 and thought to have come from Sligo, one in Aberdeenshire in the same year, one shot at Slains in the same county 10 years later, and lastly an adult male shot on Tresco on 10 September 1887.

It is a pity that the earlier name Bartram's sandpiper has been discarded in favour of upland sandpiper, and I strongly deprecate the loss of such honoured links with the past. Fortunately the great American naturalist and explorer of the eighteenth century, William Bartram (1739-1823) is still honoured in the scientific name, the type specimen having been collected near to his home at Philadelphia. The upland sandpiper is quite unlike most other waders, for it resembles a small curlew but with a sandpiper bill, small head, long wings and a wedge-shaped tail, which in flight shows a dark centre to the rump. It breeds from Alaska to the northern United States, and winters on the pampas-grasslands of central South America.

The first upland sandpiper in the British Isles was one near Warwick in 1851, a further 14 being noted up until 1957. Since then 26 more have been seen, the most in a single year being three in 1968. All save one have been in autumn, chiefly late September and October, though there have been records between July and December. Most of those recorded have been in the south-west, in Pembroke, Cornwall, and above all Scilly, where one approachable bird took worms from birdwatchers in October 1983. The only records from Scotland have been birds on Fair Isle in 1970 and 1975, and, the sole spring bird, one on St Kilda in April 1980. Ireland, rather surprisingly, since 1957 has had few records, birds at Hook Head and North Slob in 1967 and 1971, Rogerstown in 1974 and after a 12-year absence one found dead at Larne Lough in December 1986.

Although more slender, the greater yellowlegs closely resembles the greenshank in size, but note the strong bill, an important feature and of course the bright yellow legs. Non-breeding birds are grey-brown, finely spotted white above, while in flight a square white rump is immediately visible. Note carefully the bird's action when feeding, mostly picking, snatching, skimming or sweeping, but never probing. Listen for the ringing greenshank-like 'tew' call when this wary bird is flushed. The greater yellowlegs breeds in wet forests from eastern Alaska to Labrador and Nova Scotia. Winter quarters are from the West Indies to Patagonia.

The first record of the greater yellowlegs in the British Isles was one shot on Tresco on 16 September 1906, and like so many early vagrants then exhibited at a meeting of the British Ornithologist's Club. A further 11 followed up to 1957 since when 16 more have been accepted, a smaller number than might have been anticipated in comparison with the virtual explosion in the records of several other North American waders. One suspects a decline in the breeding population or a change in migration patterns has so far ruled out an upsurge in occurrences this side of the Atlantic. There are only two spring records, the remainder having occurred between early July and late November. Most have remained but a few days, but one at Blennerville which arrived in late 1982 was present until the end of the following April, at one time being joined by a lesser yellowlegs, a unique event in Europe. With so few records little apparent pattern can be discerned other than to say Ireland with five of those since 1957, East Anglia, Kent, and Flint are where most of the sightings have been.

The lesser yellowlegs being about the size of a small redshank is about a third smaller than the greater yellowlegs. The bill, although long, is shorter and finer, and is an important feature when separating this species from its close relative, for the plumage is similar, if less spotted, than in the greater yellowlegs. Another distinguishing feature is the bird's feeding actions, delicate picking and probing, methods not used by the greater yellowlegs. It breeds among woodlands from Alaska to James Bay, Canada, wintering from the southern United States to southern Chile and Patagonia.

The lesser yellowlegs is one of the more numerous of the transatlantic waders with about 200 in the British Isles since the first, a bird at Misson in the winter of 1854-5 and now preserved in the Leeds Museum. Since 1957 no fewer than 161 have been reported, the majority from August to October. The small number of spring records are probably of birds overwintering, or displaced birds from the previous autumn moving north on the wrong side of the Atlantic. The highest numbers in a single year have been 10 in 1970 and 11 in 1981. Most are from southern counties in England and Ireland, inland as well as on the coast with more scattered records north to Shetland. Some 47 have occurred in Ireland with no fewer than four together at Askeragh Lough on 6 August 1973, one of the first places in western Europe that a transatlantic wader will find, and where there is rich feeding in the shallow waters to replace fat reserves utilized during the long flight.

The solitary sandpiper, the New World equivalent to the green sandpiper, is a slim bird midway in size between that species and the smaller wood sandpiper. It has dark plumage and in flight a dark rump, a feature unique to this species amongst its relatives likely to be encountered in Europe. The solitary sandpiper breeds beside freshwater amongst the coniferous forests of North America from Alaska to Ontario. Winter quarters extend from Central America and the West Indies south to Uruguay and Argentina. It certainly deserves its name, for this is a bird generally found alone or in pairs.

The first solitary sandpiper in the British Isles was shot 'on the banks of the Clyde on the higher grounds of Lanarkshire' in the late 1860s. A further five were recorded up to 1957 and 20 since, all between mid-July and October with four in 1974 the most in any one year. Nearly half of those seen have been in Scilly, with the other records in England being from counties south of the Humber. There are three records from Ireland but none so far from Scotland or Wales.

In summer plumage the spotted sandpiper is a distinctive bird, slightly smaller than the common sandpiper to which it is closely related. Unfortunately for observers on this side of the Atlantic the famous spots are lost outside the breeding season when the plumage is pale grey brown above, white below. The bill is yellowish with a dark tip, while note that the tail only just extends beyond the closed wing. It bobs vigorously when at rest and when feeding, while in flight the wings are fluttered and flicked as it passes low over the water. In North America the breeding range is extensive, from the tree limit in the north to California and Carolina in the south. The winter range is equally extensive, from the coasts of the southern United States to northern Chile and Argentina.

A spotted sandpiper taken near Eastbourne in 1866 was the first in the British Isles to be followed by five more up to 1957. Since then a further 83 records have been accepted, and it is now looked upon as an almost annual visitor, mostly from August to October, though with evidence of spring passage in May and June. Birds are increasingly found overwintering since the first, one at Weymouth from December 1973 to the following March. It seems that the Isles of Scilly are the most likely place to encounter the spotted sandpiper in the British Isles, though there are now records from many English and Welsh counties, but rather few in Scotland. However, a pair attempted to breed on Skye in 1975, laying four eggs, though unfortunately none hatched. There are just five records from Ireland since 1957, surprisingly low for a Nearctic wader, four of these are from Cork, the other from Waterford.

Largest of the three phalaropes, Wilson's phalarope has a long, needle-like bill, long legs which are black in summer and dull yellow the rest of the year. In non-breeding plumage it is pale grey above and white below, which cannot compare with the rich summer colours when the upperparts are a striking mixture of pearl-grey, black, and chestnut. Wilson's phalarope is often tame and approachable, both on its breeding grounds and on passage. It breeds on wetlands throughout much of central North America where its range is extending eastwards. Freshwater pools are also its winter habitat, mainly in South America from Peru to Argentina.

Yet another North American wader which has made its considerable mark here, the first Wilson's phalarope for the British Isles, indeed for Europe, was discovered on a pool at the Rosyth naval dockyard in September 1954, where it remained for nearly a month. Four years later there was a spring record, a female in breeding plumage on a gravel pit near Shefford in May, to be followed a month later by one at Malltraeth. Since then Wilson's phalarope has been recorded in every year save for 1960, with the annual totals gradually increasing, the maximum being 17 in 1987. The grand total of accepted records now stands at 220. Most are recorded between early August and mid-October, though there are a sprinkling of late spring and early summer records. Are these birds which have wintered in Africa and are returning north this side of the Atlantic? Virtually all the spring records are from eastern counties with few on the west coast and until 1988 none from Ireland. In that year there was a male at Tacumshin and a female at Swords both on 11 June. The late summer/autumn records are much more widely distributed from Shetland to Scilly with a strong preponderance from west and south-western counties though disappointingly few from Wales, more especially when nearly all English counties, including the inland ones, now have at least one record. In Ireland there are autumn records from nearly all coastal counties from Derry to Clare. Probably sparse observer coverage in the north-west prevents there being reports from there also.

North Pacific

Aleutian Tern   Ancient Murrelet

The Aleutian tern is rather similar to the bridled tern, indeed they may comprise a super-species. It is slate-grey above with a black cap, a large white forehead and a white rump and tail, while the under-wing has a distinctive black bar on the secondaries. Despite its name, this is a scarce bird in the Aleutians; most choose to breed in western Alaska and eastern Siberia. The winter range is still a mystery — does it frequent Antarctic seas?

A single record, the only one in the Western Palearctic for the Aleutian tern, was on 28 and 29 May 1979 on the Inner Farne. The soft wader-like call quickly attracted the warden's attention amidst the raucous clamour of the resident terns, which to the chagrin of the island staff harried the wanderer every time it ventured near to the colonies, so that its speedy departure was not unexpected.

Another of the great surprises, some might argue the greatest of all, was an ancient murrelet in the eastern Atlantic. This small auk, the size of a little auk, has a blue-grey head, black upper parts and is white below. It breeds in colonies, some extremely large, from the Aleutian Islands to British Columbia, and from Kamchatka to Korea, birds wintering at sea for the most part at no great distance from the colonies, though some reach as far south as California.

The first ancient murrelet for the Western Palearctic occurred on Lundy on 27 May and remained there close to colonies of guillemots and razorbills until late June. Just what brought such a bird from the North Pacific to an island off Devon? It occurs as a windblown vagrant from time to time well inland in North America, but the Lundy bird presumably crossed a continent and then an ocean, remarkable for a bird whose flight is described as 'low and direct, usually for only short distances, seemingly stopping in mid flight and dropping into the ocean.' Surprised we may be, but two other auks from much the same area have reached Europe, a crested auklet in Iceland in 1912 and a parakeet auklet in Sweden in 1860, while two others, the marbled murrelet and tufted puffin, have reached eastern North America, once again providing proof that anything is possible where rare birds are concerned.

Desert and Steppe

Little Bustard
Houbara Bustard
Great Bustard
Cream-coloured
  Courser
Collared Pratincole
Oriental Pratincole
Black-winged
  Pratincole
Greater Sand Plover

Caspian Plover
Pallas's Sandgrouse
Egyptian Nightjar
Calandra Lark
Bimaculated Lark
White-winged Lark
Black Lark
Short-toed Lark
Lesser Short-toed
  Lark

Crested Lark
Blyth's Pipit
Isabelline Wheatear
Pied Wheatear
Desert Wheatear
White-crowned
  Black Wheatear
Black Wheatear
Desert Warbler
Trumpeter Finch

About the size of a female pheasant, the male little bustard in breeding dress has a distinctive pattern of a slate-grey head and throat, black neck, and an upper breast with white markings, pale sandy upperparts, and white underparts. Females and the winter male are sandy-brown above, white below. In flight both sexes show a large expanse of white in the black-tipped wings. It breeds widely in the Iberian Peninsula, in a scattering of localities in France, and at a few other sites in southern Europe, but is more widespread from the Don and Volga steppe east to Kazakhstan. In winter some of the northern birds move south.

Prior to 1958 about 92 little bustards had been recorded in the British Isles since the first in 1751, mostly in the last century and in southern England. It was then more numerous on the continent, but as its population in western Europe has declined so has the frequency of its occurrences north of the English Channel. Since 1957 there have been just 13, all in eastern England from Norfolk to Kent, save for one at Compton Down in July 1958, and one in the far west near St David's in November 1968. This one had been shot and eaten, and its occurrence only came to light when the wing, fortunately not discarded, was presented to the county bird recorder. Most have arrived betwen October and January and all have been single birds, save for a remarkable trio in December 1987 at Sudbourne. This was the first record since 1975 and further evidence of the decline in this species.

The houbara bustard, larger and longer necked than the little bustard, is mainly sandy-brown, strongly marked with black above save for the face and neck which are grey-white decorated with black plumes and frills. The female is very similar though with less flamboyant plumes. In flight both show a handsome black and white patterning.

The houbara bustard was previously known as Macqueen's bustard, though it is not known who Mr Macqueen was who brought the first specimen back from northern India, where it winters, in about 1830. The breeding range extends from the Canary Islands, across North Africa, and over much of central Asia from the Caspian Sea to Mongolia. There is some movement south by northern birds in winter. Numbers are now much reduced, partly by land reclamation and disturbance, and in much of Africa and the Middle East the bird is a major quarry of falconers.

Only five records exist of the houbara bustard in the British Isles. The first was shot in a stubble field at Kirton-in-Lindsey in October 1847. The next three were also in October, at Redcar on 5 October 1892, near Spurn on 17 October 1897, to be quickly followed by one after 10 days of severe northeasterly gales, at St Fergus on 24 October 1898. Then there was a long wait until one at Westleton from 21 November 1962. This bird spent most of the time in a field of mustard, occasionally moving to a nearby crop of winter wheat to feed, and eventually vanished during hard weather at the end of December. It was always most reluctant to fly, walked virtually everywhere, and would crouch like a huge sandy–coloured tortoise when disturbed.

The great bustard is a giant, robust bird with a blue-grey head and neck, rufous chest, cinnamon-brown upperparts strongly barred black, and white underparts. Breeding males sport a handsome white moustache, but this together with the rufous chest band is lost in winter when the sexes look similar. The flight, when the large white wing-patches are visible, is deliberate and strong.

The great bustard has declined over much of its range as a result of land reclamation and disturbance. It nested in the British Isles until the 1830s when pairs still hung on in eastern England, last nesting on Thetford Warren in about 1832, and perhaps as late as 1838. On the continent its range is now much fragmented with birds breeding in Iberia, and from parts of central Europe eastwards across Asia.

Following extinction as a breeding species in the British Isles there were hard-weather influxes in 1870-71, 1879-80 and 1890-91. Subsequently few were recorded and there were just eight between 1910 and 1936, then none until 1963. In that year, perhaps as a result of a hard weather movement, a female was found dead beneath power cables at South Creake at the end of March. There have been 20 subsequent sightings, nearly all from Norfolk, Suffolk and Kent, an exception being an adult female which reached Fair Isle on 11 January, in such a weak state that it was captured and cared for, until taken south to a wildlife park. Its arrival on the island coincided with two at St Margaret's Bay on the same day. Where was one going, indeed where had it come from, as it flew south over the Cotswold escarpment at Leckhampton on 24 May 1976? There were four great bustards in Kent in December 1981, then came almost an invasion of seven, but possibly as many as 11, in Norfolk and Suffolk from January to March 1987. These were part of a hard weather movement of great bustards across Europe.

A bird of deserts and arid grasslands, the cream-coloured courser, a starling size, long-legged bird, has mainly sandy-cream plumage with a striking pattern of blue-grey, black and white on the rear of the head. It prefers to run when disturbed. Indeed in its native habitat this is virtually the only time you see the bird, so effective is its camouflage. In flight the underwing is black with a sandy leading edge, the outer wing black above. The cream-coloured courser breeds in the desert islands of the north-east Canaries, across North Africa and the Sahara to Iraq and on to Afghanistan, and Baluchistan. Birds from some parts of the range are migratory moving south in winter into Africa and India.

Most cream-coloured coursers which have occurred in the British Isles have been during the autumn or early winter, the first being one in Kent in 1785 with a further 32 records up to 1957 including just two reports from Scotland, both from Lanarkshire, one of which was a remarkable three birds in October 1949. There is just a single record from Ireland, a bird which frequented sandhills near Raven Point in December 1952. Since 1957 there have been just six additional sightings, all of single birds, at Dawlish Warren in 1959, Aberlady Bay in 1965, Cefn Sidan in 1968, Blakeney in 1969, Ruan Lanihorne in 1980, and Hadleigh Marsh in 1984. All were October records save the latter bird which arrived at the end of September and remained for several days. The fact that such a desert species occurs in north-west Europe at all is remarkable, and it remains one of the great prizes for watchers in the British Isles.

Although a wader, the highly aerial collared pratincole more closely resembles a small tern, even a miniature skua. Note the tiny bill, short legs, long wings, and pointed tail. The upperparts are brown, while the creamy throat is surrounded by a black line, the fawn underparts giving way to a pure white underbelly. It is difficult to separate the collared pratincole from the black-winged pratincole with the result that some records can only be assigned to 'pratincole species', some 18 falling into this category between 1973 and 1987.

The collared pratincole is the most widely distributed of the pratincoles, and indeed the sobriquet 'common' would be more appropriate, especially as its closest relatives also have a collar. It breeds across southern Europe, through the Middle East to reach Pakistan and Kazakhstan, while in Africa it occurs widely south of the Sahara. Birds breeding in the northern hemisphere are strongly migratory, most choosing to winter along the southern edge of the Sahara.

The first collared pratincole in the British Isles was one which reached almost as far north as it could go, to Unst where 'Bullock procured one in September 1812'. From then until 1958 a further 29 were recorded, five more in Scotland, one in Wales, the remainder in England. The pattern since 1958 has been much the same. Of the 44 recorded most have been in England, but there have been four in Scotland, two of which reached Shetland, and there have been two in Wales, in Anglesey and Glamorgan. The sole Irish record was an immature on the Bann estuary for two days in October 1970. Most occur in late spring/early summer with much smaller numbers in autumn. In view of the small numbers they hardly merit the term 'invasion', but nevertheless in both 1973 and 1983 at least six were seen, compared to single birds, or at the most two in other years.

The oriental pratincole is very similar to the other two pratincoles seen in the British Isles, but the absence of white on the secondaries combined with chestnut underwings and the short tail with just a shallow fork are its distinctive features. It breeds from eastern India to the Philippines and Borneo, moving east to New Guinea and to north-west Australia in winter.

Despite its eastern credentials the oriental pratincole can wander far off course, and in the northern hemisphere birds have been recorded in the Aleutian Islands and twice in the British Isles. Indeed these two are the only records for the Western Palearctic. One was at Dunwich from 22 June to mid-August 1981, later moving to Old Hall Marshes, that splendid reserve of the Royal Society for the Protection of Birds on a remote peninsula beside the Blackwater Estuary, where it remained until 10 October. Interestingly the second occurrence, also of a residential nature, was also on an RSPB reserve, this time at Elmley beside the Swale in north Kent, where one was present for a month from early September 1988. It had previously been at Harty on the eastern end of Sheppey since 21 June.

The black-winged pratincole slightly larger, and some would suggest bulkier than the common pratincole, was for a period considered no more than a colour phase of this species. Note, however, the generally darker plumage, the lack of contrast in the wings, black not chestnut underwings, with an absence of white on their trailing edge. The black-winged pratincole breeds from the Danube delta, mainly in steppe country to northern Kazakhstan to about the valley of the upper Irtysh. It occasionally breeds further west in colonies of collared pratincoles. Most winter in Africa on the plains of the far south, with smaller numbers in Chad and in northern Nigeria.

The first record of the black-winged pratincole in the British Isles was one at Northallerton in 1909, to be followed by a female 'secured' on Fair Isle by Admiral Stenhouse on 18 May 1927. The first of two records from Ireland was one at Belmullet in August 1935, also 'secured' and now resident in the Belfast Museum. The next was seen by my friend J. W. Donovan on the Midrips in August 1955. If this had been seen, even shot, 50 years earlier at this locality it would have been consigned to that woeful category, the Hastings rarities. There is one other pre-1958 record, a bird at Steart Island in June 1957. Since then 20 more have been recorded with just three away from counties south of the Humber to Severn line; a juvenile near Larne in August 1974, at the Loch of Strathbeg in July 1976, and at the Inner Marsh Farm Nature Reserve on the Dee Estuary at the beginning of June 1988. That year was exceptional: there were three records when previously no more than two had occurred. These three were all in June, whereas previous ones had extended from early July until mid-October, with an exceptionally late one at Eye Brook Reservoir on 20 November 1986. One in Kent for a week in June 1988 spent part of its stay with the oriental pratincole, being described as 'just about the most amazing pair or rarities you could hope to see'.

The greater sand plover is a rather thick-set plover with long legs, pale grey upperparts and white underparts, while males have a rufous breast band. Care must be taken to avoid confusion with the lesser sand plover, which although still to be discovered in the British Isles surely will be before too many years elapse, for it has reached Austria and Norway. The greater sand plover breeds on desert and semi-desert areas from Turkey to Mongolia and parts of China. It is widespread in winter on coasts from Namibia to Australia.

The first greater sand plover in the British Isles was a bird which frequented a creek near Sidlesham Ferry, Pagham Harbour, from 9 December

1978 until the end of the month, when it probably died. The next, a bird at Sandside in June 1979 was quickly followed by another winter record, this time one which remained at Chew Valley Lake from 17 November 1979 until the following February. Towards the end of its stay it left the muddy shoreline to consort with lapwings feeding in nearby fields. There were two in 1981, birds at Breydon and one which visited both sides of the Humber to be seen at Spurn and North Coates. In the following year came the only record so far from Scotland, at Aberlady Bay. There was another Norfolk record in 1985, this time at Cley and Blakeney Harbour, two in 1988, a bird at South Walney in July and August and one at Dawlish Warren in April and early May. It was this latter individual which later in the month was discovered at St Bride's Wentlooge.

A slim, medium size plover, the Caspian plover has a fine bill and long legs. The upperparts are dark greyish brown while the breeding male has a resplendent bright chestnut breast band, edged below in black. In the female and immature this is mottled grey-brown, while the rest of the underparts are white. The long wings show a white bar and primary patch, and are dusky brown below. A bird of dry steppes eastwards from the Caspian across Kazakhstan, which winters on grasslands and dried lake shores southwards from the Sudan.

On 22 May 1890 two strange birds were observed in a market garden at North Denes, and when one was shot it was found to be a male Caspian plover. Nearly 100 years elapsed before the next, in 1988, also a male, also in May, on St Agnes. With such a rare occurrence it was remarkable that another, this time in non-breeding plumage, would occur within weeks, one spending two days in mid-July at Aberlady Bay.

Pallas's sandgrouse is a plump, pigeon-like bird with short legs and a long pointed tail. The small head combined with the long tail make the wings seem very set forward when the bird is seen in flight. Largely creamy-buff above, it has an orange-ochre head, pale grey breast and a black belly band. The steppe lands and semi-deserts of central Asia are the normal haunts of Pallas's sandgrouse. From these it occasionally makes dramatic irruptive movements away from its normal range, the reasons for which are not known, though many suggestions have been made. As one writer commented: 'Few events in the annals of ornithology have excited more interest than the irruptions of Pallas's sandgrouse.' It is surely most appropriate that such a remarkable bird should commemorate a great naturalist explorer, the German Peter Simon Pallas (1741-1811), whose name is also borne by five other species of bird — a fish eagle, grasshopper warbler, leaf warbler, rosefinch, and reed bunting.

In the past Pallas's sandgrouse regularly reached the British Isles during these irruption years, first being noted in November 1859 when birds reached Norfolk and Kent, and Caernarvon in the west. A major influx followed in 1863, with birds, sometimes in flocks, being reported from many counties, with some reaching Shetland, the Outer Hebrides, and Donegal. The last straggler of this invasion was shot in February 1864 in Pembroke. Further irruptions took place in 1872 and 1876, though they did not compare with the massive movement west in 1888 when birds first reached the British Isles in May, and spread throughout the land. It was estimated that over 2,000 were in Scotland alone, a pack of 40 being noted on Fair Isle, while again some reached the west coast of Ireland. A Special Act of Parliament was passed to provide protection for the invaders, though alas this did not come into effect until the following February by which time 'most of the survivors of the warm reception given to the newcomers had succumbed to the moisture of our climate, or had departed for more congenial regions'. Nesting, however, took place in both 1888 and 1889 at the Culbin Sands. Smaller invasions followed in several years, the last being 1908, with some birds lingering until the following spring.

The sighting of a single Pallas's sandgrouse at Stodmarsh on 28 December 1964 was an extraordinary and quite unexpected record after all this time. Was this the same bird seen earlier in the Netherlands? Equally remarkable was what can only be described as a mini-invasion of western Europe in 1969. In the British Isles one reached just about as far as it is possible to go, spending five days on Foula in May, while another, a male, was shot near Seahouses in early September. There are two further records, one on the Isle of May in May 1975, and remarkably another from a Scottish island when one was discovered near the Loch of Hillwell at the southern end of the Shetland mainland on 19 May 1990, where it remained for several weeks.

The Egyptian nightjar is slightly smaller than the nightjar, and has pale pinkish-grey plumage merging into sandy-buff with distinctive white throat patches, but no such markings on the tail or wings. It breeds in north-west Africa, Egypt, Iraq, and Iran, and from the Caspian Sea to the Aral Sea. Most winter in the sahel zone of Africa.

There are just two records of the Egyptian nightjar in the British Isles. The first was shot by a gamekeeper, attracted by its light colour, at Rainworth near Mansfield on 23 June 1883. Just over 100 years later came the next, one at Portland Bill on 10 June 1984.

A large, robust lark with a heavy bill, the calandra lark is noticeably larger than a skylark, having buff-brown streaked upperparts and off-white underparts and a prominent black patch on the side of the neck. The tail is short, the wings which are broad, show a white trailing edge, while the bill is stout, almost conical in shape. Calandra larks breed on grassland and steppe from Spain and North Africa to central Asia. The southern European population seems to be largely sedentary, though birds from the eastern parts of the range move south in winter.

Although there are early reports of the calandra lark from Devon, single birds at Devonport about 1863, and near Exeter about 1869, the first accepted record for the British Isles is of one at Portland Bill on 2 April 1961. There are just two others, again in April, at Fair Isle in 1978 and at St Mary's in 1985.

The bimaculated lark is smaller and more rufous-coloured than the calandra lark with which it shares the features of the black neck patch, though this is narrower and longer. The white trailing edge on the wing is absent, but note the narrow white terminal band on the tail. It breeds from central Turkey east to Kazakhstan, wintering from northern Saudi Arabia to Pakistan.

The bimaculated lark is another extremely rare lark in the British Isles with just three records. The first was one on Lundy from 7 to 11 May 1962, followed by one on St Mary's in late October 1975 and on Fair Isle in the following June.

About the size of the calandra lark, the white-winged lark is of more slender build, a feature accentuated by the longer tail. The crown and wing-covers are chestnut, while the underparts are mainly white. In flight the wings are black and chestnut, with a conspicuous white trailing edge. It breeds in central Asia from Kazakhstan to Mongolia, wintering from the area about the Black Sea to Iran.

The first white-winged lark in the British Isles was one caught with a flock of snow buntings near Brighton on 22 November 1869. The next two records were from the same county, at Hove, where three birds were watched at close quarters on the beach by J. Walpole Bond in November 1917, and at Rye, where the same observer located one in August 1933. These seem to have escaped being classed amongst the Hastings rarities. The next was at Hillfield Park Reservoir in August 1955, and the most recent was at King's Lynn in late October 1981.

The black lark, the largest lark in the West Palearctic, is a thick-set bird with a stumpy bill and a short tail. Males are unmistakable, being jet black, while females are dark brown with buff-white underparts. This is a bird of the steppe zone where it breeds from south-east Russia into central Asia to about Lake Balkash.

Both occurrences in the British Isles were multiple ones, and both were in the Hastings area so that, alas, the black lark lacks the necessary credentials to be accepted to the British List. Four were taken between 29 January and 18 February 1907, and there were three in a similar period in 1915. Elsewhere in Europe the black lark has occurred as close to our shores as Belgium and Germany.

The short-toed lark is a small rufous or grey bird with whitish underparts, a short yellow bill, a rather square head, and a small dark crescent on the shoulder, though this is not always visible. The call note should be noted and learned, it being a sharp, dry 'chichirp'. This is a bird of dry open plains from Iberia and north-west Africa east to Manchuria, which winters mainly in Africa south of the Sahara.

The short-toed lark is by far the most numerous of all the rare larks seen in the British Isles, with some 40 from the first, a bird netted near Shrewsbury on 25 October 1841, up to 1957. There have been nearly 300 since, during which time it has occurred annually, with a small spring passage, mostly during mid-May. The majority, however, are autumn birds, the peak being during late September and October. The only months for which records are lacking are from January to March. Recently in most years about 12 short-toed larks have been seen, with a peak of 17 in 1979. Interestingly the vast majority have been from opposite ends of the country, in Shetland, and in Scilly. Is this a true reflection of the bird's distribution, or is it the wealth of ornithological expertise, and binocular power, gathered in these two favoured localities, which has resulted in the sightings? Certainly elsewhere with sparse coverage such a drab, rather unremarkable bird must surely be easily overlooked. There have been a small number of sightings from other counties, mostly in England, though several birds have reached both Wales and Ireland.

The lesser short-toed lark is very similar to the short-toed lark from which it is best identified by its voice, a loud rattled, or rippled 'chirrit'. The shoulder mark is lacking, and generally the short-toed lark is more heavily streaked brown on the upperparts and chest. The pale supercilia meet in front of the eyes and form a white forehead. It breeds from Spain and north-west Africa eastwards around the Mediterranean and across Asia to the Yellow Sea, eastern populations moving south in winter.

Almost a mystery, the lesser short-toed lark is easily overlooked, and so far in the British Isles only recorded from Ireland, and then only for a brief period in the 1950s. The first, a flock of 30 no less, was seen though not identified until later by Frank King, a leading ornithologist, on a grassy area on Derrymore Island in early January 1956. Two months passed and the same observer, with others, found five on the Great Saltee, and this time identification was possible. A further two months, and Frank King with a fresh companion found two more near Belmullet. The only other record is of five on Great Saltee in March 1958.

Another member of the lark family which is difficult to identify is the crested lark, which is slightly stouter built than the skylark, with a shorter broad tail, and a much plumper head and body. The plumage is primarily pale buff, streaked on the upper-parts and on the breast, while there are dark facial markings and a rather spiky crest. No fewer than 24 races of the crested lark have been recognized in a range which extends across north Africa, southern Europe, the Middle East, and Asia to Korea.

The first crested lark in the British Isles was at Littlehampton some time prior to 1845, to be followed by 12 others, including a remarkable record of two feeding on the bank of the Thames at Chiswick Eyot, London, during hard weather in early March 1947. Since 1958 when one overwintered at Exmouth there have been five, all single birds, at Marazion in April 1965, Steart Point in April and Tunstall in June 1972, Dungeness in October 1975, and Bardsey in June 1982.

Blyth's pipit is one of the most difficult of all rare visitors to identify, and to convince those who adjudicate on such matters of the veracity of the record, however convinced you are of your observations. It is very similar to and only separated with extreme care from both Richard's pipit and the tawny pipit, though this can be achieved, and no doubt as experience and confidence grows so will the number of accepted records, though not before much debate, even controversy. Note particularly the short legs and tail, the shorter hindclaw (that is if you can get that close) and the short bill. The main calls are a distinct 'psscheoo' and a double alarm note 'cherp-cherp'.

The first Blyth's pipit in the British Isles was shot at Brighton on 23 October 1862 but remained mis-identified as a Richard's pipit in a drawer at the British Museum until its true identity was revealed in 1972 by Kenneth Williamson, perhaps the best known in a line of distinguished wardens of Fair Isle. Even then, doubts were expressed as to whether this bird would ever occur again in western Europe, doubts happily dispelled when one reached Fair Isle, appropriately enough, in mid-October 1988 where it remained, elusive for much of the time, for ten days. Finally, as far as this book is concerned, was one at Portland Bill from 16 March to 3 May 1989. Despite its long stay, it proved a most difficult bird to obtain clear views of, and this, together with some divergence of opinion, indeed hot debate, has resulted in some observers claiming it to be a Richard's rather than a Blyth's pipit. Clearly there is much more to learn of this most frustrating of birds. Hopefully the words of the late Peter Grant will prove correct when he said: 'As is invariably the case with "difficult" rarities, I suspect that a real Blyth's will be obvious and non-controversial, and hopefully trapped and photographed to confirm the identification'.

The isabelline wheatear, largest wheatear in the Western Palearctic, is also as the name suggests one of the palest, having a sandy-coloured plumage. It breeds in small numbers in the extreme south-east of Europe from where its range extends eastwards, the bird frequenting grassy steppes and steppe-desert to Manchuria, Mongolia, Tibet, and the high plains of Afghanistan. Winter quarters are in the Sahel of Africa, the Arabian peninsula, Pakistan, and north-west India.

The first record of an isabelline wheatear in the British Isles was one at Allonby on the coast of Cumberland on 11 November 1887. There were 90 years to the next, to 28 May 1977, when one frequented the dunes at Winterton for the day. Subsequent records, like the first, have all been in the autumn, one on a golf course at Girdleness on the south side of Aberdeen remained from 17 October to 10 November. The next, at Bamburgh in September 1980 has been followed by just one other, at St Mary's at the beginning of October 1988.

By way of contrast the pied wheatear is the smallest of the West Palearctic wheatears, a lightly built, often rather shy bird, though it frequently hunts from a perch rather than from the ground. It usually breeds in stony areas in the extreme south-east of Europe, extending from there to central Asia and northern China. The winter quarters are from Aden and the Yemen, and through eastern Africa from the Sudan to Tanzania, where it seems to lose its shyness, even coming to frequent towns and villages.

The first two records of the pied wheatear were both from Scotland. A female on the Isle of May on 19 October 1909 was shot by the 'two unforgettable heroines' of Scottish ornithology, Evelyn Baxter and Leonora Rintoul. The second was on Swona in the Pentland Firth on 1 November 1916, and the third at Portland from 17 to 19 October 1954, since when there have been 14 other records, most birds remaining for several days. The longest was one on a boulder beach at the mouth of the River Don from 26 September to 7 October 1976. There is just one spring record, a first-summer male at Winterton at the end of May 1978. The others, all coastal records, have been between late September and early December, from Boulmer to Paignton, with one in Wales, at Skokholm in October 1968, and two in Ireland, at Knockadoon Head in November 1980 and Ballynaclesh in November 1963. Most remarkable of all in 1988 were the three pied wheatears recorded in the period 16 to 19 October, at Stronsay, Flamborough Head, and Blakeney Point.

The name desert wheatear is somewhat misleading, for although it frequents a range of dry habitats the desert wheatear rarely penetrates beyond the desert edge in a range which extends from north-west Africa along the southern shore of the Mediterranean, in parts of the Middle East, and through central Asia to Sinkiang, and Mongolia. The desert wheatear often winters at no great distance south of the breeding areas.

The first desert wheatear to be seen here was a male at Alloa on 26 November 1880, with just 10 further records up to 1958 in which year a male was located in mid-January at the mouth of the River Colne. There have been a further 16 records, the majority like this one in the winter, though there have been sightings from mid-September to mid-April. All were seen on the coast, at localities from Shetland to Scilly, with just one in the west, at South Walney in November 1986.

The white-crowned black wheatear is a large, oval-shaped black wheatear, with a white crown in the adult. It breeds across the Sahara and in parts of the Arabian Peninsula.

A machinery dump close to the coast at Kessingland was a most unlikely spot to discover the first, and so far only white-crowned black wheatear, in the British Isles. One was there for several days in early June 1982. But what brought such a sedentary bird over 1,000 miles (1,600 km) north of its normal range? A strong southerly airflow originating from North Africa which raised temperatures over much of southern Britain was probably the reason why this Saharan wheatear arrived here.

A large wheatear, almost thrush-like in flight, the black wheatear (the male black, the female brown) inhabits stony areas in the extreme southwest of France, through Iberia, and in north Africa from Libya to the Rio de Oro. It is largely sedentary in habit, save for a post-breeding season dispersal, and in mountainous areas where some birds will move to lower levels.

Just four black wheatears have been recorded from the British Isles, the first being a male seen on Fair Isle on 28 September 1912 by the Duchess of Bedford and W. Eagle Clarke; it must have been an elusive bird to avoid their guns. Fair Isle had its second record on 19 October 1953, the others being at Altrincham on 1 August 1943, and at Dungeness on 17 October 1954. The sole Irish record (though the possibility of it having been a white-crowned black wheatear cannot be ruled out) was at Portnoo on 10 June 1964.

The desert warbler is a tiny grey/sand-coloured warbler which breeds on the steppe desert lands from the Caspian east to Mongolia, and also in the north-west of the Sahara. Winter quarters extend from Africa south of the Sahara to Arabia and south-west Asia.

A desert warbler at Portland from 16 December 1970 to early the following January was the first for the British Isles. There were two in 1975, at Spurn from 20 to 24 October, and at Frinton-on-Sea in late November. The next was at Meols for nearly a month from late October 1979, and finally there was one at Bembridge Pools on 30 October 1988.

Linnet size, with a large head and pink bill, the trumpeter finch gets its name from the nasal, far-carrying call, once described as 'like a rather poor effort on a child's trumpet'. It is a bird of dry ravines and rocky areas from the Canaries, across north-west Africa and the Sahara to the Sudan and Egypt and on to Sind. Most are sedentary, but some local movements can occur, and birds began to colonize southern Spain in the late 1960s.

The arrival of the trumpeter finch on the British List was a major surprise when it occurred at Minsmere from 30 May to at least 19 June 1971. It was a good thing that it stayed, for at least it avoided confusion with the second, a bird at Handa on 8 June the same year. Ten years later the next was also in the north, a male on Sanday in May 1981. One at Church Norton in May 1984 had the misfortune to be taken by a sparrowhawk. Two further records were both late in the year, at Foulness on 21 September

1985 and Holy Island on 1 August 1987. Is this a species which with changing climatic conditions we are likely to see much more frequently in the years to come? Beware, however, that trumpeter finches are kept in captivity, and the possibility of escapes cannot be ruled out.

The Mediterranean Region and Beyond

Great Spotted
  Cuckoo
Red-necked Nightjar
Pallid Swift
Alpine Swift
Little Swift
Bee-eater
Roller
Crag Martin
Red-rumped Swallow
Alpine Accentor
Rufous Bush Robin
Black-eared
  Wheatear
Rock Thrush
Blue Rock Thrush

Fan-tailed Warbler
Moustached Warbler
Great Reed Warbler
Olivaceous Warbler
Marmora's Warbler
Spectacled Warbler
Subalpine Warbler
Sardinian Warbler
Ruppell's Warbler
Orphean Warbler
Bonelli's Warbler
Collared Flycatcher
Wallcreeper
Short-toed
  Treecreeper

Penduline Tit
Lesser Grey Shrike
Woodchat Shrike
Masked Shrike
Rose-coloured
  Starling
Spanish Sparrow
Rock Sparrow
Snow Finch
Citril Finch
Rock Bunting
Cretzschmar's
  Bunting
Black-headed
  Bunting

The great spotted cuckoo is distinctly larger than the cuckoo, being dark above, spotted white on the wings, and creamy white below. Adults have a blue-grey crown with a crest which is frequently raised. In the slightly dipping flight, the rounded wings with chestnut primaries and the long, white-edged tail give a rather magpie-like silhouette. It breeds from the Iberian peninsula to Iran, and also in southern Africa, parasitizing members of the crow family, in southern Europe most frequently the magpie. In winter the northern populations move to Africa, mainly south of the Sahara.

The first great spotted cuckoo in the British Isles was found alive but in an emaciated condition on the island of Omey off the coast of Connemara in about March 1842, and is now in the Museum of Trinity College, Dublin. There were a further five before 1958, in Northumberland in 1870, Kerry in 1918, Merioneth in 1955 and two in Norfolk, in 1896 and 1941. Since another great spotted cuckoo found freshly dead at Winterton on 6 August 1958, 21 more have been recorded, mostly single birds in a year, but with two in 1978 and 1982. Occurrences range from one found dead at Ballajora on 12 March 1963 to a juvenile which remained at Easington from mid-October to early November 1982. Most of those recorded are from England with two from Ireland, at Mahee Island, Strangford Lough, in September, and another early bird found dead, this time on 13 March 1983

Bridled Tern, Cemlyn, July 1988 *(Steve Young)*.

Ocean Nomads

Wilson's Storm-Petrel, 50 miles south-west of Mizen Head, Cork, August 1985 *(Anthony McGeehan)*.

Arctic Birds

King Eider, Ythan Estuary, May 1987
(Steve Young).

Ross's Gull, Filey,
February 1983 *(D. W.
Burns)*.

Ivory Gull, Sumburgh, November
1980 *(Dennis Coutts)*.

Snowy Owl, Unst,
June 1987 *(Steve
Young)*.

White-billed Diver, Hartlepool,
February 1981 *(D. W. Burns).*

Gyr Falcon, North
Slob, Wexford
Harbour, April 1986
(Anthony McGeehan).

Arctic Redpoll, Fair
Isle, September 1987
(Tim Loseby).

Eurasian Waterbirds

Night Heron, Magor Marsh, May 1983 *(Richard G. Smith)*.

Cattle Egret, New Mills, Derbyshire, January 1987 *(Steve Young)*.

Slender-billed Gulls, Cley, May 1987 *(Steve Young)*.

Little Bittern, Oreham
Common Pond, April
1988 *(Tim Loseby).*

Black Stork, Walney
(Tony Broome).

Little Crake,
Cuckmere, March
1985 *(D. W. Burns).*

Baillon's Crake,
Sunderland, May 1989
(Tim Loseby).

Whiskered Tern,
Radipole Lake, April
1987 *(D. W. Burns).*

White-winged Black
Tern, Cuckmere,
August 1984 *(D. W.
Burns).*

North American Waterbirds

Pied-billed Grebe, Kenfig, 1987/8
(David M. Cottridge).

Sora Rail, Pagham
Lagoon, November
1985 *(Barry Wright).*

Blue-winged Teal,
Tamar Reservoir,
August 1989 *(Barry
Wright).*

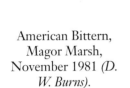

Bonaparte's Gull, Cardiff, April 1986
(Richard G. Smith).

American Bittern,
Magor Marsh,
November 1981 *(D.
W. Burns)*.

American Wigeon, Fair Isle,
September 1986 *(Alan Roberts)*.

Ring-necked Duck,
Llanelli, April 1988
(Richard G. Smith).

Surf Scoter, Southerness, 1980 *(Alan Roberts)*.

Laughing Gull, Lerwick, September 1989 *(Dennis Coutts)*.

Franklin's Gull, Plymouth, January 1982 *(Richard G. Smith)*.

Hawk Owl, Lerwick, September 1983 *(Dennis Coutts)*.

Birds of Prey

Red-footed Falcon, Walls, Shetland, June 1989 *(Dennis Coutts)*.

Black-winged Stilt, Holme, June 1987 *(Tim Loseby).*

European and Asian Waterbirds

Long-toed Stint, Teeside, September 1982 *(D. W. Burns).*

Great Snipe, Fair Isle,
September 1981 *(Tony
Broome)*.

Little Whimbrel, Sker
Point, September
1982 *(D. W. Burns)*.

Marsh Sandpiper,
Cley, August 1984
(Richard G. Smith).

North American Waders

Least Sandpiper, Porthscatho, April
1986 *(Richard G. Smith)*.

Lesser Yellowlegs,
Drift Reservoir,
August 1989 *(Barry
Wright)*.

American Golden Plover, Drifts
Dam, September 1980 *(Alan Roberts)*.

Killdeer, Bo'ness, January 1983
(D. W. Burns).

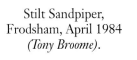
Stilt Sandpiper,
Frodsham, April 1984
(Tony Broome).

Long-billed Dowitcher, Unst, April
1989 *(Dennis Coutts)*.

Upland Sandpiper, St
Mary's, October 1983
(D. W. Burns).

Black-winged Pratincole, Clevedon, June 1988 *(David M. Cottridge)*.

Desert and Steppe

Greater Sandplover, Walney, July 1988 *(Steve Young)*.

Oriental Pratincole *(Tim Loseby)*.

Desert Wheatear, Penclawdd, November 1989 *(Richard G. Smith)*.

The Mediterranean Region and beyond

Penduline Tit, St Agnes *(Richard G. Smith)*.

Lesser Grey Shrike, Aberdaron, October 1986 *(Tim Loseby)*.

Alpine Accentor, Isle of Wight, May 1990 *(David M. Cottridge)*.

Great Spotted Cuckoo, Shoreham,
April 1990 *(Barry Wright)*.

Isabelline Shrike,
Berry Head *(Richard
G. Smith)*.

Rose-coloured
Starling, St Mary's,
October 1986 *(Tim
Loseby)*.

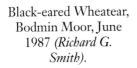

Black-eared Wheatear,
Bodmin Moor, June
1987 *(Richard G.
Smith)*.

Citrine Wagtail, Blakeney Marshes, September 1986 *(Barry Wright)*.

North-east and Central Europe

Little Bunting, Adswood Tip, April 1983 *(Alan Roberts)*.

Blyth's Reed Warbler,
Fair Isle, September
1987 *(Dennis Coutts)*.

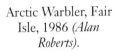

Arctic Warbler, Fair
Isle, 1986 *(Alan
Roberts)*.

Nutcracker, Westleton,
1985 *(Tim Loseby)*.

Parrot Crossbill, Catfirth, Shetland, October 1982 *(Tim Loseby)*.

Rustic Bunting, Fair Isle, September 1987 *(Tim Loseby)*.

Yellow-breasted Bunting, Fair Isle, September 1987 *(Tim Loseby)*.

Central Asia

Dusky Warbler,
Happisburgh, Norfolk,
November 1987 *(Steve
Young)*.

Rufous Turtle Dove,
Spurn Point,
November 1975 *(Tony
Broome)*.

White-throated
Robin, Skokholm,
May 1990 (*J. W.*
Donovan).

Paddyfield Warbler,
Fair Isle, September
1986 (*Alan Roberts*).

Siberian Forests and Taiga

Pallas's Warbler, Spurn Point, October 1988 *(Steve Young)*.

Dusky Thrush (Naumann's Thrush), Chingford, February 1990 *(David M. Cottridge)*.

Needle-tailed Swift, Quendale, 1984 *(Dennis Coutts)*.

Olive-backed Pipit,
Bracknell, February
1984 *(Tim Loseby)*.

Eye-browed Thrush,
Fair Isle, October
1987 *(Dennis Coutts)*.

Pallas's Grasshopper
Warbler, Fair Isle,
September 1981 *(Tony
Broome)*.

North American Landbirds

Veery, Lundy, 1986 *(David M. Cottridge)*.

Yellow-billed Cuckoo, St Mary's, October 1986 *(Tim Loseby)*.

Black-billed Cuckoo, St Mary's, October 1985 *(D. W. Burns)*.

Grey-cheeked Thrush,
Tresco, October 1986
(Tim Loseby).

Swainson's Thrush, St
Agnes, October 1984
(D. W. Burns).

Yellow-bellied
Sapsucker, first winter
female, Cape Clear,
October 1988
(Anthony McGeehan).

Golden-winged Warbler, Larkfield, Kent, February 1989 *(David M. Cottridge)*.

Northern Parula, St Mary's, October 1985 *(Barry Wright)*.

Black and White Warbler, How Hill, December 1985 *(Tim Loseby)*.

Yellowthroat, Fetlar, 1984 *(Dennis Coutts).*

Tennessee Warbler, Fair Isle, September 1975 *(Tony Broome).*

Savannah Sparrow, Portland, Dorset, April 1982 *(David M. Cottridge).*

Indigo Bunting, Wells Wood, October 1988 (*Barry Wright*).

Song Sparrow, Fair Isle, April 1979 (*Dennis Coutts*).

White-throated Sparrow, Lerwick, May 1989 (*Dennis Coutts*).

Rose-breasted
Grosbeak, Cape Clear,
October 1987
(Anthony McGeehan).

Bobolink, St Mary's,
October 1983 *(D. W.
Burns)*.

Northern Oriole,
Roch, 1989 *(J. W.
Donovan)*.

Radde's Warbler (1st WP).
Porthgwarra.
-17th -19th Oct. "88".
E. A. Fisher.
Neat Version of original field
Sketches :-

Head: Large; long yellowish Supa
Starting finely at base of
uppermandible, broadest over
eye. Often upcurved. Eye-
Stripe broadest at rear (as
upperparts) - bordering ear covs.
Ear covs. dusty- mottled grey/
yellow.

Majority of upperparts
olive brown.

Bill: broad based +
blunt ended -
culmen + tip dark
horn, rest orangey.

"Bulky looking-
"Pot billed",
Robust.

Generally an
olive and yellow
bird.

Large headed.

Majority of
underparts
yellow / buff.

Tail: Sub-stantial length,
broader + longer than
Chyg-Chaff.(Square
ended).

Under diff. lighting etc,
the upperparts appeared
browner and the under-
parts buff.

Wings: Short + rounded,
with no obvious markings.

tail often
raised.

Legs: Sturdy looking
with v. large feet
(orangey).

"Wren like" posture.

Rusty-
undertail
coverts +
vent.

At range uppermandible
appeared all dark.

V. Skulking
behaviour, usually
found in low cover.

wings usually
held below tail.

Radde's Warbler, Porthgwarra, October 1988. *(Field sketch by E. A. Fisher)* at North Bull. There have been single records from Scotland, an immature which remained at Rendall from 14 to 30 August 1959, and in Wales at Malltraeth in August the following year. One near Truro remained from late April until the end of June 1968, while most recent of all was one at Shoreham for the whole of April 1990.

A robust bird, slightly larger than the nightjar, the red-necked nightjar is further distinguished by its reddish-brown, more variegated plumage, the large white throat, rufous nape collar and large white spots on the tail and outer wing. It breeds in Iberia and in north-west Africa from Tunisia to Morocco, with most wintering in west Africa. The only record of the red-necked nightjar for the British Isles occurred on 5 October 1856 when John Hancock recognized a bird killed at Killingworth, the same Hancock whose collections are now based in the famous museum in Newcastle-upon-Tyne which bears his name.

The pallid swift is most easily confused with the swift and for that reason may well be overlooked, though it has broader wings, a blunt tail fork and larger head. the plumage is paler, more milky brown, not unlike that of a sand martin, with a white face and throat. It breeds at the Canaries, and in Madeira where many nest in sea cliffs, around the Mediterranean, in north-west Africa, the Middle East, and around the Persian Gulf. Wintering birds occur throughout much of the northern tropics in Africa.

We hear much about sponsored bird counts as a means of raising funds towards bird protection measures, though few who take part can expect to add a new bird to the British List whilst doing so. What price such an event in sponsorship terms? However, this did happen on 13 May 1978 to D. Raine and W. G. Harvey at the Stodmarsh National Nature Reserve when a pallid swift was identified during a passage of swifts across the reedbeds and lagoons. It remained until at least 21 May, was photographed and was seen by many observers, so that a bird which had been claimed in the past was at last accepted. The next, at Farlington Marshes in May 1983 remained for a mere 15 minutes, leaving one excited observer to spread the word amongst numerous disappointed colleagues. The remaining records, all from November 1984 are intriguing, two at Portland on the 10th and one at Strumble Head on the 12th and 13th, and one at Warden Point, Sheppey, from 14th to 16th. What prompted such a northward movement by birds which should at that time have been foraging low over the Sahel zone of Africa?

The alpine swift is a powerful bird, larger and more thick-set than the swift, though with a comparatively shorter tail. The plumage is umber-brown with a white throat, brown breast band, and white belly. Holes in buildings, as well as natural sites in cliffs are the nesting site of the alpine swift in a range which extends across southern Europe and as far as India, and Ceylon in Asia, and in east and southern Africa and Madagascar. This is an extremely mobile species whose flights often take birds long distances from the colony, some flying up to 600 miles (960 km) in a day. Birds from European colonies winter largely in southern Africa.

The first alpine swift in the British Isles was shot off Cape Clear about 1829, with about 50 others having been noted up to 1957, and no fewer than 267 added since. Birds are now being seen annually with occurrences likely at any time from mid-March to early November. There are distinct peaks of movement in May and again in late September. The annual totals vary, reaching a maximum of 20 in 1987 and 18 in 1988. Whether in spring or in autumn, the occurrences show much the same distribution, most alpine swifts occurring in southern and eastern counties with smaller numbers in Ireland where there have been 22 birds, with 17 in each of Scotland and Wales since 1957.

The square tail of the little swift is a feature unique among West Palearctic swifts. Its name is appropriate, for this small compact bird is only three-quarters the size of a swift, having sooty-brown plumage with a pale face and rump. The flight is more fluttering than other swifts, with frequent steady glides when the wings are held straight out from the body. Widely distributed in Africa, where there has been a marked expansion of range in the north-west, and across southern Asia to Indonesia and north to Japan.

One at Cape Clear on 12 June 1967 was the first little swift in the British Isles. The next occurred on 6 November 1973 at Llanwrst, while in 1981 there were two sightings, one at Skewjack in mid-May, followed by one on Skokholm at the end of the month. In 1983 there was the second November record, this time even later on the 26th at Studland. In 1984 one at Seaforth in late May was followed by two in 1985, at St Andrews also in May, and Slapton Ley in mid-August. Most recently was the one at Flamborough Head in July 1988.

Another unmistakable bird, the bee-eater is a resplendent mixture of chestnut in various hues, blue-green, a white forehead and a vivid yellow throat. Much of the bright colour is lost by late summer, though the yellow throat and brown head are retained. The call of migrating bee-eaters, a romantic 'quilp' is immediately recognizable, especially if you have been fortunate to hear it previously in some part of the birds' breeding range. This extends from Iberia and north Africa to central Asia, and also in South Africa. Northern populations move to Africa south of the Sahara for the winter.

The bee-eater is one of the more frequent rare visitors to the British Isles, certainly once seen attention is bound to be drawn to its presence here. As early as 1668 it was described as a rare visitor, though not until 1793 was a specimen obtained, this a bird taken in Norfolk. The 154 records up to 1957 include a pair which attempted to nest in a sandbank on the River Esk at Musselburgh in 1920. Unfortunately the female was caught by a local gardener and confined in a greenhouse where, not surprisingly, it died, though not before laying an almost fully developed egg. The male also suffered ill-fortune, being caught and eaten by a cat. More success surrounded no less than three pairs which took up residence in a Sussex sand-pit in 1955. Here two reared a total of seven young, the nest of the third pair being accidentally destroyed by an excavator.

Since 1957 nearly 300 bee-eaters have been recorded in the British Isles with records in every year except 1975. The number seen each year has increased with 21 in 1983, 26 in 1985, 34 in 1987 and 37 in 1988. Warmer summers may well have lured more bee-eaters north. Will we see more breeding attempts? Most occur in the spring from mid-April until June, with a smaller passage in the autumn, some stragglers remaining until December. Quite a few multiple occurrences have been reported; three in Orkney in June 1966, seven at the Mumbles in June 1983, four at Kendal in

June 1981. Were the seven at Valencia Island in May 1983 the same seven seen several days previously at St Agnes? Even more impressive were the 15, though it could have been as many as 27, at Porthgwarra on 26 May 1985. Although most reported are in southern England, some have reached Shetland where as one observer noted this must be the only place in the world where the snowy owl and bee-eater meet. In the west some 15 have reached Ireland since 1957, with 11 in Wales.

The size of a jay and equally dramatically coloured, the roller has a blue-green head, neck, and underparts, chestnut brown upperparts, and wings a mixture of blue and of black. It often perches in prominent positions like telegraph wires, or in dead trees, from where it may drop swiftly on to its largely insect prey. The roller breeds from Iberia and north-west Africa to central Asia, most wintering in east Africa.

Some 135 rollers had been recorded up to 1957, the first being described as a visitor here from a specimen taken in Norfolk in May 1864, though there is a reference to its occurrence in Orkney as early as 1700. Subsequently there have been a further 78 birds being seen almost annually between the end of April and late October, most in May and June with a smaller peak in September. Quite often birds remain for several days before moving on. Indeed one in Orkney in the Deerness area in May 1958 stayed for two months. Most rollers occur in eastern and southern counties, as well as regularly from Scotland north to the Shetlands, and from Wales, but so far there have only been two from Ireland since 1957, a bird found freshly dead at Castlegregory in late May 1958, and one seen at Castlederg in July 1976.

A stoutly built hirundine, the crag martin is about the size of the swallow but lacks the long tail streamers; indeed the tail is almost square. Dusky brown in colour with black underwing coverts and white spots under the tail, its flight is distinctive, a few easy wing beats with frequent leisurely glides. It breeds widely in Iberia, and from there across southern Europe and Asia to China, and also in north Africa. In Europe the crag martin is slowly extending its range northwards, with nesting first reported in Jura, Switzerland, in 1970 and Bavaria, Germany, in 1981, with an expansion of ranges in both Austria and Romania. Most are sedentary, but there is some movement south in the autumn.

There are just two records of the crag martin in the British Isles, and indeed despite the expansion in range already referred to the only other records in northern Europe are of single birds in Finland and in East Germany. One at Stithians reservoir on 22 June 1988 was followed by another — or was it the same bird? — at Beachy Head on 9 July. On both occasions just a single observer was fortunate to be present, who after taking note of all salient features rushed off to alert others, but on return the bird had gone.

The red-rumped swallow is about the same size as a swallow, but has a bulkier build, shorter, more rounded wings, and shorter, blunter, tail streamers. There are no white spots in the tail, while the dark chest band of the swallow is also absent. The rump is a creamy-buff, and the nape is chest-nut. Note the different style of flight, the deliberate, slower wing-beats than the swallow, with much more gliding. Beware of swallow/martin hybrids, and if you encounter what you believe to be a red-rumped swallow, please take full field notes, though this action should be *sine qua non* whenever you encounter a rare bird.

Although it uses houses, mosques, bridges and other man-made structures, the red-rumped swallow is much less dependent on such sites than the swallow. It breeds in the Iberian peninsula and in south and south-eastern Europe, with a tiny population in Italy and France where it only became established as a breeding bird in the mid-1970s. Elsewhere the red-rumped swallow occurs across Asia, south to Ceylon and north to the Amur River, while in Africa a series of races occupy large tracts of the continent south to Zaire and Malawi. Northern birds leave the breeding areas in late summer, though winter quarters are hard to determine in view of the southern resident populations.

The first red-rumped swallows in the British Isles were described as three waifs when they appeared at Fair Isle during a rush of migrants on 2 June 1906. Before 1958 there were only seven additional records, but since then the total has risen by a further 167, with birds being seen annually since 1964. No fewer than 64 arrived in 1987, including flocks of seven in Flint and Scilly. Most red-rumped swallows occur in the British Isles in April and May, but surprisingly during the 1987 invasion the majority were in November and December. This is primarily an English bird, largely seen from Yorkshire to Scilly, with comparatively few elsewhere. There are only 15 records from Scotland since the first trio on Fair Isle, including three, possibly four, in Shetland during the 1987 invasion. There are just five records from Ireland, all since 1952 and three of these were in 1987, at the Old Head of Kinsale in April, and November records from Loop Head and Hook Head. Are these occurrences the precursor of even more frequent visits by the red-rumped swallow to the British Isles? Indeed, might we see it breeding here during the next century?

The alpine accentor is the largest accentor, distinctly larger than the dunnock, with a pale blue-grey head and breast, mottled brown back, a white throat speckled black, and a white-tipped tail. The wings show a black patch between two white wing-bars. It breeds in upland regions from Spain across southern Europe and through central Asia, making only local movements of an altitudinal nature.

The first alpine accentor was one at Walthamstow in August 1817, followed in late November 1822 by two birds noticed climbing about the buildings or feeding on the lawns in King's College, Cambridge. There followed a further 26 records, mostly in the last century or the early part of this. One on Fair Isle in June 1959 was only the second alpine accentor in Scotland, the other having been at the same locality in October 1908. Recent records have all been during the 1970s, at Ramsgate in May 1975, Dungeness the following year almost to the day, on St Mary's at the end of October 1977 and then two in 1978, both spring records and both trapped and ringed, at Sheringham and Portland. When will the next be? Is this a bird which because of changing climate will not be seen again in the British Isles during our lifetime? The answer is, fortunately, no, for much to everyone's surprise and quite unbounded pleasure, one was discovered on the cliffs at West High Down at the western end of the Isle of Wight on 27 May 1990.

The rufous bush robin or rufous scrub-robin, formerly known as the rufous warbler, is slightly larger than a robin, slimmer built but with a distinctly longer, fan-shaped tail, and longer legs. The upperparts are a bright brown, sometimes grey-brown, the underparts buff-white, while there is a conspicuous creamy stripe above the eye, and a double white wing-bar. It should be unmistakable as it cocks its tail up over its back, or jerks it nervously while drooping the wings until they nearly touch the ground. The rufous bush robin breeds around the Mediterranean, in North Africa, east to Lake Balkhash in central Asia, and to Baluchistan. Some reach east Africa in winter.

A rufous bush robin obtained near Brighton on 16 September 1854 was the first in the British Isles, with just 10 others subsequently recorded. These were at Start in 1859 and at Slapton in 1876, the same year that one was shot at the Old Head of Kinsale, and which posed for some 20 years as a nightingale; then came two in a year in 1951, at Great Saltee and Dungeness, followed by one at Prawle Point in 1959, and another, this time trapped at Butlin's holiday camp, at Skegness in 1963. One at Cape Clear in April 1968 is the only spring record, with just two subsequent sightings of the rufous bush robin in the British Isles, Flamborough Head in 1972 being the furthest north so far, and finally another Devon record, this time at Prawle Point in August 1980.

An elegant and agile wheatear with a long conspicuous tail, the black-eared wheatear breeds from Iberia and north-west Africa around much of the northern Mediterranean, through Turkey and parts of the Middle East to Iran. The savannahs and semi-desert regions of Africa from Senegal to Ethiopia are its winter quarters.

The first black-eared wheatear in the British Isles was a male near Bury in May 1878, and subsequently it has proved to be the most frequent of the rare wheatears to arrive. There were 14 others up to 1957 and some 30 since, being now not quite annual in its occurrence. Most are reported between mid-April and early July, with others from the end of August until early October. In most years just a single bird is reported, but in 1987 there were an exceptional six. The majority of black-eared wheatears are seen in the British Isles on east and south coasts from Shetland to Scilly. More westerly records have been two on Lundy, single records from the Calf of Man and Bardsey, and two from Ireland, both in 1987, at Great Saltee and Newcastle, the first in that country since the first ever, one found at Tuskar Rock Lighthouse in May 1916. During the mini-invasion of 1987 there was a single inland record, one on Bodmin Moor for two days in mid-June.

A plump, short-tailed thrush, the rock thrush is a shy bird, which despite its striking appearance in summer of grey-blue upperparts and orange underparts can be confused with several related species which are kept in captivity. It usually breeds in rocky areas in north-west Africa, and from Iberia across southern Europe, Asia Minor, parts of the Middle East, and Asia to Mongolia, and China. Winter quarters are in tropical Africa, mainly just north of the equator.

The first rock thrush in the British Isles was shot at Therfield on 19 May 1843, with five other early records, two on the Pentland Skerries in May 1910, at Fair Isle in 1931 and 1936, and in Kent in 1933. Since 1957 16 more have occurred, usually one in a year, but in 1969, 1983 and 1984 there were two reported. All except two have been between mid-April and the end of June. Outside this period were the bird at Minster in February 1983 which remained until April, and the sole autumn record, a first-winter male on St Mary's in mid-October 1984. Most of those recorded since 1957 have been in southern counties with just two from Scotland, birds on St Kilda and Fair Isle, two from Wales, at Ynyslas and Llyn Alaw, and just one from Ireland, a fine adult male at Clogher Head.

About the size of a redwing, the blue rock thrush is another handsome bird, which not surprisingly is frequently kept in captivity. It breeds on sea cliffs and on inland crags, quarries and in large ruins, from Iberia and Morocco eastwards, largely along the north side of the Mediterranean, through the Middle East and southern central Asia to Japan. Winter quarters extend from east Africa, Arabia, India, and south-east Asia to Indonesia.

The four records of the blue rock thrush in the British Isles have never been accepted as confirmed migrants. They remain as Category D species, those where escape from captivity cannot be ruled out. There are, however, accepted records elsewhere in northern Europe, at much the same time as our own birds, so that the whole question of its status in this country is somewhat overdue for consideration. The first for the British Isles was one on North Ronaldsay on 29 August 1966, a suitable date and a more than suitable landfall for a vagrant, though its damaged tail feathers suggested a captive origin. The others were at Rye in August 1977, one found dead at Skerryvore Lighthouse in the South Minch in June 1985, and finally one at Moel-y-cest near Porthmadog in June 1987.

The fan-tailed warbler is a tiny warbler, tawny-buff above with heavy streaking, and white below, with a long bill and roundish tail which, as the name suggests is frequently fanned or cocked. Usually only the singing male reveals the presence of this bird for it has most secretive habits except when making short but sometimes towering display flights. It is a bird which has extended its range north in Europe so that the fan-tailed warbler now breeds on the Biscay coast of France. Elsewhere it occurs around the Mediterranean, over much of Africa south of the Sahara, and from north-west India across Asia north to Japan, and through the East Indies to Australia. Most are sedentary, though there is some evidence of migration in the western Mediterranean.

The first fan-tailed warbler in the British Isles was seen in a sedge clump on Cape Clear on 23 April 1962. There are just three further records, at Cley, then at Holme in August 1976, Lodmoor in June the following year, and a second at Cape Clear in April 1985. Despite the northward extension of range, and a prophecy in 1977 that the fan-tailed warbler would soon colonize the southern counties of England, Ireland and Wales, such hopes have alas so far not been realized.

The moustached warbler closely resembles the sedge warbler in appearance, though it has shorter wings and a more rounded tail. Even the voices are similar. This is a bird of reed and *Typha* beds rather than the scrub favoured by the sedge warbler, in the Mediterranean region, east across Asia to Turkestan, and north-west India, most remaining within the breeding range throughout the year.

There are just five records of the moustached warbler in the British Isles, the first being among the most remarkable of all rare bird occurrences, for in 1946 a pair nested at the Cambridge sewage farm and reared three young. Despite the observations made, there was still much controversy in the aftermath of the event in view of the similarity with the sedge warbler, while as one authority astringently commented: 'The chance of a lone female and a lone male meeting in a Cambridgeshire reedbed seem rather remote.' There were two at Totton in August 1951. Had they possibly nested somewhere as well? There are just three other records, Kent in 1952, Buckingham in 1965 and Sussex in 1979. This must be a candidate species for northward expansion due to climatic change, so that its establishment here as a breeding species, despite such faltering efforts in the past, cannot be ruled out.

The largest warbler to occur in the British Isles, the great reed warbler is olive-brown above and orange-buff below. If it chooses to sing attention will be quickly drawn by the loud, harsh, almost frog-like notes. It breeds widely in Europe from southern Sweden and the Baltic states to Iberia and east through much of Europe, and across much of Asia, wintering mainly in Africa.

One of the most frequent of rare warblers to reach the British Isles, the majority of great reed warblers occur in spring and early summer, undoubtedly birds which have overshot breeding grounds just across the English Channel and southern North Sea. The first was obtained near Newcastle on 28 May 1847, with a further 22 up to 1957. Since then 124 others have been recorded, with the bird only being absent in 1968 and 1983. Numbers vary, with nine in 1978 being the highest annual total.

Hopes must rise whenever this noisy songster establishes a territory for a few days in a reedbed, but alas so far they have all moved on. The small number of late summer and autumn records extend as late as mid-November, though most are seen in August. Although there is a strong southerly bias in spring, birds do extend north to Shetland, where the first for Scotland was heard singing at Loch Brow in early June 1958, and to the west coast, with just two in Ireland, both at Cape Clear. In autumn most occur south of the Humber to Severn line.

Another difficult warbler to identify, the olivaceous warbler is very similar to the melodious warbler, being olive-grey above, buffish-white below but with a longer bill. It breeds in southern Europe and north Africa east to Kazakhstan and Pakistan, with winter quarters south of the Sahara.

The first olivaceous warbler for the British Isles was one seen and subsequently caught above South Haven, the main landing place on Skokholm on 23 September 1951. The next was at Portland Bill on 16 August 1956. Again the bird was caught, and so that identification could not be doubted was taken to the British Museum (Natural History) for comparison with skins, before being released in Richmond Park, where perhaps not surprisingly 'it was very shy and soon lost to view'. Since 1957 there have been 12 further records, all in the autumn, the earliest on 27 August being at Portland in 1967, the latest being one that remained on St Mary's from 17 to 27 October 1985, incidentally the last to have been recorded.

The sole record for Scotland was one which spent two days on the Isle of May in September 1967 before being killed by a great grey shrike. In England the olivaceous warbler has been recorded in Yorkshire, Kent, Dorset (2), Cornwall, Scilly (4), and in Ireland in Donegal and Cork.

Marmora's warbler is very like the Dartford warbler save for grey rather than red-brown upperparts. It has one of the most restricted ranges of all warblers, breeding only in Corsica, Sardinia, the Balearics, and on the Mediterranean coast of Spain. Winter quarters are in Tunisia and Libya. Records away from these areas are extremely rare, the most northerly previously being in north-west Italy.

How then did a Marmora's warbler come to appear 1,200 miles (1,920 km) further north? One at Mickledon Clough, high in the Pennines near Langsett on 15 May 1982 is the only record for the British Isles. It remained in this upland valley, giving joy to hundreds of birdwatchers, until late July. The arrival of this Mediterranean species seems to have been linked with one of the occasional and, for the naturalist, exciting flows of warm air from the south which brings unexpected gems north, not only for the ornithologist, but also, on occasions, for the entomologist as well.

The spectacled warbler is like a small slim whitethroat, having a slate-grey head and nape, rufous wings, and a white throat which contrasts with the pinkish breast. Do not be mistaken: the white spectacle is not always visible. It breeds on the Cape Verde Islands, Canaries, Madeira, and in north-west Africa, and Egypt, and on the north side of the Mediterranean in parts of Iberia, Italy, and Sicily.

Although the spectacled warbler has been claimed as having occurred in the British Isles on several occasions, the first being at Spurn Point in October 1968, all the records have been rejected save that for Fair Isle where a male was present on 4 and 5 June 1979. Even this is under review, so one earnestly hopes that before too long a spectacled warbler will arrive and be recorded without any doubt, in order that its place, some would say rightful place, on the British List can be assured.

Like a tiny lesser whitethroat in shape but with a longish tail, the subalpine warbler is a rich mix of grey upperparts and pinkish underparts, with white moustachial stripes. It is a skulking species of scrubby areas around much of the Mediterranean basin from Iberia and Morocco east to Syria, with winter quarters in west Africa south of the Sahara.

The first subalpine warbler in the British Isles was shot on St Kilda on 14 June 1894. There were 11 further records up to 1957, and some 211 subsequently, with birds occurring annually since 1966 save for 1973. Birds have been seen from early April until mid-November, though most are in May, the classic period for overshooting when *en route* to summer quarters in southern Europe. Recently occurrences have been increasing, with an unprecedented 32 in the spring of 1988. The distribution in spring is surprising with far fewer in southern counties than might be expected, and with a higher proportion in the north and west, with Fair Isle having a quarter of the records. Some birds have summered; a female on the Isle of May remained there from 24 June to 4 October 1985. The small number of autumn records are distributed from Shetland to Scilly, where most are seen, with one in the Isle of Man and three in Cork.

A most handsome bird, the male Sardinian warbler has a dark hood and conspicuous red eye-ring, while females are brownish above and white below and have a brown eye-ring. Largely sedentary, it breeds in the Canary Islands, and around the Mediterranean basin to Asia Minor and Syria.

The first Sardinian warbler in the British Isles was a male on Lundy on 10 May 1955. There have been 17 further records, all since 1967, with most occurring in spring between mid-April and the end of June. Several of the autumn birds have remained for several weeks, while one on St Agnes is thought to have wintered there. There have been just three for Scotland, birds on Fair Isle in 1967, the Isle of May in 1981 and Birsay in 1988. One for Wales, that on Skokholm on 28 October 1968, is also the latest so far. The others have been in coastal counties from Yorkshire to Sussex, and in Scilly where the total now reaches four. All but two have been males, the only females being those at Dungeness in 1973 and St Agnes in 1988.

The male Ruppell's warbler, named after the remarkable German naturalist and explorer of the Middle East and of Africa south to Ethiopia, has a striking black head and throat, with white moustachial stripes, blue-grey upperparts and pinkish white underparts; females are grey-brown above, buff below, and both have reddish eye-rings. Its breeding range is restricted to southern Greece, Crete, some Aegean islands, and the west and south coasts of Turkey. Winter quarters are in Chad and the Sudan.

A male at Dunrossness on 13 August 1977 was the first Ruppell's warbler for the British Isles and remained in the area for a month, frequenting gardens where there were dense willows and rose scrub, and where it might be lost for several days at a time due to its secretive nature. There has been just one other, also a male and this time on Lundy from 1 to 10 June 1979.

A large warbler, like most other members of its family the orphean warbler is a handsome bird, grey-brown above, pinkish white below, and with a striking white eye-ring. It breeds in open woodland around the Mediterranean, and eastwards to north-west India, wintering in tropical Africa, Arabia, and India. Despite its wide range and migratory habits few have wandered far north in Europe.

A female orphean warbler shot at Wetherby on 6 July 1848 was thought to have been breeding because a male was observed nearby. There are just four other records, all males, and all in the autumn between 20 September and 22 October, at Portland in 1955, Porthgwarra in 1967, St Mary's in 1981 and Aberdeen in 1983, this one being caught in a city park.

Bonelli's warbler is slightly larger and bigger-headed than a chiffchaff which it closely resembles, and has a yellowish wing-panel and rump. Franco Andrea Bonelli was an Italian naturalist and Professor of Zoology at Turin during the early part of the nineteenth century, and was instrumental in obtaining the first specimen of this leaf warbler, to which was given his name. It breeds from north-west Africa, through Iberia and across southern Europe, and Asia Minor to Syria, winter quarters being in Africa, south of the Sahara. The breeding range has been expanding northwards in Europe throughout the present century and it now breeds as close to the British Isles as northern France.

The first Bonelli's warbler in the British Isles was a female caught on Skokholm on the last day of August 1948 and, in the days before the outstanding field guides and identification papers now so readily available, presented a major problem for its discoverer, island warden Peter Conder. It was followed by two others up to 1957, and a further 98 since. Perhaps surprisingly for a bird which migrates north to within a short distance of the English Channel, few overshoot in spring. So far only 17 have been recorded at that time of year, none penetrating further north than Spurn Point and South Walney, except for one which reached Islay where its short trilling song was heard for two days in May 1976. Most occur from August to early November, and are presumed to be migrants carried westwards in classic movements from the south-east of the breeding range. Six in 1981 and seven in 1984 are the peak totals. Although Bonelli's warblers regularly reach Fair Isle, the majority of autumn records are in coastal counties south of the Humber to the Mersey, with no fewer than five having occurred on Bardsey and once elsewhere in the county, with just one other in Wales, a bird at Lavernock Point at the end of August 1963. In Ireland all 12 records have been from Cork, Waterford, and Wexford.

Collared and pied flycatchers are very similar in appearance, the males being boldly marked black and white birds, females and winter males being brown and white, the latter with a black wing panel. To add to confusion interbreeding occasionally takes place where the ranges overlap. The collared flycatcher breeds in open forest, well-timbered parks and orchards from eastern France and Italy, to the Ukraine. Migration takes the birds across the eastern Mediterranean south to Zaire, Zambia, and Malawi.

The first collared flycatcher in the British Isles was an adult male, but unfortunately it was shot, as recently as 11 May 1947 at Skaw, Whalsay. The next, 10 years later, was in the famous Nant withy bed on Bardsey, well-known as a place for migrant birds, on 10 May 1957. Since then there have been a further 14, never more than two in any one year, and all save two between late April and early June. Similarities in the autumn to the pied fly-catcher means that birds can easily be overlooked, and so far the only records are of one at North Fambridge in September 1962 and at Fair Isle in October 1986. Spring birds have reached Shetland on three occasions, Orkney on two, with single records from Yorkshire, Norfolk, Suffolk, Essex, Kent, Scilly, and just one from the west coast, a male found dead near Ravenglass on 2 June 1964.

There can be few more handsome birds than the wallcreeper, about the size of a nuthatch and with remarkable plumage of grey and black, and with large, rounded wings mainly red in colour. The bill is long and curved and used to probe into crevices for food on the steep rock walls which it inhab-its, often up to the snow line. Its haunts are in mountain ranges from Iberia to the high Himalaya. During the winter months wallcreepers will descend to lower habitats, and at such times are equally at home on churches, castles and in quarries.

The first reference to the wallcreeper in the British Isles is its name in a list of birds published in 1667. However, the first definite occurrence was one shot while flying round a house at Sutton Strawless on 30 October 1792, and first reported in a letter to Gilbert White of Selborne. There were two records in the late nineteenth century, one flying round a mill in May 1872 at Sabden, where it attracted the attention of mill hands by its crimson-banded wings, the other at Winchelsea in 1886. Birds at Mells in 1901, Dorchester in 1920, and Rottingdean in 1938 were eventually fol-lowed by two long-staying individuals. A male stayed in disused stone quar-ries near Worth Matravers from at least 19 November 1969, but possibly as early as September, to 18 April the following year; and one at Cheddar from early November 1976 to April 1977, which amazingly returned the follow-ing November and was last seen on 9 April 1978. There was also one at Ecclesbourne Glen near Hastings in April 1977, and finally one at St Catherine's Point in May 1985.

Almost identical to the treecreeper, the short-tailed treecreeper is almost impossible to identify with certainty even in the hand. As the authors of a detailed paper in 1976 said: 'The odds are very much against observers suddenly faced with just one strange bird.' It breeds from north-west Africa, and Iberia, east to Asia Minor, and north to the southern shores of the Baltic, North Sea, and English Channel.

A treecreeper trapped at Dungeness on 27 September 1969 on close examination proved to be the first short-toed treecreeper for the British Isles. The next was at Hornsea on 26 October the following year. Other than one in Epping Forest in May 1975 the remaining six occurrences have all been in Kent, with two at Dungeness in October 1978 and two at Sandwich Bay in the same month in 1988. This is destined to remain a bird of mystery in the British Isles. Possibly more arrive and are simply overlooked, or identified as treecreepers. Is there even the exciting possibility that a small breeding population is established in the south-east?

The penduline tit is a tiny bird with a long tail and a striking plumage of grey and black on the head, russet back, and pinkish-buff underparts. It builds its remarkable bottle-shaped nest in reed beds and thickets from southern Europe to northern China, Manchuria and Outer Mongolia. Some migratory movements take place, and there is a tendency for occasional population explosions, which have no doubt aided the range expansion which has taken place in north-west Europe during the last 50 years or so.

The first record of a penduline tit for the British Isles was one at Spurn Point on 22 October 1966 where it joined a group of other small birds mobbing a fox in a thicket of sea buckthorn. Here it remained until 28 October. The next in October 1977 was on St Agnes. A further 22 have been recorded since, and the penduline tit has been almost annual since 1980, with five in 1987 and seven in 1988. Several have remained for lengthy periods in likely habitats like the pair at Blacktoft Sands in the winter of 1981-2, and a male at Stodmarsh in the winter of 1983-4. Other than one on Bardsey in May 1981 and at Moreton in September 1986, records have been in coastal counties from Yorkshire to Scilly, with two inland, one at a gravel pit at Ditchford in 1983 at a time when there were over 100 reported on the coast of Brittany, and one in a similar habitat at Brumpton in 1988. A bird caught and ringed at Pett Level in October 1988 was recovered in southern Sweden the following May. Clearly the penduline tit is a bird to pay special attention to, and could well cause some revision of distribution maps and county avifaunas by the next century.

The lesser grey shrike is like a small version of that more frequent visitor to the British Isles the great grey shrike, being a boldly marked black, grey and white bird with a longish tail and short, rounded wings. In its breeding haunts it is a bird of open forests, orchards and vineyards, using trees as observation posts and open ground for hunting. It breeds from France and Italy east to Afghanistan and Turkestan, winter quarters being in Africa, south of the Sahara.

A lesser grey shrike near Christchurch in September 1842 seems to have been the first for the British Isles, with some 31 others up to 1957. Since then it has occurred almost annually, with a further 97, peak years being 1961 and 1977 both with six birds, while since 1986 there have been only single records. Some 60 per cent of those reported are in spring from mid-

May, while the remainder are on autumn passage between mid-August and November. The east coast from Shetland to Sussex is where most sightings are reported, though some birds do extend inland like those at Haslemere, Glastonbury, Fan Pool, and Stanlake. There are records from west coast counties from Carmarthen to the Outer Hebrides, where one reached Loch Druidibeg in South Uist at the end of May 1964, and in Ireland, where two have occurred in Cork and one in Wexford. One was found dead, drowned in a water tank, on North Ronaldsay in May 1965, while another actually fed at a bird table at Abersoch on the Lleyn Peninsula during the late autumn of 1986.

Surely the most handsome of the shrikes to occur in the British Isles, the male woodchat shrike is a brilliant combination of black, white and chestnut. Females have much the same pattern though in not quite such bright hues. Open parkland, olive groves and orchards are its habitats from Iberia and north-west Africa east to Asia Minor, Iran, and Baluchistan, most moving south to winter quarters from Senegal to Dharfur.

One of the most frequently recorded of all the rare visitors to the British Isles, the woodchat shrike had been recorded on no fewer than 101 occasions up to 1957, with the massive total of 413 since. It is likely to be encountered between early April and early November with a slight preponderance in the spring when the main passage occurs in May. Annual totals vary, but there were 21 in 1981, 24 in 1968 and 1988, and 25 in 1986. There is little variation in the geographical distribution of records between spring and autumn, though in the latter period smaller numbers extend to the far north. At both seasons the woodchat shrike is likely to be encountered in virtually any coastal county of England and Wales except in the north-west, and not infrequently inland. Except for Orkney and Shetland, most records for Scotland are from the east coast with occasional ones in the west, like those which have reached Skye and South Uist. Some 36 have occurred in Ireland since 1953, most in Cork and Wexford, with single records from Waterford and Down. One remarkable occurrence was a female ringed on Skokholm on 3 June 1976 and retrapped at Walberswick 17 days later.

The masked shrike is a small, slim shrike with a long tail, and the only one with a broad white forehead and blue-black crown. Females are much paler, but still have the white forehead. A shy and often inconspicuous bird, the masked shrike breeds in forests, scrub and orchards from south-east Europe to the delta of the Euphrates and Tigris. Winter quarters are in north-east Africa.

There is just one record of the masked shrike from the British Isles, a male at Woodchurch on 11 July 1905, though this is no longer accepted to the British List.

The adult rose-coloured starling is a handsome mosaic of pink and black. Small wonder that it is frequently kept as a cage bird, but this can cause a problem as to the authenticity of some records. Are they of genuine migrants, or are they escaped cage-birds? Its occurrence as a breeding bird within some parts of its range is sporadic and much dependent on locust numbers, its main food supply. When food is abundant the rose-coloured starling may become established in new areas for short periods. Normally it breeds from south-east Europe to Iran, and to the upper Irtish of central Asia.

About 160 rose-coloured starlings had been recorded in the British Isles up to 1957 since the first in 1743, with 179 subsequently, during which period it has been annual in its visitations, 12 in 1975 being the maximum in a single year. Although there are records for every month, most are seen between mid-May and the end of October. Rose-coloured starlings are likely to be seen anywhere in the British Isles with records from coastal and inland counties, even to the far north and west, including Ireland. Mid-winter records are nearly all south of the Humber–Severn line, with single records from Shetland, Orkney, Pembroke, and Devon. Some birds have remained for long periods like the juvenile on St Mary's from 14 September to at least 26 October 1981, one at Market Deeping from mid-January to 8 March 1983, and one which died in St David's in late December 1986 after a stay in a garden for about two months.

Very similar in appearance to the house sparrow, the Spanish sparrow has a chestnut crown and much whiter cheek patches. Often a colonial bird, it breeds in scrub and thorn thickets in the Canaries and Cape Verde Islands, from Rio de Oro to Libya, and from southern Spain to Turkey, and then eastwards to Afghanistan and into Chinese Turkestan.

The first Spanish sparrow in the British Isles was one on Lundy on 9 June 1966 where it remained for three days. The other two records were both in October and both on Scilly, one on St Mary's in 1972, the other on Bryher in 1977, where it shared the same field as an Arctic redpoll. There can be few occasions when these species have met.

The rock sparrow resembles the female house sparrow though it has a more distinctive striped head and a generally plumper appearance. This largely sedentary bird breeds in north-west Africa, and across southern Europe, then eastwards to the Himalayas, China, and Mongolia.

The only record of the rock sparrow in the British Isles, and this as brief as such occurrence can be, was at Cley on 14 June 1981. It was seen at 08:00 hrs, but had gone by 08:30 hrs, leaving five satisfied but somewhat incredulous observers who had good views as it fed on the ground or perched on a fence. The thoughts of the many who arrived later in the day are best not dwelled upon.

One of the largest finches, the snowfinch is easily distinguished from the snow bunting, the only other species with which it might be confused, by the grey head in all plumages. It is a bird of upland regions, always close to the snow line in southern Europe, parts of the Near East and to the high Himalayas. Some movement to slightly lower altitudes occurs in winter when birds will often associate with man.

The first snowfinch for the British Isles was seen by Michael Nicoll at Rye Harbour on 21 February 1905 and was shot the next day. Michael Nicoll will be further remembered for his book *Three Voyages of a Naturalist*, an account of his 72,000-mile travels in 1902-1906 on Lord Crawford's yacht *Valhalla*, during which no fewer than 11 new species were described. He lived for many years in Egypt where he wrote the definitive Handbook to the birds of that country, before dying tragically young at the age of 45. This sighting was followed by two at Paddock Wood on 28 December 1906, during severe weather over Europe when one of the most remarkable daylight migrations ever witnessed in the South of England took place. Three were present at Rye Harbour on the last day of February 1916.

Despite the impeccable reference to the first, the fact that it and the others were all in the area encompassed by the 'Hastings Rarities' of Kent and Sussex means they have been deleted from the British List.

The handsome citril finch with its unstreaked greenish-yellow underparts, ash-grey nape and yellow wing-bars is a bird of upland coniferous woodlands, often occurring close to the tree-line in Spain, south-east France, southern Germany, Austria, Sardinia, and Corsica. A primarily sedentary species, the only example from the British Isles was an adult female caught by a birdcatcher at Yarmouth Denes on 29 January 1904.

The rock bunting, with its black-striped head, grey throat and chest, and orange underparts, is one of the easiest of buntings to identify. Warm uplands with rocky outcrops, walls, and crags, with small trees and scrub are its habitat from north-west Africa and Iberia across southern Europe, and central Asia to China where it occurs in mountain ranges up to 17,000 ft (5,180 m). It is a largely sedentary bird save for altitudinal movements.

An extreme rarity in the British Isles, the first rock bunting was one of two netted by birdcatchers near Shoreham in late October 1902, though an earlier record is sometimes claimed of one near Dover in 1859. There have been just four others, at Faversham on 14 February 1905, at Dale Fort on 15 August 1958, at Spurn Point from 19 February to 10 March 1965, and lastly one on Bardsey on 1 June 1967.

Another extremely rare bunting in the British Isles, Cretzschmar's bunting takes its name from the German naturalist of 1786-1845, and resembles the ortolan bunting, a scarce passage migrant in north-west Europe, save for its blue-grey head and orange throat. It breeds, usually in rocky areas with sparse trees and scrub, in Greece, Cyprus, Turkey, and the near East, wintering mainly in the Sudan and Arabia.

The first Cretzschmar's bunting in the British Isles was a male discovered on Fair Isle on the evening of 10 June 1967, though not positively identified until it was rediscovered, trapped and ringed on 14 June. Subsequently it was seen on several occasions up to 20 June. The second and so far only other record was also on Fair Isle, and also in June, this time in 1979.

One of the most handsome members of its family, the black-headed bunting is frequently kept as a cage bird, and thus has caused confusion to those who assess records and some agony to observers. It breeds from eastern Italy to Iran, and winters in north and central India.

The first black-headed bunting in the British Isles was a male at Brighton in early November 1868. Indeed the vast majority of records right up to the present day have been males. Is the nondescript female overlooked, or is it less prone to wander? There were eight other early records, and since 1957 a further 73. Although these extend from mid-April to late November most are seen in May and June, presumably northward migrants overshooting their Mediterranean breeding grounds. In both spring and autumn the majority of records are from Shetland, though the black-headed bunting is likely to be seen in any coastal county, with occasional sightings inland, like birds seen in Nottingham, Leicester and at Bromley-by-Bow in London.

North-east and Central Europe

Red-throated Pipit
Citrine Wagtail
Thrush Nightingale
Red-flanked Bluetail
Lanceolated Warbler
River Warbler
Blyth's Reed Warbler

Booted Warbler
Greenish Warbler
Arctic Warbler
Nutcracker
Two-barred Crossbill
Parrot Crossbill

Pine Grosbeak
Pine Bunting
Rustic Bunting
Little Bunting
Yellow-breasted
   Bunting

The red-throated pipit, a bird of tree pipit size though of plumper build, is very heavily streaked above, with buff underparts, spotted on the breast and flanks. In the breeding season males have a red-buff face, throat, and even chest, traces of which may remain into the winter. Females have pink rather than red colouration, being replaced in winter by buff-white. The call note is a striking drawn out 'pseeh' and will help separate this bird from either the tree pipit or meadow pipit. It breeds on mossy tundras from northern Scandinavia to the Bering Strait, with some in western Alaska, and chooses to winter in tropical Africa and south-east Asia.

The red-throated pipit was first recorded in the British Isles when one was captured on Unst on 4 May 1854, with a further 29 up to 1957. Since then it has been noted annually except for 1962, and the number has grown by a further 181. There are two quite distinct passage periods, in spring from mid-April to mid-June, and in the autumn from late August until November when slightly more are seen. Spring records are mostly in eastern counties, while those in the autumn are more widespread, a few reaching the west and even Ireland, where it has occurred in Cork and Wexford.

Slightly larger and longer tailed than the yellow wagtail, the plumage of the citrine wagtail seems to be a combination of that species and the white wagtail. With one exception, all those seen in the British Isles have been immature birds which have slate-grey upperparts, grey sides to the breast, and buff underparts. The forehead is pale cream, the supercilium yellow or white, there are double white wingbars, and a variable breast band which can even be absent. The breeding range extends from northern Russia and Siberia into central Asia south to Iran, and the Himalayas, with some evidence of a western expansion of range into southern Russia. Winter quarters are in India and south-east Asia.

The first citrine wagtail in the British Isles was caught in the Gully Trap, Fair Isle on 20 September 1954, to be quickly followed by another on 1 October. The third record, also at Fair Isle, was in October 1960, since when a further 43 have been recorded. Indeed it has occurred here annually since 1966, though never more than four in any one year, and this total has only been reached once, in 1986. Citrine wagtails occur in the British Isles from late August until late October. About half have been in Shetland, the remainder distributed in eastern and southern counties to Scilly with two in Ireland, both at Ballycotton.

One quite extraordinary record of the citrine wagtail was when a male was discovered in July 1976 on an Essex salting carrying food to a nest of four young wagtails. These eventually fledged, though no female was seen, but the consensus of opinion was that the brood were hybrid yellow/citrine wagtails.

The thrush nightingale is very similar to the nightingale, but has more pointed wings, and a marginally longer tail. The plumage is olive-grey-brown above, paler beneath, with a mottled chest and flanks. The dull rufous tail has little contrast with the upperparts. Damp woodlands from southern Scandinavia, and central Europe east into central Asia are the breeding haunts of the thrush nightingale, which has been slowly expand-ings its range westwards during this century, with quite large population increases in some areas. Wintering birds are found from Ethiopia south to Natal Province.

There seems to be a little confusion as to which was the first thrush nightingale in the British Isles. Eagle Clarke refers to himself obtaining 'the first undoubted one' on Fair Isle on 15 May 1911 during 'a great rush of migrants on their passage north', and then goes on to mention one at Smeeth in October 1904, thought to have been an escape. But why? Another, shot in Norfolk in June 1845, was erroneously considered for many years to be a Savi's warbler. However, there is no confusion over the next, again on Fair Isle and 47 years to the day since Eagle Clark's bird. Although reference was made at the time to the exciting possibilities in the wake of the range expansion westwards of more frequent occurrences, it was not until 1965 the next arrived, again in spring, and again on Fair Isle. That same autumn came the first two birds further south, both caught and ringed at Low Hauxley. A further 73 have now been seen, and except for 1980 and 1982 the thrush nightingale has been seen annually since 1972 with up to seven in a year. By far the main passage is in spring. Does this augur well for future breeding even this far west? Certainly singing birds have been heard on several occasions. Spring records are all from east coast counties, from Fair Isle with about half the sightings south to Kent. The smaller number of autumn birds are much more widespread, with birds away from the east coast in Sussex, Devon, Scilly and Caernarvon.

The red-flanked bluetail, save for the longer tail, is very similar in build to the robin. The male is a resplendent dark blue above, white and grey below, with orange flanks. Females and immature birds are olive-brown above, dull white below, but still retain the orange flanks, blue rump and tail. This is a bird of coniferous woodlands with watercourses and swamps from Finland to Kamchatka, and Japan, and also from Afghanistan to cen-tral China. Those which have extended their range west during the present century undertake one of the longest migrations of any small bird, to winter quarters in south-east Asia, reaching Assam, Burma, and Thailand.

CITRINE WAGTAIL; FAIR ISLE
8th SEPT 1988

Call: harsher than
Yellow Wagtail

dark shadow
above
supercilium
wide superc.

wispering grey back, hint of
olive sheen in good
light

a few dark
streaks on breast

white vents

2 large white wingbars
+ fringes on tertials visible at long
range

whiter
throat

Typical
wagtail
posture.

pinkish
wash
on breast

grey flanks

"hollow" centred ear-coverts
(complete pale surround)

dark streaks
inside earcoverts
and darkish
surround.

General impression of a neat "greyish" wagtail with well
defined head pattern, pale broad supercilium contrasted
with dark grey ear coverts. White wing bars very obvious
as was pinkish flush on breast at short range.
Ted in short grass occasionally with other wagtails
Andrew Birch 1988

Copy of field notes.

Citrine Wagtail, Fair Isle, 8 September 1988. *(Field sketch by Andrew Birch)*

A red-flanked bluetail at North Cotes in September 1903 was the first in the British Isles. The next was on Whalsay in 1947, while the third was found dead at Sandwich in 1956. Since 1957 there have been seven further records, six in the autumn, the exception being a male on Fetlar in May 1971. Four of the seven have been from Shetland, the others in Fife, Northumberland, and Lincoln.

The lanceolated warbler, like a small, heavily streaked grasshopper warbler — indeed it was once known as Temminck's grasshopper-warbler — skulks in thick cover and normally only reveals its presence with a deep churring song. Probably more occur in the British Isles than the records suggest. It breeds eastwards from central Russia to Kamchatka and Japan, with winter quarters in southern Asia from India to Vietnam.

The first lanceolated warbler in the British Isles was initially considered to be a grasshopper-warbler when it was shot on Fair Isle on 9 September 1908. It was quickly followed by further examples at North Cotes in 1909, and on the Pentland Skerries in 1910, with a further six up to 1957. Since then 36 more have been accepted, all between early September and mid-November, though by far the majority are in mid-September. After three in 1960-61 there was a gap until 1972, since when there has been at least one lanceolated warbler in all but four years. Shetland is the place to see this tiny bird in the British Isles, with most of the records being on Fair Isle where one on 23 September 1982 was found around the milk pails at the Observatory door, and later walked into the nearby trap, straight into the catching box and, of course, the record books. The only birds outside Shetland since 1957 have been those at Damerham in 1979, Prior's Park in 1984, and the Isle of May in 1987.

Another skulking warbler is the river warbler, though even in the British Isles birds are occasionally heard in a song, which is said to resemble the fast shuttling rhythm of a sewing machine, and usually delivered from the top of a bush under a tree at dawn or at dusk. It has unstreaked olive-brown upperparts with sparse streaking on the breast, and pale underparts. This is another bird which has extended its range westwards, and now occurs in Denmark, Sweden and East Germany from where it extends to western Siberia. The wintering area is in east Africa.

The first river warbler in the British Isles was one trapped at Fair Isle on 24 September 1961. Of the nine subsequent records, four have been at the same locality, including one found dead there on 25 May 1981. The exceptions are one at Bardsey in September 1969, and still the only west coast record, and one ringed at Spurn Point in August 1981. Two records are especially noteworthy, birds in song at Roydon in late May and June 1981, and 'somewhere in Suffolk' in July 1984. Are these pioneers the forerunners of eventual colonists?

It is said that 'no group of warblers in the West Palearctic presents more identification problems than the unstreaked *Acrocephalus*', and Blyth's reed warbler is one of these. A more recent paper lists no fewer than nine features, a combination of many of these, or preferably most, being essential for certain identification. It breeds from the Baltic States and Finland, across Russia and Siberia as far as the basin of the Lena, and south to Iran, Afghanistan, and Mongolia. Wintering birds extend throughout the Indian sub-continent.

Despite advances in identification techniques and skills, and the opportunities now available to catch and examine migrant birds, the occurrences of Blyth's reed warbler in the British Isles are no more frequent than earlier in the century. The first was obtained on Fair Isle by the Duchess of Bedford on 30 September 1910, to be followed by a mini-invasion in the autumn of 1912. In that year there were single birds at Spurn Point, Holy Island, the Dudgeon Lightship, and four, possibly five, on Fair Isle. There was a single bird at this locality in September 1928, then no more records until one at Cape Clear in October 1969, and at Filey Brigg at the end of August 1975. There have been five further records, at Holm in October 1979, Spurn Point in May 1984 and two in 1987, at Fair Isle, and at Priors Park.

Smallest of the *Hippolais* warblers, the booted warbler is more like a pale *Phylloscopus* in appearance, something which has caused much confusion even in the hand. Grey-brown above and whitish below with a rounded head and a tiny bill, it breeds from north-west Russia east to the Yeneisi, northern Mongolia, and western Sinkiang south to Iran. Wintering birds are found throughout India and in southern Arabia.

The first booted warbler recorded in the British Isles was one on Fair Isle on 3 September 1936 where it was taken by a remarkable combination of the islander George Stout, and George Waterston, through whose unstinting efforts the future of the island was assured after the 1939-45 war. It was to the same locality that the next arrived, this time trapped, on 29 August 1959. Since then the number of sightings has risen to 26, all in the autumn. The earliest was another Fair Isle bird, on 20 August 1977, the latest at St Alban's Head on 23 October 1984. Since the mid-1970s the booted warbler has been almost annual in occurrence, the maximum in any one year being four in 1981. Early records were for the most part all from Shetland, but strangely there has been none there since one on the Out Skerries in 1981, indeed only one recent Scottish record, that on South Ronaldsay in 1988. The emphasis has switched south, with six records from Scilly, three from Yorkshire, two from Dorset, and single birds in Lincoln, Norfolk, and Kent.

The greenish warbler so closely resembles the chiffchaff that before the similarities were appreciated, especially the presence of a wing-bar in some races of the chiffchaff, there was much confusion, and some misidentification. The greenish warbler frequents mixed forests with good undergrowth in a breeding range from north-east Europe through central Asia to western China, moving south to winter in India and south-east Asia.

The first greenish warbler in the British Isles was shot at North Cotes on 5 September 1896, the next was on Whalsay in 1945. Since then a further 166 individuals have been accepted, and it is now an annual visitor, only absent in 1980 in recent years. Totals are very variable, though there has been a definite upsurge in late summer and autumn records, with 18 in 1987 and 15 in 1988. Indeed the majority are seen during this passage, mostly from mid-August to the end of September. Spring and early-summer birds extend from mid-May until July, about 20 having been reported, all in counties from Fife to Devon. The autumn emphasis is in the east from Shetland to Norfolk, with much smaller numbers along the south coast to Scilly, and in the west where birds have been recorded from Lundy, Skokholm, Bardsey, and the Calf of Man. The nine records from Ireland, seven since 1957, have all been in the autumn, and only from Cork and

Wexford. Greenish warblers have extended their breeding range slowly westwards in Europe throughout the present century, and there has been at least one instance of possible breeding in the British Isles, when a singing bird was located at Aberfeldy from 21 May to 26 June 1983.

A large but slim *Phylloscopus*, the Arctic warbler has a distinct pale wing-bar with a second often just visible, and a longer, heavier bill than the greenish warbler with which it may easily be confused. It breeds in northern birchwoods from Swedish Lapland to Kamchatka, and Alaska, with birds wintering in south-east Asia, so that this is another small passerine of which the western populations undertake quite extraordinary migratory movements.

The first Arctic warbler in the British Isles was killed at the lighthouse lantern on lonely Sule Skerry, 40 miles (64 km) west of Hoy on 5 September 1902, with 18 others being recorded up to 1957. Since then it has occurred annually except for 1963, and the number has now risen by a further 140 records. Fewer than eight are seen in most years, but in 1981 there were 16. All have occurred between early July and mid-November, with most during September. Shetland and not surprisingly Fair Isle have accounted for nearly half, the distribution of the remainder being mainly in eastern counties south to Kent, and in south-west England. Single birds have occurred in Cheshire and on Bardsey. In Ireland just six have been recorded, single birds on Tory Island, Loop Head, and Toe Head, with three on Cape Clear.

A jackdaw-size bird, the nutcracker is dark chocolate-coloured, speckled white, and with a large, pointed bill. It is a bird of coniferous woodlands from southern Scandinavia and central Europe east in a great swathe across Asia, to Kamchatka, and Japan. A separate population occurs in the Himalayas, parts of China, and Formosa.

So closely associated is the nutcracker with its pine seed food supply, especially that of the arolla pine, that when this fails vast movements take place as birds rapidly move out of their normal range. Such a mass exodus often brings birds far west so that some reach the British Isles, where the first was one in Flint in 1753. At least 45 others were recorded up to 1957, with 358 since, of which 315 were in the great invasion of 1968. In that year the first birds arrived in Norfolk on 6 August and in Kent the following day, the last during October with some remaining over winter. Some 15 were seen the following year, with no more than three in any year since, except for five at Eddleston on 28 August 1971. Single birds at Holland-on-Sea in February 1961, and Cherry Hinton in February 1987 are the only ones which have arrived outside the autumn period. Most nutcrackers are located in the British Isles in England south of Yorkshire, with East Anglia the main area. Birds occasionally reach Scotland, though even during the great 1968 invasion there was just a single record, a bird in Shetland. Some reach as far west as the borders and southern counties of Wales, though as yet none has made the additional sea crossing to Ireland.

Smallest of the crossbills, the two-barred crossbill is very similar to the crossbill, save for two white wing-bars which are present in all plumages, males a handsome red and black, females and immatures a yellow-green. It is a bird of northern larch and spruce forests from Scandinavia to the basins of the Lena and Amur Rivers, and also in North America from Alaska to Newfoundland.

The first two-barred crossbill in the British Isles was one obtained near to Belfast on 11 January 1802, with about 40 further examples of this nomadic species up to 1957. Some 53 have been recorded since, in all months from early July to April, the peak being from July to September. It seems highly likely that some of those seen early in the year are most probably overwintering birds rather than new arrivals. Mostly only single stragglers are seen, but in 1966 there were four, in 1972 six, then an unprecedented 27, nearly all immature birds, in August 1987. All save one was in Shetland, the exception being on North Ronaldsay. Away from these northern islands there are records from a number of counties south to Devon since 1957, but none during this period from either Wales or Ireland.

The large and powerful bill gives the parrot crossbill an almost top-heavy look when compared to the slightly smaller crossbill and Scottish crossbill. All three species have virtually identical plumage, a crimson orange in the adult male, yellow-green in the female and immature. It breeds in dry pine forests in Scandinavia, the Baltic States and northern Russia to the Ural Mountains. For the most part this is a sedentary bird, only making movements west and south when the seed crop fails.

Records of the parrot crossbill in the British Isles have been masked to a large extent by the difficulties of identification. The first was a bird at Blythburgh in 1818, nine others being recorded up to 1957, including one from a party of four killed by a car on the Newcastle to Jedburgh road in mid–September 1954. Subsequently 221 have occurred in nine years.

An invasion in 1962 brought in 63 birds, nearly half on Fair Isle, with others early in 1963. A single bird was killed by a cat at Grutness on 22 October 1975 on the same day that an adult male was at Spurn Point, and the following day a female was found dying at Tophill Low Reservoir. At least seven were discovered at Gladhouse on 26 October and were to remain until the following January. Such events seemed to herald an invasion, though alas no more were recorded until 1982. In the autumn of that year 82 swept into eastern Britain, with 50 in 1983, 16 in 1984 and nine in 1985. Some of the latter birds may well have been associated with the main movements, but had remained previously undiscovered. There has been just one subsequent record, a first-winter male in the north of Scotland in February 1987.

The main movements take place from late September to mid-November, and parrot crossbills during invasion years have occurred largely in east coast counties from Shetland to Suffolk. Only two have been recorded from the west coast, both from the Outer Hebrides, one in Lewis in 1962, and a female and four juveniles at Langass on North Uist in 1982. A few have reached inland counties, notably Derbyshire where up to 25 were present at Howden Reservoir on the borders with Yorkshire during November and December 1982, remaining until at least February 1983, while rather intriguing was the occurrence of three juveniles in the same county in June and July 1985. Elsewhere birds have been noted in Berkshire and Surrey.

In the aftermath of the two main invasions parrot crossbills nested successfully in north Norfolk in 1984 and 1985, and in Suffolk in the same period, while elsewhere a pair remained at Hartsholme until the end of

1963, and two pairs attempted to nest in northern England in 1983.

A gigantic, long-tailed crossbill-like bird, the pine grosbeak is the size of a starling, and, seemingly unafraid of man, allows a close approach. The male is a raspberry red with a greyish back, and brown wings with double white wing bars, in the female the red is replaced by a greenish gold. It breeds in coniferous woodlands from central Scandinavia east to Kamchatka, and over much of Alaska and Canada, and in the United States south through the western mountains to Arizona. Some populations are migratory and irruptions occasionally occur.

The first pine grosbeak in the British Isles was one in Durham, sometime before 1831, with single birds in Middlesex and Yorkshire, and two in Nottingham up to 1890. Many others have been claimed but not accepted as genuine migrants, as the pine grosbeak was regularly imported as a cage bird. The next was one on the Isle of May during a severe south-west gale on 8 November 1954, when many migrants battled to seek shelter on the island. It was during this year that a small invasion brought pine grosbeaks to southern Sweden, Norway and Denmark. A male at Charing in April 1955 may have had its origins in this invasion. There have been just three others, two more from Kent in 1957 and 1961, and lastly a male on Holy Island in May 1975.

The male pine bunting is a handsome bird, easy to recognize with its white and brown head markings, white breast and underparts. The females are not so distinct but still show the white underside, while the crown is more prominently streaked than in the female yellowhammer with which it can easily be confused. It breeds in bushy coniferous country from eastern Russia to Sakhalin and south into central Asia. Wintering birds occur from northern Iran to southern China.

The first pine bunting in the British Isles was one on Fair Isle on 30 October 1911, the next on Papa Westray on 15 October 1943, followed by one on North Ronaldsay on 7 August 1967. There are just 13 subsequent records, with two in 1980, 1985 and 1988, and four in 1987. Does this upsurge in occurrences suggest a change in status here? Is the pine bunting about to become a regular rather than an extremely scarce vagrant? Most of those seen have been from August until early November, with one mid-winter record, and three in April. All have been in Orkney and Shetland save for single birds in Sutherland, Yorkshire, Dorset and Scilly.

The male rustic bunting has a striking black and white head pattern and reddish-brown chest band. It is an abundant bird in swampy coniferous forests from northern Scandinavia to Kamchatka, moving south in winter to India, Ceylon, China, and Japan. This is one of some 27 species and sub-species from the Western Palearctic which makes a south-easterly migration into Asia, rather than one south or south-west into Africa, a route taken by most summer visitors to northern Europe.

The first rustic bunting in the British Isles was one near Brighton on 23 October 1867, with 33 others up to 1957. A further 181 have been seen since, some in every year, so establishing its claim as a rare but regular passage migrant, with an almost equal division of records between spring, chiefly May, and the autumn, when October is the peak month. In spring the majority of rustic buntings occur in Shetland, with occasional ones in Orkney, and east coast counties from Fife to Kent, and in the west in a few counties from the Outer Hebrides to Pembrokeshire, but strangely none yet in Ireland or in Scilly. Shetland still takes the lion's share of rustic buntings in autumn, at which season the bird is also frequently recorded in Scilly which claims about a quarter of the records, while elsewhere Orkney and counties from Fife to Dorset share the remainder. The only west coast records are of a bird on Lundy in 1986 and three from Ireland, Loop Head, in 1985, and Cape Clear in 1959 and 1988. There is just one inland record, a bird at Upton Warren on 7 November 1987. Although rare birds are frequently caught and ringed, the chances of recovery is small, so that the female on Fair Isle in June 1963 recovered in October the same year on the Greek Island of Khios is worthy of special note.

A rather dull-plumaged bird, the little bunting is not dissimilar to the female reed bunting, but distinctly smaller and more compact. This is a bird of the shrub and willow tundra zone from Lapland to eastern Siberia, wintering in tropical Asia from India to China.

Most frequent of the rare buntings to occur in the British Isles, the first little bunting, at Brighton on 2 November 1864, was to be followed by nearly 100 others up to 1957. Despite its small size and inconspicuous habits a further 357 have been recorded subsequently, and it now occurs annually, with the vast majority in the autumn between early September and the end of October. Some are recorded right through the winter suggesting that they remain here on occasions. Annual totals have reached as high as 40 in 1984 and 42 in 1987. Nearly half the autumn records are from Shetland, but birds have been encountered in virtually all east and south coast counties, though strangely not from Kent as yet. There are sightings from several west coast counties and in Ireland from Clare, Cork, and Donegal. Spring passage is mainly in April and May with the small number of records fairly evenly distributed across the country, with no place at that season where one is more likely to encounter a little bunting. It is then there have been a number of inland records with birds occurring at places like Adswood Tip on the outskirts of Manchester in April 1983, Perry Oaks Sewage Farm in May 1965 and at Sandbach in April 1976.

Smaller than the yellowhammer, the adult male yellow-breasted bunting is easily recognized by its black face and yellow underparts. An extension westwards in range means that it now breeds in Finland and Russia, from where it reaches eastwards, mainly in birch and willow forests, to Sakhalin and Kamchatka, moving to south-east Asia for the winter.

A female yellow-breasted bunting at Cley on 21 September 1905 was the first for the British Isles, being followed by two other early records from north Norfolk in the 10 seen up to 1958. Except for 1960 and 1970 the yellow-breasted bunting has occurred annually ever since, the total having risen to 131. Most are autumn visitors between late August and October. There are just four records outside this period, at Spurn in June 1975, Gibraltar Point in May 1977, Fair Isle in July 1890 and a male discovered singing in northern Scotland in mid-June 1982. It could not be found subsequently, and there was no sign of a female. Shetland again is the place, with 96 of those seen since 1957. Elsewhere it has occurred in a scattering of coastal counties from Orkney to Scilly, also in Argyll, Somerset, Caernarvon, Donegal and Cork.

Central Asia

Rufous Turtle Dove
Blue-cheeked Bee-
  eater
White-throated
  Robin

Paddyfield Warbler
Thick-billed Warbler
Green Warbler
Dusky Warbler
Brown Flycatcher

Brown Shrike
Isabelline Shrike
Daurian Starling
Red-headed Bunting

With broader wings and a heavier build than the rather similar turtle dove, the rufous turtle dove is the largest of its family in the Western Palearctic. However, it lacks the blue-grey in the wings, while a further difference, at least in the western race, is the grey rather than white rim to the tail, the underside of which shows much less contrast to the black and white pattern of the turtle dove. A variety of woodlands, groves and gardens are its habitat, in a range which extends east from the Ural Mountains to Japan and south to India and Burma. Although resident in southern parts of the range, northern populations move into the Arabian peninsula and parts of south-east Asia for the winter.

An immature rufous turtle dove at Scarborough on 23 October 1889 was not followed until another, again an immature, was shot during a pheasant shoot at Castle Rising at the end of January 1946. There have been a further six records, two of which were in May, those on St Agnes in 1960 and near St Ives in 1978. One of the four autumn records was also from Cornwall, a bird at Land's End in early October 1973. The observer D. I. M. Wallace suffered the distress of having his coloured drawings made at the time of observation lost in the post, but nevertheless the record was accepted after due consideration of the detailed field notes. The remaining records are all from the east coast, at Fair Isle at the end of October 1974, Donna Nook in October 1975 and at Spurn in early November the same year.

Slightly larger than the bee-eater and with much longer tail-streamers, the blue-cheeked bee-eater has an irridescent green plumage with a striking head pattern of blue, black, yellow, and chestnut, while in flight the wings will be seen to be a glorious copper-chestnut. It breeds in a variety of habitats in scattered localities through Africa, and from the Middle East to central Asia and north-west India. There are two distinct wintering areas, birds from north-west Africa winter from Senegal to Nigeria, those from central Asia from Ethiopia to South Africa.

There are just four records of the blue-cheeked bee-eater for the British Isles, the first being one shot at St Mary's in July 1921. Thirty years later came the next, also from Scilly, where Miss H. M. Quick, pioneer naturalist of the islands, first saw it as it skimmed past as she walked up a lane on St Agnes 'for the milk' on 22 June 1951. Later she was called by a neighbour who said that he had seen a most wonderful bird 'sitting on the wires and eating my bees as fast as it can'. The next by contrast was in a Peterborough lorry park on a foggy September morning in 1982. The last was in June 1987, on the Otter estuary at Budleigh Salterton.

A robust bird, distinctly larger than the robin, the male white-throated robin has lead-grey upperparts, a white supercilium and throat patch, and black cheeks, while the underparts are a rich rufous orange. Females are browner, but still retain the white throat and warm orange underparts. It is a skulking bird breeding in scrub thickets from southern Turkey to Iran, wintering in Kenya and Tanzania.

In northern Europe the white-throated robin has occurred in Norway and Sweden and its arrival in the British Isles was forecast in 1980. Three years later it was here briefly when a male spent 22 June 1983 on the Calf of Man. At the end of May 1990 the second, a female, which fortunately was far from 'skulking' as described in the handbooks, spent several days on Skokholm.

The paddyfield warbler has the shortest bill, shortest rounded wings, and longest tail of any of the unstreaked *Acrocephalus* warblers. The creamy supercilium is noticeably broad behind the eyes, while on landing after their short whirring flight on distinctly rounded wings birds often raise a small crest. Dense marshland vegetation is its habitat from southern Russia east to central Mongolia and in the south to Iran, and Afghanistan. Winter quarters are in the southern part of the breeding range, and on into India, and southern China.

The first paddyfield warbler was on Fair Isle from 26 September until it was shot on 1 October 1925 by Admiral Stenhouse. Without recourse to such a measure it was necessary to trap and ring the next, also on Fair Isle, in mid-September 1953 to elucidate its identity. There were no further records until one at Hartlepool in September 1969, also trapped and ringed. Subsequently there have been just 13 more, all but three in the autumn between mid-September and early December, the exceptions being on Fair Isle on 13 May 1984, and two in 1988, the first on the Isle of May on 31 May, followed by another 11 days later at Landguard Point. In autumn there have been three more on Fair Isle. One on 26 September 1986 shared a ditch with a Pallas's grasshopper warbler. The other records have been in Fife, Northumberland, Durham, and Cumberland, and Hertfordshire where the only inland record is of one photographed at Tring Reservoirs. The sole record from the west is of one at North Slob in December 1984.

Another massive warbler, the thick-billed warbler when seen briefly in the field may initially be confused with the great reed warbler, but the bill shape, absence of a supercilium, shorter and rounded wings, and a long tail soon clarify matters. It breeds in southern Siberia, northern Mongolia, and Manchuria, and winters in the Yunnan, south-east China, Burma, Thailand and eastern India.

There are just two records of the thick-billed warbler from the British Isles, both from Shetland. The first was trapped and ringed on Fair Isle on 6 October 1955, the second was on Whalsay in late September 1971.

The green warbler is one of a series of 'green' warblers which present special problems for the ornithologist with their similar but variable plumages. The green warbler most closely resembles the greenish warbler, but note the broad wing bar in the former species, and the yellow underparts. It breeds in forested regions from eastern Turkey to Afghanistan, wintering in southern India and Ceylon. There is just one record of the green warbler from the British Isles, a first-winter bird on St Mary's from 26 September to 4 October 1984.

The dusky warbler is very similar to Radde's warbler, but has a narrower bill and finer legs, a short tail, and rusty cheeks and flanks, though its general shape and actions suggest a small chiffchaff. It breeds in central Asia from the valley of the Ob to the Pacific, and winters in northern India and southern China.

William Eagle Clark discovered the first dusky warbler in the British Isles on Auskerry on 3 October 1913, the next was caught on Fair Isle in mid-October 1961 at the same time that a Siberian stonechat, a race of the stonechat, was on the island, a great coincidence because one was also on the Isle of May at the same time that the dusky warbler was collected on Auskerry. It has been seen annually in the British Isles since 1978, the grand total having risen to 71. An adult at Bamburgh on 18 August 1980 was especially early, as birds do not normally arrive until late September, with none after late November. There are just two spring records. One trapped and ringed on the Calf of Man on 14 May 1970 was found dying in Limerick on 5 December the same year. But where had it been in the meantime? The other was at Holkham in May 1985. Although dusky warblers have occurred in many east coast counties from Shetland to Scilly, the majority have been from Norfolk and Scilly. On the west coast in addition to the Calf of Man/Limerick bird already referred to, there have been two dusky warblers on Bardsey, one at Strumble Head, one at the Old Head of Kinsale, and one on Cape Clear, both in 1987.

The brown flycatcher is distinctly smaller than the spotted flycatcher with which it might just be confused, but note the ash-coloured underparts, the broad black bill with yellow at the base and, at close range, the white eye-ring. It breeds in Siberia eastwards from Lake Baikal to Japan, wintering largely in southern India.

An adult male shot on Romney Marsh on 21 May 1909 and exhibited five days later at a meeting of the British Ornithologists Club and accepted without demur at the time as a genuine vagrant has, like several other species already referred to, been classed as one of the 'Hastings Rarities' and as such has been deleted from the British List.

The brown shrike is closely allied to the isabelline and red-backed shrikes though it is more strongly built. It breeds in central Asia and China, wintering in India and south-east Asia. One at Sumburgh on 30 September 1985, which remained for two fleeting days, is the only record of the brown shrike in the British Isles.

For many years the status of the isabelline shrike was to say the least confused, and it was not until the late 1970s that it was re-established as a separate species, previously having been considered a race of the red-backed shrike. It is largely grey-buff above, white below with some pinkish-buff on the flanks, and with a rusty tail. The breeding range extends from Iran to

Isabelline Shrike   Portland Bill   15th - 23rd September 1985

Field Description

In flight orange brown tail and rump immediatly obvious, contrasting with uniform pale mantle. White wing flashes very noticable at some range.

Head - pale tan colour on crown divided from darker brown ear coverts by a narrow whitish line running above eye and above bill. Lores unmarked whitish.

Nape, mantle and scapulars as crown.

Bill - horn colour with dark tip and culmen.

Chin and throat - uniform whitish

Closed wing: lesser and median coverts as mantle; some contrast on greater coverts due to dark centred fresh outer three and worn, faded inners. Alula quite dark brown; primary coverts brown. Primaries - brown narrowly edged buffish and with broad white bases (8th-9th) forming distinct white patch on closed wing; secondaries as primaries. Tertials dark brown centred with broad buffish fringes.

Underparts - rather uniform buffish. Breast and flanks could appear quite peach coloured in certain lights.

Legs and feet greyish

Rump + upper tail coverts - pale washed out orange colour.

Belly and undertail coverts pale whitish

Tail - orangey brown although darker on last third and with noticable pale tips to all feathers

Structure - Compared with Red Backed Shrike this bird appeared distinctly longer tailed. Tail shape somewhat narrow and well rounded. Bill deeper based than Red Backed. Otherwise generally slimmer overall than Red Backed.

Action - Very active most of the time, taking quite large prey items such as bush crickets. Had a habit of wagging its tail from side to side thus highlighting its length. Typical undulating flight.

Dave Beadle
BEADLE

Isabelline Shrike, Portland Bill, September 1985. *(Field sketch by Dave Beadle)*

Mongolia, with birds wintering in south-west Africa and in the north-east of Africa.

The first isabelline shrike in the British Isles was an adult male on the Isle of May on 26 September 1950 when it was seen and sketched by Miss M. I. Kinnear and Miss W. Flower. With clarification of its status and a better understanding of key identification features the number seen has now risen to 27, and since 1975 occurrences have been almost annual. Most have been between August and mid-November with just two in spring, at Fair Isle in May 1960, and a male at West Sidlesham from 1 March until 20 April 1975, where it was occasionally even heard in song. Shetland claims four of the records, the others have been from Flamborough Head to Scilly with one inland, at Hemingford Grey in 1978, and just one on the west coast, at Holyhead in October 1985.

The Daurian starling is a small starling, hardly larger than the Greenland race of the wheatear, with a pale head and underparts, dark back and wings, so there can be little confusion with other species. It breeds east from northern Mongolia to Korea, and winters in the Malayan peninsula, Sumatra and Java.

An adult male Daurian starling in immaculate plumage which arrived on Fair Isle on 7 May 1985 and remained until the 28th, one of the biggest surprises of the 1980s, was the first for the Western Palearctic, though it was followed by an immature a few months later in Norway.

Of all the rare birds to occur in the British Isles the red-headed bunting is the most numerous of those which, because they might be escaped cagebirds, are placed in Category D. The male is a handsome bird with a reddish-brown head and breast, a yellow neck and underparts and a yellow rump. It breeds from Kazakhstan eastwards to China, and winters largely in India.

The first red-headed bunting in the British Isles was procured on 19 June 1931 on North Ronaldsay. There can now be few coastal counties, certainly in the east, where further examples have not occurred at some time, while smaller numbers are reported on the west coast, and from Ireland. One that reached Fair Isle carried an avicultural ring, and it is thought that all records are of escaped cage birds, and for that reason the red-headed bunting is not yet admitted to the full British and Irish Lists. One day I am sure a bird will surprise us. Meanwhile . . .

Siberian Forests and Taiga

Needle-tailed Swift
Pacific Swift
Olive-backed Pipit
Pechora Pipit
Siberian Rubythroat
Daurian Redstart
White's Thrush
Siberian Thrush

Eye-browed Thrush
Dusky Thrush
Black-throated
 Thrush
Pallas's Grasshopper
 Warbler
Two-barred Greenish
 Warbler

Pallas's Warbler
Radde's Warbler
Pallas's Rosefinch
Yellow-browed
 Bunting
Chestnut Bunting
Pallas's Reed Bunting

T he needle-tailed swift is a powerful bird, much larger than the swift, with a short rather square tail and a generally broad appearance. A white chin and throat and a large white area below the tail contrast strongly with the rest of the plumage which is dark brown, glossed green on the upperparts. Holes and crevices in rocks and trees provide nesting sites for the needle-tailed swift from central Siberia to Japan, and south to Burma and western China. Most winter in Australia.

One at Great Horkesley in July 1846 was the first needle-tailed swift in the British Isles, the next being one at Ringwood in the same month in 1879. There was one at Cape Clear in June 1964 then a further gap, this time of nearly 20 years to 11 June 1983 on South Ronaldsay, with one at Quendale which remained for some two weeks from 25 May the following year. There was one at Fairburn Ings on 27 May 1985, then there was a two year gap until the next, another Orkney record, this time from Hoy where a bird remained for some days from 28 May 1988. This is a quite exciting sequence of records which has those who monitor such events wondering whether the same individual has been involved since 1983. If so, where else did it go, and remain unremarked upon?

The Pacific swift is a medium size, rather elegant swift, sooty-grey in colour with a large white rump, and a distinctly forked tail. Indeed, an alternative name is the fork-tailed swift. It breeds in rock crevices and in buildings, from Siberia to Japan and south to Thailand and Burma, wintering largely south to New Guinea and Australia.

There is just one record of the Pacific swift from the British Isles. One found exhausted on the Leman Bank gas platform, some 27 miles (43 km) off the Norfolk coast on 19 June 1981 was brought ashore and released at Beccles. On the following day it was seen at Shadingfield just to the south. Its arrival at Beccles heliport was fortunately reported to a local ornithologist, an employee there, who on seeing the swift lying on an office worker's cardigan and recognizing it as something special surprised his colleagues, 'who were somewhat startled when I reacted by running around closing all the windows'. Its occurrence in the British Isles places the bird in Category E of the national List, one that has occurred more than 3 miles (5 km) but not more than 200 miles (320 km) offshore, or the median line between Great Britain and Ireland and neighbouring countries. Such points seem trivial when appreciating just how far this, and many other small migrants travel from their normal haunts to reach us.

The olive-backed pipit is the size of a tree pipit, with dark olive-green, relatively unstreaked upperparts and mainly white underparts suffused with yellow-buff and with some heavy black spots and streaks. The supercilium is orange in front of the eye, white behind, and contrasts with a dark eye-stripe. The tail is continually pumped, more so than in any other pipit. It breeds across much of Siberia and central Asia, wintering in India and in south-east Asia.

The first occurrence of the olive-backed pipit in the British Isles has a curious history worth retelling. A bird trapped and photographed on Skokholm on 14 April 1948 was not identified until skins were examined in the British Museum the following autumn. On discovering its identity, the island warden, Peter Conder, hesitated to submit the record of then such a little known bird, and only did so when other examples began to appear during the 1960s. Alas his hopes were dashed with the comment, 'Probably, but not sufficient evidence.' There the matter rested until the Editor of the journal *British Birds* on sorting through old files in 1977 came across a photograph with the words written on the back 'Skokholm pipit'. Realizing its true identity but not knowing the origin of the photograph, it took a little more detective work eventually to give this bird its rightful place in the annals of British ornithology. Subsequent records were on Fair Isle in 1964 and 1965, then a second spring record, one at Portland in May 1970. From 1973 the olive-backed pipit has occurred in every year, and the grand total of birds seen is now 69. The majority occur in autumn between late September and November, with just four in spring. Fair Isle and Scilly make the running with the majority of records, though birds have been recorded in Orkney and in most coastal counties from Fife to Dorset. No more have occurred in Wales since the now famous first one on Skokholm, and there is only one from Ireland, a bird on Great Saltee on 21 October 1978. The sole inland record is a quite amazing bird which spent from 19 February to 15 April 1984 in a Bracknell garden, again showing that anything is possible with rare birds.

One final point about the olive-backed pipit. The name is an appropriate one, as is its scientific name *Anthus hodgsoni*. Hodgson was one of the great pioneers of Indian ornithology, who is rightfully commemorated in several other Indian birds names, including a frogmouth, flycatcher, and redstart.

The pechora pipit is one of the smallest of pipits, less bulky than the tree pipit and with a shorter tail and a rather long bill. The warm buff upperparts are well streaked, while the belly is white. There is a white stripe on each side of the mantle, and a thin double white wing-bar. Note especially the broadly streaked rump and buff-white outer tail feathers. It breeds on bushy taiga and in taiga swamplands across much of Siberia, wintering in the Philippines and in Borneo.

Unlike most pipits, the pechora pipit is a remarkably shy and skulking bird, difficult even to flush, so that its occurrence in the British Isles may to some extent be overlooked. The first was taken on Fair Isle on 24 September 1925 by Rear-Admiral Stenhouse. Indeed all subsequent records, up to 1957, 12 in all, were from the same locality. The number of pechora pipits seen in the British Isles has risen since by another 17, and of these 11 have been on Fair Isle, the exceptions being single birds on Whalsay, Spurn, Minsmere, and Portland. All have occurred in September and October, save that at Minsmere which arrived in April 1975.

The Siberian rubythroat is slightly larger than a robin, though with a longer tail and legs. The upperparts are mid-brown, the underparts creamy-buff. A rufous panel is visible on the closed wing, while the rump is also slightly rufous. A white supercilium and eye-ring are distinctive, but only the adult male has the striking ruby throat. It breeds east of the Ural Mountains to the Kamchatka Peninsula, usually in scrub, or among stands of small trees on the taiga. In winter, birds reach south-east Asia and the Philippines.

There is just one record for the British Isles, a Siberian rubythroat on Fair Isle on the morning of 9 October 1975. It is occasionally kept as a cage-bird, as are near relatives like the Himalayan rubythroat, but the first-winter male on Fair Isle was considered a genuine migrant, the star of the year in which so many other Siberian vagrants reached the far west of Europe.

The Daurian redstart resembles the redstart, but has an orange rather than white belly and undertail coverts. The male has a broad white down-curving supercilium, while the wings show a white flash on the secondaries. It breeds in woodlands from central Siberia eastwards to the Pacific, wintering in Japan and southern China.

There is just one record, which at the time of writing is not accepted to the British List, a male first seen on 29 April 1988 on the Isle of May and found dead there the next day.

Largest of the thrushes, White's thrush is more stoutly built than the mistle thrush, and in flight has an almost woodpecker-like appearance. A superb golden-brown above, yellow-white beneath, with numerous black crescent markings, this is a secretive bird, spending its time on the forest floor amongst the spruce and pines of northern Asia east of the Yenisei. Other populations occur in the Himalayas, southern India, Ceylon, and from Malaysia east to New Guinea. Those from the far north winter in south-east Asia.

Gilbert White, the Hampshire curate after whom it was named would not have seen one, indeed probably did not know of its existence, as it was only described in 1790, three years before his death. The first White's thrush in the British Isles was shot by the Earl of Malmesbury near Christchurch in January 1828, and named by Thomas Eyton in White's memory. A further 28 were recorded up to 1957, mostly in the last century or in the early part of this century. Since then there have been just 12 more, all but one in the autumn or winter, the exception being a bird at Weaverham on 7 May 1964. Perhaps this was one which had successfully overwintered and remained unnoticed. Of the others five have been in Shetland, the others in Lanarkshire, Durham, Yorkshire, Gloucestershire, Cornwall, and Scilly.

The Siberian thrush, about the size of a song thrush but with a flatter head, has conspicuous bands on the underwings similar to those on White's thrush, with which it also shares skulking habits. The male is mainly a handsome slate-grey, females are olive-brown above with brown crescent markings below. It breeds in coniferous woodlands in Siberia east to the Sea of Okhotsk; wintering birds reach India and Borneo.

Although an adult male Siberian thrush which was trapped on the Isle of May on 2 October 1954 is regarded as the first for the British Isles, there is a record from a century earlier which deserves attention. One was shot on St Catherine's Hill near Guildford at the beginning of February 1855 and first considered a melanistic redwing. Only when Edward Blyth, of pipit and reed warbler fame, examined the skin was its identity revealed. It is a pity when such early and apparently genuine records are lost sight of, and high time that a thorough review was made in the light of current knowledge. The work of pioneers must not be neglected.

There are just four other records of the Siberian thrush, single birds in Hampshire in December 1976, Great Yarmouth on Christmas Day 1977, one at Widewall on the west coast of South Ronaldsay in November 1984 and a year later the only record from Ireland, an immature female on Cape Clear in October.

The eye-browed thrush most closely resembles the redwing, having rich orange-buff flanks and the creamy-white supercilium. Note the grey head and throat of the male and grey-brown of the female and the unmarked pale underparts. It breeds in the taiga forests from about the Yenisei to the Sea of Okhotsk, wintering from Japan to south-east Asia, and in India.

The first eye-browed thrush in the British Isles was not recorded until 1964 when no fewer than three arrived, birds in a garden at Oundle on 5 October, at North Rona on 16 October, and at St Agnes on 5 December. There were eight subsequent records in just four years, autumn birds in Shetland, Orkney, Renfrew, and three from Scilly, and two in spring, at Aldeburgh in April 1981, and another – or was it the same bird? – at Newburgh a month later.

The dusky thrush is very like the song thrush in build, but with a stouter, rather dagger-shaped bill. The northern race is black-brown above with chestnut, the underparts creamy-white with dark markings on the upper breast and flanks. Known as Naumann's thrush, the southern race has grey-brown upperparts, the underparts a pinkish-red with darker markings, red on the underwing and in the tail. Northern birds breed in sparse woodlands close to the tree-line in northern Siberia, Naumann's thrush occupies the area immediately to the south extending east to Sakhalin. Both winter from Japan and Korea to northern Borneo and Assam.

The dusky thrush has occurred as a vagrant in many European countries, the first for the British Isles being one at Gunthorpe on 13 October 1905. The next, a first-winter male, frequented a school playing field and nearby bowling green at Hartlepool from 12 December 1959 to 24 February 1960. This was followed by three, all in Shetland, at Fair Isle in October 1961, Whalsay in September 1968 and Firth in November 1975, then an inland bird, at Shirley from 17 February to 23 March 1979. Had it arrived the previous autumn and remained at first undetected? There have been just three more, at Bude in November 1983, Skomer in December 1987, and finally one at Chingford in February 1990, which also resorted to a playing field. This latter bird is the first example of Naumann's thrush in the British Isles, the other eight having all been the dusky thrush.

The black-throated thrush is an upright bird about the size of a black-bird, with a striking black or spotted throat and chest, replaced by a dull red in the eastern race. It breeds from the upper Kama to Lake Baikal and south into Tibet, while winter quarters are from Iraq and Arabia east to northern Burma and south-west China.

The first black-throated thrush in the British Isles was at Lewes on 23 December 1868, to be followed by one near Perth 11 years later. The next, at Fair Isle on 8 December 1957, was not followed until 1974 when one was located at Toab also in Shetland. The report on this makes reference to the small number of records in the British Isles, despite its more westerly range than the other Siberian thrushes. Subsequently there have been 13 more records, all between early October and February. Six of those since 1957 have been in Shetland, but surprisingly there has been none elsewhere in Scotland. The others have been in Northumberland, Yorkshire, where one frequented the Botanical Gardens in Sheffield in January 1987, Norfolk, Cheshire, and Staffordshire.

Pallas's grasshopper warbler is slightly larger than the grasshopper warbler which it closely resembles, except in song, not that this feature is likely to be of assistance to observers fortunate enough to encounter this bird in the British Isles. It breeds from western Siberia to Kamchatka, and south to Manchuria and Japan. Wintering birds are found in India, southern China and the Philippines.

The first Pallas's grasshopper warbler was found dead at Rockabill Lighthouse on 28 September 1908. This is just one of many valuable records of birds found dead at lighthouses, a source which now that few lights are manned seems unlikely to produce more. The next, one studied at close quarters in a Fair Isle turnip patch, was on 8 October 1949. Since then 10 more have arrived, the earliest on 13 September 1976 at Cley, the latest on 26 October on the Farne Islands. In most cases there were just single birds in a year, but in 1976 there were two, and in 1988 an unprecedented three, all on Fair Isle. This really is the place to see Pallas's grasshopper warbler, for eight of the 12 have been there, the exceptions birds at Out Skerries, also in Shetland, and those in Northumberland and Norfolk.

The two-barred greenish warbler is distinguished from the greenish warbler as its name suggests by the presence of two white wing-bars. It breeds from eastern Siberia to Mongolia and northern China, wintering in south-east Asia. There is just one record, and it is still under consideration for admission to the British List, a first-winter bird on Gugh from 21 to 27 October 1987.

Pallas's warbler is a tiny goldcrest-like bird which resembles the slightly larger yellow-browed warbler, with its double wing-bar, but note especially the dark crown, yellow central head stripe and supercilium, and the yellow rump. Its habits are goldcrest-like as it flutters amongst the vegetation, even hanging upside down on occasions. Coniferous and mixed woodlands east from the Altai Mountains of Siberia, and south to Afghanistan and central China are its breeding haunts, while wintering birds occur from India to southern China.

Few of the rare birds which visit the British Isles have changed their occurrence here quite as dramatically as Pallas's warbler. It was first recorded in 1896 when one was taken at Cley on 31 October, then there were two further records, in 1951 and 1957, since when only five years are without one, none more recent than 1973. The total of birds seen has risen to 469, with a staggering 127 in 1982, so that surely Pallas's warbler must rank as a scarce visitor to our islands rather than a rare vagrant. The increase in records, especially those of 'invasion' years is attributed to weather conditions over Asia giving rise to strong easterly airflows at a critical time of the birds' departure from the breeding grounds. All arrivals have been in a very compact period commencing in late September, with a peak during the first half of October, to be followed by a rapid decline to the last in late November. Where do they all go then? East and south coasts from Shetland to Scilly are the main areas to receive Pallas's warbler, but some penetrate inland, like those which have reached Loch Rannoch, Wandsworth Common, and Pelwell. Others reach the west coast, being recorded from the Isle of Man, Caernarvon and from Wooltack Point. There have been just four in Ireland, two in Cork, the others in Dublin, and Wexford.

Radde's warbler is a dark, skulking warbler which feeds largely on the ground. Note the broad buff supercilium, and the stout bill and legs. It breeds in central Siberia east to Amurland and Sakhalin, wintering mainly in Burma and south-east Asia.

A Radde's warbler at North Cotes on 1 October 1898 was the first recorded in the British Isles. The next was caught at Blakeney on 3 October 1961, and was subsequently followed by 81 more, all occurrences in a compact period between late September and the beginning of November. Peak years have been 1982 with 14, and 1988 with 21. Although occurring north to Shetland, the majority of records are further south, largely between Norfolk and Scilly, with just two on the west coast, Bardsey and Skokholm, and two in Ireland at Hook Head and Helvick Head.

Pallas's rosefinch, similar to but paler and with more red than the scarlet rosefinch, with white streaks on the crown and chin, was discovered by Pallas during a journey to the Mongolian border in 1771. He collected the first specimens on the banks of the Uda River in Transbaikalia from where it breeds east to Sakhalin, wintering to the south in China and Japan. A first-summer male Pallas's rosefinch on North Ronaldsay from 2 June to 14 July 1988 was the first for the British Isles, though it still awaits admission to the British List.

A small bunting, the yellow-browed bunting has a distinctive head pattern of black, white and yellow, and white underparts. It breeds in a comparatively small area of Siberia east of Lake Baikal, and winters in south-east China. The first yellow-browed bunting in the British Isles was at Holkham on 19 October 1975. The second was a male at Fair Isle from 12 to 23 October 1980, during one of those spells of weather which bring so many good migrants to the island. On this occasion these included both pine and rustic buntings.

The chestnut bunting is a common cage-bird, the male having bright chestnut red upperparts, while in the female this colour is confined to the rump. It breeds in southern Siberia, wintering in Burma, southern China and south-east Asia. The four records of the chestnut bunting are all classed in Category D, as escapes from captivity cannot be ruled out. The first was a male on Foula from 9 to 14 July 1974, while the others were all in June, on the Isle of May in 1985, and on Fair Isle and Bardsey in 1986.

Pallas's reed bunting is a small bird rather similar to the reed bunting, the adult male being boldly streaked black and white on its upperparts. It breeds in the lowland tundras and river valleys of central Siberia, Manchuria, and Chinese Turkestan, wintering immediately to the south. The first Pallas's reed bunting in the British Isles was one seen on 29 September 1976 on Fair Isle and although seen briefly over a period of some days it was not positively identified until caught and ringed on 10 October. There is just one further record, also from Fair Isle on 17-18 September 1981.

North American Landbirds — Doves to Grosbeaks

Mourning Dove
Black-billed Cuckoo
Yellow-billed Cuckoo
Common Nighthawk
Chimney Swift
Belted Kingfisher
Yellow-shafted
 Flicker
Yellow-bellied
 Sapsucker
Eastern Phoebe
Tree Swallow

Purple Martin
Cliff Swallow
American Pipit
Cedar Waxwing
Brown Thrasher
Gray Catbird
Varied Thrush
Wood Thrush
Hermit Thrush
Swainson's Thrush
Grey-cheeked
 Thrush

Veery
American Robin
Golden-crowned
 Kinglet
Ruby-crowned
 Kinglet
Red-breasted
 Nuthatch
Red-eyed Vireo
Philadelphia Vireo
Evening Grosbeak
American Goldfinch

The mourning dove, most widespread and numerous of the North American doves, is somewhat smaller than the turtle dove and has a long tapered tail. Largely pinkish-buff in colour its long wings show pale grey in flight. Birds in the northern part of its range which extends from south-east Alaska and southern Canada, move south in winter. Otherwise it occurs throughout the year in the United States, Central America and the West Indies.

On the last day of October 1989 a mourning dove was caught in a Heligoland trap on the Calf of Man, the first for the Western Palearctic. Unfortunately it was in an exhausted state and died in the Observatory garden later that same day.

An almost dove-shaped bird, the black-billed cuckoo, slightly smaller than our own cuckoo, is bronzy-brown above and white below in all plumages. As the name suggests, the bill is grey-black. Look carefully for the small white spots on the outer tail feathers, and the fine white speckling on the upperparts, a key feature when separating this species from the next. It breeds in central North America, wintering south to northern South America.

The first black-billed cuckoo in the British Isles was shot at Killead on 25 September 1871. Of the others up to 1958, one was on Tresco in October 1932, and two were in Scotland, the only ones so far from that country, at Southend in Kintyre early in November 1950, and on Foula in October 1953. The eight since have been in England, all between 1965 and 1985, six of which were in October, the others at the end of August and the end of September. The south-west has provided the majority of records, three from Scilly, two from Devon and one from Cornwall, the exceptions being birds much further north at Redcar in September 1975, and Red Rocks on 30 October 1982, the year in which there amounted to almost an 'invasion' with no fewer than four, of which both of those located on Scilly were eventually found dead.

The yellow-billed cuckoo is similar in size and general appearance to the black-billed cuckoo, though perhaps is bulkier in build. The main differences are the yellow base to the bill, the rufous wing-patches, the bold white spots on the black outer tail-feathers, and the absence of white speckling. It breeds from southern Canada to the Caribbean and winters in South America.

The first yellow-billed cuckoo in the British Isles, indeed in the Western Palearctic, was killed near Youghal in the autumn of 1825. There were two in 1832, at Stackpole and at Bray, with 19 more up to 1958, including no fewer than four in the autumn of 1953 of which three were in Scotland, the other in Yorkshire. There have been a further 28 subsequently, all but one in the period mid-September to mid-November, the exception being a bird found freshly dead on 14 December 1960 at Middleton-on-Sea. Indeed the majority of yellow-billed cuckoos seen in this country have been found dead or dying, so that a juvenile at Portland for five days in September 1979 was a real bonus, and entered into the life lists of several hundred grateful observers. In the 13 years since 1957 in which yellow-billed cuckoos have been seen in the British Isles, there are single records in four years, two in seven years, while there were no fewer than five in 1985. Most are seen in south-west England, though there are records north to Caithness, but none for Wales, surprisingly since three of the early records were from that country. Also surprising for a transatlantic vagrant is the scarcity of records from Ireland, with only four since 1957, on Achill Island in 1964, Cape Clear in 1969, Lecarrow in 1979 and another on Cape Clear in 1986.

The common nighthawk is smaller than the nightjar, largely on account of the shorter tail, though it has longer rather pointed wings. The upperparts are dark brown, almost black, paler beneath, with white spots on the close wing forming in flight a bold band. It breeds in North America from south-east Alaska to Panama, wintering south as far as Argentina.

The first common nighthawk in the British Isles was one shot on Tresco on 17 September 1927. The next three were from the same islands, two on St Agnes in September 1955 to be followed by one at the same locality, first seen by birdwatchers standing outside the snooker room at dusk on 12 October 1971. Equally dramatic, and certainly more surprising was one later the same month, which hawked insects around gardens at Bulcote. There have been a further eight since, all but one from England, this being trapped at Kirkwall on 12 September 1978, the earliest to have arrived, for virtually all are seen during October. Four were from Scilly, the others were at Studland, Barnes Common, and lastly one found exhausted at Moreton in October 1985. Nursed back to health, it was subsequently transported to winter quarters in Belize, courtesy of the Royal Air Force.

The chimney swift is a small, plump, sooty-brown swift with a torpedo-shaped body, long wings and slightly rounded tail. At close quarters this will be seen to have several small protuding 'spines', the hardened tips of feathers used to help the bird cling to vertical surfaces. In flight the chimney swift is agile and almost bat-like. It breeds in eastern North America, wintering in central America and north-eastern South America. The first chimney swift in the Western Palearctic was one observed at Porthgwarra on 21 October 1982, where the delight and surprise of birdwatchers knew no bounds, for it was joined by another on the 23rd, with a final sighting four days later. In 1986 one was seen for three days in early November on St Mary's and in 1987 there was one near Truro on 18 October.

A powerful kingfisher, the belted kingfisher is a magnificent bird the size of a jackdaw, with a large dusky-blue crested head, upperparts and neck collar, and white underparts which in the female have a rufous chest band. The loud rattling calls often advertise the bird's presence. It breeds through much of North America from the tree limit south to California and Florida with some movement south to winter in the Caribbean.

A belted kingfisher was shot near Sladebridge in November 1908, though not accepted to the British List until 1980 by which time there had been a second occurrence, one on the River Bunree. This bird was first seen in December 1978 and remained in the area until it was shot in the following February. Fortunately the perpetrator of the crime was prosecuted, and the mounted specimen passed on to the National Museum of Ireland. By one of those strange coincidences which surround the occurrences of some rare birds, the third belted kingfisher was from Sladebridge, a male discovered there in November 1979, and which remained until the end of August the following year. The second record from Ireland, a female, so no confusion with the Cornish bird, was alas also shot, this time at Dundrum Bay. The only other, also in Ireland and also a female, was first seen at Ballyvaughan in October 1984, then it moved to Killaloe where it remained until late March 1985.

The yellow-shafted or northern flicker is the largest of the medium sized North American woodpeckers. It has a grey crown, pinkish cheeks with a black 'moustache' and a red nape, barred brown upperparts, a black breast band and strikingly mottled buff underparts. In flight the underside of the wings and tail show a golden yellow, while the rump is white. It breeds in woodland from Alaska south to the Gulf of Mexico, northern populations moving south in autumn, especially along the east coast.

A yellow-shafted flicker shot in Amesbury Park in the autumn of 1836 has never been accepted to the British List. Why? It seems a perfectly respectable record, certainly no less doubtful than earlier records of some other rare birds. The only other records are of known ship-assisted birds, for this is a frequent ship-borne passenger each autumn in the western Atlantic. One of some 10 that came on board the RMS *Mauretania* in October 1962 during a crossing from New York was seen to fly ashore at Cobh. In July 1981 the corpse of another which is thought to have died on board ship was found in Caithness.

The yellow-bellied sapsucker is a small woodpecker, mainly black and white above, with a white wing-patch and rump, red crown and throat, black breast and yellow-white undersides. Immatures are a mottled brown, though still show the white wing patch and rump. It breeds from central Canada to the northern United States, and winters to central America and the West Indies.

The yellow-bellied sapsucker has occurred on two occasions in the

British Isles. The first, an immature male, spent nearly two weeks on Tresco during the great autumn for American visitors in 1975, having been first located amongst willows beside the Great Pool on 26 September. The second, a female, was trapped on Cape Clear in mid-October 1988.

The eastern phoebe is a large American flycatcher, larger than the spotted flycatcher, grey above, darker on the wings and tail, with creamy white underparts and strong black bill and legs. The long tail is constantly flicked downwards in a leisurely fashion. It breeds from central Canada to the south-east United States, wintering in the Gulf States, Mexico and Central America.

There are just two records from the British Isles, indeed the only ones from the Western Palearctic, though conceivably the same bird was involved. One at Slapton on 22 April 1987 was followed by one at Lundy on the opposite side of the county on 24 and 25 April.

The tree swallow is a small swallow, the only one with blue-green upperparts contrasting with the white underparts, and a slightly forked tail. Immature birds with brown upperparts rather resemble a sand martin. It breeds across a huge tract of North America from Alaska south to California and east to Labrador and parts of the West Indies.

Just two records for the British Isles. The first is a bird shot from amongst sand martins near Derby in 1850, a record subsequently placed in square brackets and not admitted to the British List, though there seems no reason why it should not have arrived unaided. It is after all not very suitable as a cage-bird. No doubt surrounds the male tree swallow which delighted birdwatchers for five days in June 1990 as it hawked insects over Porth Hellick on St Mary's.

A large swallow, the male purple martin has brilliant blue-black plumage, while females are duller and greyer. Few now nest in natural sites, nearly the whole population chooses nestboxes in the 'martin houses' provided across much of North America from Central Canada to the Gulf of Mexico. The winter is spent in South America south to Bolivia and northern Argentina.

Has the purple martin occurred in the British Isles? One is said to have been shot at Kingstown in 1839 or 1840, another at Brent Reservoir in September 1842, with one at Colne Bridge near Huddersfield in 1854. None of these is currently accepted, though clearly deserving further consideration.

About the same size as the familiar swallow in Europe, which to avoid confusion might possibly be called the barn swallow, the cliff swallow has brown upperparts, an orange rump and buff forehead, while the wings are broad and rather martin-like, and the square tail lacks streamers. It breeds over much of North America, choosing nest sites on buildings, under bridges and culverts, even occasionally still on cliffs, before moving south to Brazil and Argentina for the winter.

The first cliff swallow for the British Isles was a juvenile which appeared on 10 October 1983 on St Agnes but quickly moved to St Mary's, where it remained until 27 October. The only other, also a juvenile, was seen at South Gare on 23 October 1988.

Formerly considered a race of the rock and water pipit, but now classed as a separate species, the American pipit is another of that difficult family for birdwatchers to wrestle with when it comes to identification. It is slimmer than the rock pipit, and has olive-brown rather than plain upperparts, buffish underparts with black streaks, and dark legs. The loud, and frequent 'pippit' call is also distinctive. This is a bird of the tundra edge and upland meadows in east Greenland from the Arctic circle north to about Upernivik, and across much of northern North America to Alaska and south through the Rockies. Its range also extends westwards across Siberia from the Bering Strait to about Lake Baikal. Winter quarters extend south to the Caribbean and Central America.

The first American pipit in the British Isles was a young male, captured on 30 September 1910 at the margins of a small stream near the village on St Kilda. William Eagle Clarke who made the discovery recalled: 'It is doubtful if it would have been detected, in its immature dress, among the numerous Meadow-Pipits, but its unfamiliar note betrayed it.' The other records so far accepted are of birds at the Great Saltee in October 1951, Fair Isle in September 1953, Newcastle (County Wicklow) in November 1967, and St Mary's in October 1988.

Slightly smaller than the waxwing, the cedar waxwing lacks the conspic-uous yellow and white markings on the wings of that species, while the underparts are a brighter yellow and the undertail coverts white instead of cinnamon. It breeds across much of central North America moving, often in irregular irruptions, to the southern United States and Central America in winter.

Just one record, though so far not accepted to the British List, is a bird on Noss on 27 June 1985.

The brown thrasher is one of two members of the mockingbird family to have reached the British Isles, the other being the next species, the gray cat-bird. The thrasher is as large as a mistle thrush, though the long rounded tail makes up half the length. The upperparts are red-brown with a double white wing-bar, the underparts white, spotted black. In flight its shape resembles a small but nimble magpie, while the tail is raised (thrashed) as it runs about on the ground where it spends most of the time. It breeds in wooded and thick scrub areas in central and eastern North America from southern Canada to Texas and Florida, and most winter in the southern United States.

The first and so far only record of the brown thrasher in the British Isles was one which was present on Durlston Head from 18 November to early February 1967. There is just one other record from the Western Palearctic, one on Heligoland in the autumn of 1836.

The gray catbird is about the size of a redwing, and like the previous species the tail takes up nearly half its length. The plumage is generally dark grey with a slightly darker cap, and dark chestnut undertail coverts. The tail is frequently flicked, while the name comes from the cat-like mewing call. It breeds in dense scrub and thickets from southern Canada to the Gulf States, where it winters in a range south to Panama, and through the Caribbean.

There are just two records of the gray catbird from the British Isles, the first seen briefly on Cape Clear on 4 November 1986, the second in Cot Valley in October 1988.

The varied thrush is one of the most handsome of the North American thrushes, having blue-grey upperparts and orange-red underparts. The presence of an orange eye-stripe, orange wing-bars, and a grey breast band, help avoid confusion with the American robin. Varied thrushes breed in moist coniferous forests in the Pacific north-west of America from Alaska to northern California. In winter the range, still hugging the Pacific, extends into southern California. Small numbers do, however, move eastwards, and it has recently been described as 'a scarce but regular winter visitor to bird-tables along the eastern seaboard, chiefly from Maine to New York'.

This surely is a species as unlikely as any passerine to reach the British Isles, though such records continue to occur to astound us. Indeed surely by now we realize anything, or very nearly anything is possible when it comes to rare birds. The only record for the Western Palearctic so far is a bird at Nanquidno which fed on fallen apples and cotoneaster berries from 9 to 24 November 1982. Much confusion initially occurred, something not unknown with first records, but on this occasion it was amplified as the bird was in aberrant plumage with all the orange areas whitish, a feature occasionally recorded in parts of the normal range.

The wood thrush is a small robust bird rather similar in appearance to the song thrush but with a rusty head and white eye-ring, tawny-brown upperparts and pure white underparts heavily marked with large dark spots. It is a common bird in damp broad-leaved woodlands and town parks in eastern Canada and the United States, and winter quarters are south from Mexico to Panama.

A wood thrush on St Agnes on 7 October 1987 is the only record, with just one other in the Western Palearctic, a male in Iceland 20 years previously.

The hermit thrush is considered by many to be the finest songster of all North American birds. Smallest of the North American thrushes, it has been likened to a small song thrush with a red tail, or a thrush nightingale with a spotted breast. Note the distinctive feature of cocking then slowly lowering the tail. It breeds in coniferous woodland across much of North America from central Alaska to New Mexico and east to Newfoundland and Long Island. Most winter in the southern part of the breeding range south to Central America.

The first hermit thrush in the British Isles was found on 2 June 1975 in a newly ploughed field on Fair Isle. The other two records have both been in October, and both from Scilly. One on St Mary's in 1984 was especially elusive, though it was eventually seen during its brief stay of a day by all observers. The other remained for two days in October 1987 on St Agnes.

Swainson's thrush, also known as the olive-backed thrush, is another small thrush with olive upperparts and a bold buff eye-ring. It breeds in forested regions from Alaska to the northern United States, wintering from Mexico to Argentina.

Although Swainson's thrush was recorded in Europe on no fewer than seven occasions between 1843 and 1906, the first British record was not until 1956. On 26 May that year one was found dead at the Blackrock Lighthouse, loneliest of the rock lighthouses off the Irish coast. The next was trapped and ringed on Skokholm where it remained for five days in October 1967. Since then a further 11 have been recorded, all in October save for one that just missed out, a bird on 30 September 1984 at St Agnes. Five have been from the Isles of Scilly, the others being in Cork, Cornwall,

Devon and Kent, with just a single northern record, a bird at Scatness at the southern tip of Shetland in October 1980. a Swainson's thrush at St Mary's from 20 to 28 October 1979 was joined at the end of its stay by a gray-cheeked thrush, the first time surely that two species of this genus have occurred together in the Western Palearctic.

Despite its specific name *minimus*, the grey-cheeked thrush is the largest of its genus. The upperparts are oliver-grey with a grey face and rather indistinct eye-ring, the underparts grey-white, spotted on the throat and breast. This is a shy bird of northern woodlands often near to the tree line in Alaska, Canada and the northern United States. Most winter in northern South America south to Ecuador.

The grey-cheeked thrush is the most frequently recorded of the North American thrushes in the British Isles. There have been 32 since the first, one on Fair Isle on 5 October 1953, with records in 14 years, all but one in October. The exception was one found dying at Lossiemouth on 26 November 1961, though several of the October birds have remained until November. Five birds in 1976 and a staggering 12 in 1986 were particularly exciting years for any transatlantic vagrant. Although south-west England is the most likely place to encounter the grey-cheeked thrush, in addition to the Moray individual birds have occurred in Shetland on two further occasions, and on St Kilda, in Durham, and on three occasions in the 1960s on Bardsey. There have been just two from Ireland, both from Cape Clear, where the first, in 1982, was caught by hand after it had been knocked to the ground by a sparrowhawk.

Another North American thrush, the veery gets its name from the fluty notes of its song, though observers in the British Isles are hardly likely to hear this and need to note the uniform tawny-brown upperparts, and the rather indistinct breast spots. One of the more southerly of the thrushes, its breeding range, largely in broad-leaved woodlands, extends right across southern Canada, and south to Arizona and Long Island, while winter quarters are in southern South America.

Just two veery have been recorded in the British Isles. The first was discovered and eventually trapped at Porthgwarra, the secluded valley at the south-westerly tip of Cornwall, on 6 October 1970. The second stayed for a month from 10 October 1987 on Lundy.

A large and robust thrush, the American robin is about the size of a blackbird with much the same active manner, the wing and tail flicking. The breast and underparts are a bright brick-red, with a white throat, streaked black, the upperparts dark grey, the almost black head having a striking white eye-ring. Juvenile birds are heavily spotted below, and paler grey above with mottles and streaks. It breeds over much of North America from about the tree line to southern Mexico. Winter quarters extend from the southern United States to Central America.

There have been 10 early records of the American robin in the British Isles since the first, one at Dover in April 1876. Doubts were expressed over such records at the time, for this handsome bird was regularly kept as a cage-bird, while there was at least one attempt at introduction, that by Lord Northcliffe near Guildford in 1910. Since 1957 there have been 19, mostly between mid-October and mid-February, these later sightings suggesting that some birds have been capable of overwintering. Are these also the origin of late spring records, three occurrences in May and early June? Although mostly there are just single records in a year, in 1963 and 1982 there were two, and in 1966 three. Sightings have been from Shetland, Orkney, Outer Hebrides, Caithness, and Kincardineshire in Scotland, from Surrey, Dorset, Devon, and Scilly in England, and from Down, Cork, and Kerry in Ireland, with none so far from Wales. One of the five from Ireland was a bird which came aboard a trawler off the Skelligs on 28 January 1965. Was this a transatlantic passage nearing completion? Why make such a journey at the end of January? One of the two records from Surrey, from Haslemere on 12 October 1984, was also the earliest, though the bird, an immature, had the misfortune to be a magpie's meal, being identified only from a few feathers.

The golden-crowned kinglet with its vividly striped head of red, yellow, black, and white, might easily be mistaken for a firecrest, for it even has the two white wing-bars of that species though lacks the bronzy-green shoulders. It breeds in Alaska and Canada, further south than the ruby-crowned kinglet, though like that species its range extends south through the mountain ranges of the United States, where it winters throughout much of the country and in South America.

There is a single intriguing record of the golden-crowned kinglet in the British Isles. One shot at Wharmton Clough near Oldham on 19 October 1897 remained unrecognized in a private collection for nearly a quarter of a century, and when 'discovered', its identity seemed so unlikely that the suggestion was even made that it was possibly an undiscovered Asiatic race of the firecrest rather than of North American origin. Clearly it is a golden-crowned kinglet, and a reinvestigation in the light of present knowledge nearly 100 years later is therefore overdue.

The ruby-crowned kinglet is a tiny bird, goldcrest size with olive-green upperparts, the wings having a double white bar, a white throat, greenish breast and white underparts. The ruby crown is only present in the male, and then it may be concealed. It breeds largely in coniferous woodlands, from the tree line in Alaska to Labrador and south in the Appalachians and in the Rocky Mountains. Many move south in winter to reach the southern United States and Central America.

Although the ruby-crowned kinglet has not been accepted to the British List, two records most certainly deserve consideration. One was shot in Kenmore Wood on the west shore of Loch Lomond in the summer of 1852. Had it arrived the previous autumn? There has been just one further record, on 21 September 1871, a likely date, at Highnam.

In Scotland, John Mitchell has made a singular contribution to the history of rare birds in the British Isles, by carefully examining all the evidence surrounding the Loch Lomond ruby-crowned kinglet. It is a fascinating story, well worth briefly summarizing, and deserving of a wider audience.

The bird shot by Donald Dewar, then a student, while seeking goldcrests for his collection was considered by him to be a firecrest, a major prize none the less. Not until six years later when Robert Gray, a noted ornithologist, saw the skin at a natural history meeting in Glasgow was its true identity revealed. As a result the specimen was presented to the artist John Gould and eventually the British Museum collection, where it is now housed at Tring.

Over 30 years elapsed before quite unjustified doubts were expressed, first by Henry Seebohm in his *History of British Birds* published in 1883. Alas these doubts were perpetuated by later authors, some even going beyond and causing more confusion by referring to two birds having been shot. Only the great T. A. Coward stood out against these opinions and concluded that the ruby-crowned kinglet from Loch Lomond was genuine. Alas even his comments have been neglected, and his great work largely forgotten amongst the plethora of modern handbooks and field guides.

Fortunately the evidence, the facts so ably marshalled by John Mitchell, can hardly be ignored. The ruby-crowned kinglet clearly has a strong case to be given its rightful place on the British List. Let it be ignored no longer, but re-admitted with acclamation. Surely a bird which has crossed the North Atlantic unaided, especially one of such a diminutive size, deserves no less.

The red-breasted nuthatch about the size of a blue tit, is distinctly smaller than the nuthatch, but has the same blue-grey upperparts. However, the underparts are a rusty orange-brown, while the crown and nape are black with a distinct white eye-stripe, a combination of features peculiar to this nuthatch. A bird of coniferous woodlands throughout much of southern Canada and the western United States, wintering birds, often the result of occasional irruptive movements, occur south almost to the Gulf of Mexico.

A single record only for the British Isles, a male red-breasted nuthatch was sighted at Holkham Meals, the extensive belt of Corsican pines close to the shore just west of Wells-next-the-Sea, from 13 October 1989 to the spring of 1990. It proved extremely elusive, disappearing high in the canopy, only occasionally showing itself, or coming nearer to ground level. One other for the Western Palearctic was a bird on the Westmann Islands on 21 May 1970.

About the size of a great tit, the red-eyed vireo is like a thick-set warbler with a stout bill, and, as its name suggests, a red or rather brownish-red eye. The blue-grey crown, white supercilia, and olive-green upperparts contrast with the white underparts. It is said to be the most abundant bird in the deciduous woodlands of eastern North America, moving to South America as far as Argentina for the winter.

The first red-eyed vireo in the British Isles was found dead at the Tuskar Rock Lighthouse on 4 October 1951. The next, indeed there were two, an adult and an immature together, was on St Agnes in October 1962. From such modest beginnings this has now become the most frequent North American passerine on this side of the Atlantic, being recorded annually since 1980. The grand total now stands at 55 of which no fewer than 11 were recorded in 1988. All have been in autumn, between 21 September and 27 October, most from Scilly, with others regularly in Cornwall and Cork. Other southern counties visited are Devon, Dorset, Kent, Suffolk, Caernarvon, Pembroke, and in Ireland in Waterford and Wexford. Further afield there are records from Caithness, South Uist and Northumberland.

The yellow breast and unmarked wings of the Philadelphia vireo, features unique among the vireos, can cause confusion with the wood warblers, but note the thick, dark bill. The upperparts are dark olive, while the crown is greyish. It is an elusive bird of woodland margins and scrub in southern Canada, which winters in Central America.

There are just two records. The first Philadelphia vireo for the Western Palearctic was at Galley Head from 12 to 17 October 1985. Two years later there was one on Tresco from 10 to 13 October.

A handsome, unmistakable bird, the evening grosbeak is about the size and shape of a hawfinch, with a striking combination of yellow and black in the male, and with large white wing patches. Females are paler but still have the black wings and tail and the white patches while both have massive bills. It breeds through much of central North America south to Mexico in the west, with some movement south in autumn.

The first evening grosbeak for Europe was a male in the old village on Hirta, St Kilda, on 26 March 1969. During the preceding winter huge movements of evening grosbeaks had been witnessed in eastern North America from Nova Scotia to Florida, and the arrival of one in western Britain may be associated with these. One subsequent record was a female at Nethybridge from 10 to 25 March 1980.

The male American goldfinch is a bright canary yellow with a black cap and wings and whitish rump. The female is more greenish and although it lacks the black cap it retains the other features. It breeds commonly across much of Southern Canada and the Northern United States, moving south as far as the Gulf States in winter.

The sole record of the American goldfinch is on Achill Island on 6 September 1894, though this is not accepted on to the Irish List, as its feathers showed sign of wear suggesting a possible captive origin.

North American Landbirds — The Wood Warblers

Black and White Warbler	Cape May Warbler	Ovenbird
Golden-winged Warbler	Magnolia Warbler	Northern Waterthrush
Tennessee Warbler	Yellow-rumped Warbler	Yellowthroat
Northern Parula	Blackburnian Warbler	Wilson's Warbler
Yellow Warbler	Blackpoll Warbler	Hooded Warbler
Chestnut-sided Warbler	Palm Warbler	
	American Redstart	

A lmost the size of a garden warbler, the black and white warbler was described by one fortunate observer as a 'beautiful, unmistakable, near apparition'. It feeds, treecreeper-like, largely on the trunks and branches of trees, and is a common bird in deciduous woodlands from northern Canada to the Gulf States, from where it winters south to Ecuador.

The first black and white warbler in the British Isles was found dead during stormy weather in October 1936 at Scalloway and sent to the Royal Scottish Museum. So unexpected was such a bird in Europe that many thought it could only be an escape from captivity. Next came two records from Scilly, on St Mary's in 1975 and 1977, to be followed by the only one in spring, at Tavistock at the beginning of March 1978. In October the same year there was the first in Ireland, one on Cape Clear. One on Skomer in September 1980 remains the only record for Wales, and was followed by birds in Cornwall in 1982 and 1983. The first found dead was handed to Dr G. W. Davis who the following year found the live one on the Lizard peninsula. There was one in Loughermore Forest in 1984, then the only east coast record, at How Hill in 1985, and lastly a bird at Prawle Point in 1986.

No other warbler has the unique combination of a black throat, grey in the female, and yellow wing-bars found in the golden-winged warbler. Note also the yellow crown, white head stripes, and grey-white underparts. A not very numerous warbler breeding mainly in birch woods in the north-east United States, it winters in the south-east and into Central America.

When Paul Doherty left home on the afternoon of 7 February 1989 to post some letters on the Lunsford Park Estate, Larkfield, the last thing he expected to encounter during the walk of some 200 yards was a rare bird, let alone one new to the Western Palearctic. A brief but close view of a yellow and black warbler in a cotoneaster bush followed by consultation with the field guides at home a few minutes later revealed the bird's identity, a golden-winged warbler. The following day, and much to the discoverer's relief, because, as he was later to write 'I simply couldn't believe I was being handed a first for the Western Palearctic on a plate', the bird was rediscovered in the car park of a nearby Tesco's store. Three days later, on a Saturday morning, some 3,000 birdwatchers were present to see the bird. Fortunately it remained in the area, attracting large numbers of watchers, many of whom partook of coffee and cakes sold from a stall by enterprising Girl Guides. The last sighting seems to have been on about 9 April. Subsequent investigations were to reveal that it had been present on the Larkfield Estate since at least 24 January. Perhaps it had even arrived the previous autumn, and certainly it found Kent much to its liking as winter quarters.

The Tennessee warbler is a dumpy warbler, and when in winter plumage not unlike a willow warbler, though it is brighter green above. Its persistent and repeated 'zit-zit' call is quite unlike that of any other warbler, and resembles the call-notes of a firecrest. Aspen and spruce forests across much of Canada and the north of the United States are its breeding haunts, from where it moves to winter in Central and northern South America.

The first two records of the Tennessee warbler in the British Isles were remarkably both in the same year and at the same location, Fair Isle in 1975. One was present from 6 to 20 September, being caught and ringed, to be followed on the 24th by a second bird. There is just one further record, a bird on Holm from 5 to 7 September 1982.

The northern parula is a small but robust, striking blue-grey and yellow bird with two white wing-bars and broken eye-rings. It is almost tit-like in habit as it forages on tree trunks, or hangs below branches in the damp woodlands which are its home in eastern North America, from about the Great Lakes to the shores of the Caribbean. Winter quarters extend to Nicaragua and through the West Indies.

The first northern parula was one found with willow warblers and goldcrests in the trees by Great Pool, Tresco, on 16 October 1966. A further 11 were subsequently recorded, all between late September and the beginning of November, mainly single birds, with two in 1988, and three in 1983 and 1985. Except for one found dying at Wigan Infirmary on 2 November 1982, all have been in south-western counties from Dorset to Scilly, with just one in Ireland, at Firkeel from 19 to 24 October 1983.

The only all-yellow wood warbler, of which even the immature is distinctive though less bright than an adult, the yellow warbler is also one of the most widespread. It breeds across much of North America from Alaska and Labrador to Baja California and North Carolina from where its winter range extends south to northern Brazil and Peru.

There is just one record of the yellow warbler, a bird on Bardsey on 29 August 1964. It was first seen by Hugh Miles, newly arrived assistant warden as he carried his belongings from the beach to the Observatory, and subsequently by all the other residents. What a start to one's ornithological career! There is also an unaccepted record from Axwell Park in May 1904.

The chestnut-sided warbler has, as the name suggests, chestnut sides, a feature shared only with the bay-breasted warbler, though this lacks the yellow-green head and streaked back. It is a common resident of scrub woodland in south-east Canada and the north-east United States from where it moves to Central America in winter.

There is just one record from the British Isles, a first–year chestnut-sided warbler found on Fetlar on 20 September 1985.

The Cape May warbler (Cape May being at the mouth of the Delaware River, New Jersey) is a heavily streaked, indeed striped, yellow warbler, a feature recorded in the specific name *tigrina*. Males have chestnut cheeks, a large white wing patch, and a yellow-green rump, characteristics shared with both the female and immature. It is a rather uncommon bird, subject to fluctuations in the spruce bud worm population, found in the coniferous woodlands of central and south-eastern Canada and adjoining parts of the United States. Winter quarters seem largely to be in the West Indies.

There is one quite remarkable record of the Cape May warbler in the British Isles, a male singing in Paisley Glen, an area of parkland on the outskirts of Paisley, on 17 June 1977. As the two fortunate observers point out in their subsequent report, Alexander Wilson who named the bird was born within sight of Paisley Glen. But what wanderings must have brought such a bird to this place in mid-summer, a feat which again underlines that anything seems possible where rare birds are concerned.

The magnolia warbler shares with the Cape May warbler the prominent white wing-patch, but it is the only yellow-throated warbler to have a broad white tail-band. Note also the grey head and bright yellow rump. A common bird in moist forests from north-west Canada to the Great Lakes, and the maritime provinces, it winters in Central America and the West Indies.

There is just one record of a magnolia warbler on St Agnes on 27 and 28 September 1981.

Previously known as the myrtle warbler, its favourite food being myrtle berries, the yellow-rumped warbler is a rather dark bird, having a pattern of four yellow patches — on the crown, on each flank, and on the rump — except in the juvenile. Coniferous woodlands from Alaska through central Canada to Labrador, Newfoundland, and the north-eastern United States are its summer haunts. Although it can winter well north of any other wood-warbler, some nevertheless reach the West Indies and Panama in the east and Baja California in the west.

The first yellow-rumped warbler in the British Isles was one which fed at a bird table at Newton St Cyrs near Exeter from 5 January until it was found dead on 10 February 1955. The next, also from Devon, was on Lundy in early November 1960. Subsequently a further 15 have been recorded, of which just two are spring records, both in May, from Fair Isle in 1977 and the Calf of Man in 1985. The rest have all been between mid-September and the end of October, eight in Ireland, of which seven were at Cape Clear and one at Loop Head, four from Scilly, and one in the Outer Hebrides at Newton, South Uist, in October 1982.

Named after the English botanist Anna Blackburn (1740-93) the Blackburnian warbler has a double wing-bar and two white longitudinal stripes on the back. Adult males have a bright orange throat and head markings, in the female these features are yellow, and in the immature pale buff-yellow. It is a bird of the conifer tops in southern Canada east of the Great Plains, to Nova Scotia and south through the mountains to Georgia. In winter birds are found from Costa Rica to Columbia, Venezuela, Ecuador, and in central Peru.

The first Blackburnian warbler in the British Isles, indeed in the Western

Palearctic, surprised, mystified and delighted myself and my wife, two lone observers on Skomer, on 5 October 1961, as it fed on the ivy-covered cliffs above the North Haven. In the absence of a field guide, or other literature on North American birds on the island at the time, it was some weeks before the bird could be identified from the description taken. So improbable did the record seem that it was not accepted until long after, when the scale of transatlantic vagrancy had become fully appreciated. There is just one further record, one on Fair Isle on 7 October 1988.

The palm warbler is a ground-feeding, tail-wagging bird, with bright yellow under-tail coverts, a yellow rump and throat. Boggy areas eastwards from central Canada to the Atlantic seaboard and Newfoundland are its summer home, winter quarters extending from the south-east United States, through Central America and the West Indies.

The only record of the palm warbler in the British Isles is a woeful one, the remains of an adult found on the tide line at Walney Island on 18 May 1976, and as such only admitted to Category D of the British and Irish Lists.

The blackpoll warbler is a large black and white warbler, the summer male having a distinctive black crown. The dark olive-green upperparts are heavily streaked, the pale underparts less so. This is one of the most abundant wood warblers in North America, frequenting coniferous woodlands from Alaska and northern Canada to New York State. Winter quarters are in northern South America to Brazil.

The first blackpoll warblers in the British Isles arrived at the same time in October 1968, one being present on St Agnes from 12 to 20 October, while another was on Bardsey on the 22nd. There have been 24 since, all between mid-September and the end of October. Single birds on Scilly in 1970 and 1975 were followed by no fewer than eight there in 1976, when Bardsey had its second, while in the far south there was one at Prawle Point. In the years since, Scilly with a further six has continued to be the most likely place to encounter the blackpoll warbler this side of the Atlantic, while single birds have visited Porthgwarra and Lundy. Three in Ireland have all been at Cape Clear, with a fourth and most recent bird being at Hook Head in 1985. There has been just one away from southern Britain, on Whalsay in 1985.

One of the most handsome of the wood warblers, the male American redstart is black above and white below, with large salmon-pink patches in the wings and tail. Females and immatures are grey and brown above, with the same patches, this time in pale yellow. All have the habit of continually drooping their wings and of fanning the tail. It breeds in deciduous woods from northern Canada to the south-east United States, wintering in the West Indies and in parts of South America.

The first American redstart in the British Isles was discovered in willow scrub above Porthgwarra on 21 October 1967. In October the following year there was one on Cape Clear, though it was not until 1982 that any more were recorded. A female at Portnahaven, Islay, on 1 November was followed by a first-winter male at Gibraltar Point where it remained for almost a month. There was also one at St Just in October 1983, and then two in October 1985, at Winchester College and at Galley Head.

A large and handsome warbler, the ovenbird has a heavily spotted white underside, olive-green upperparts with an orange-red crown, white eye-ring, and pink legs. Most of its time is spent on the ground where it actively dashes about like a small thrush. The unusual name is derived from its domed nest of leaves and grasses which resembles an old-style oven. It can be found from southern Canada south to Georgia, Oklahoma and Colorado, wintering birds reaching through the West Indies and Central America.

The first record of an ovenbird in the British Isles was a strand line corpse at Formby on 4 January 1969. The next was trapped on the Out Skerries on 7 October 1973. One freshly dead at Lough Carra on 8 December 1977 is the only record from Ireland, while the last, also found dead, was at Wembury on 22 October 1985. The chances of seeing a live bird therefore seem rather slim.

The northern waterthrush has a superfluous resemblance to a pipit, having olive-brown upperparts, streaked underparts, and pink legs, and in the way it walks and runs on the ground with much tail-wagging. Note, however, the bird's plump build and the short tail. It breeds near to fresh water from Alaska, throughout Canada and the north-eastern United States, the winter range extending from Florida to northern South America.

The first northern waterthrush for the British Isles was one which fed among rotting seaweed at the head of a small cove on the east side of St Agnes from 30 September to 12 October 1958. The next two birds were also from Scilly, on Tresco in October 1968 and Bryher at the end of September 1982. One at Cape Clear on 10 September 1983 was by far the earliest, while the latest was at Gibraltar Point on 22 October 1988.

The yellowthroat is an abundant warbler, olive-brown above, the male having a handsome black mask; both sexes and first-winter birds have the yellow throat. It has several wren-like characteristics, skulking and hiding, appearing briefly then just as rapidly disappearing, often uttering sharp chattering and scolding notes. It breeds from south-east Alaska and Labrador, to Mexico and Georgia, and winters throughout Central America and the West Indies.

A yellowthroat on Lundy on 4 November 1954 was the first for the British Isles. So extraordinary was the record of a small American passerine at the time that the report of its occurrence dwelt heavily as to whether such a bird could cross the North Atlantic unaided. Two more have subsequently made the journey, both by coincidence in the same year, 1984, a male on Fetlar from 7 to 11 June, and a first-winter male at Bryher from 2 to 17 October.

Another very yellow warbler, the adult male Wilson's warbler has a thin glossy black cap. It breeds from Alaska, across much of Canada, and in the United States south through the western mountains. Winter quarters are in Central America.

The only record of a Wilson's warbler in the British Isles is of a male at Rame Head on 13 October 1985.

The male hooded warbler with its resplendent black hood contrasting with a bright yellow face and underparts clearly provides the name for this species. Females are not nearly so brightly coloured, and lack the black hood. It is a common visitor to the eastern United States, and the Canadian border, wintering in Central America.

There is one record of the hooded warbler for the British Isles, a female or possibly an immature, from 20 to 23 September 1970 in the vicinity of the Pool, St Agnes.

North American Landbirds — Tanagers to Orioles

Summer Tanager	White-throated	Eastern Meadow
Scarlet Tanager	Sparrow	Lark
Rufous-sided Towhee	Dark-eyed Junco	Red-winged
Fox Sparrow	Rose-breasted	Blackbird
Song Sparrow	Grosbeak	Rusty Blackbird
Savannah Sparrow	Blue Grosbeak	Northern Oriole
Lark Sparrow	Indigo Bunting	
White-crowned	Painted Bunting	
Sparrow	Bobolink	

The male summer tanager is a resplendent scarlet bird, while the females and immatures are equally striking, though this time the plumage is mustard and gold. It breeds from the east-central United States south to Florida and Mexico, wintering south to Peru. There is just one record of the summer tanager in the British Isles, a first-winter male which gave observers tantalizingly brief views on Bardsey on the morning of 11 September 1957, before it was caught and full details taken. It remained on the island for some 15 days, feeding largely on the abundant blackberry crop, before moving on.

Although the adult male scarlet tanager is easily separated by way of the dark wings on otherwise scarlet plumage from the summer tanager, females and immatures are much more difficult, being olive-green above, yellow below, with darker wings. Woodland habitats in southern Canada and the eastern United States are its breeding haunts while birds move to South America from Columbia to Peru for the winter.

The first scarlet tanager in the British Isles was a female at the Copeland Islands on 12 October 1963, the next, a first-winter male, on St Mary's on 4 October 1970, followed by others at Tresco on 28 September 1975, Nanquidno on 11 October 1981, and St Mary's from 12 to 18 October 1982. This one shared a bush for a short while with a Pallas's warbler, surely a unique event. Finally there are two further records for Ireland, a female at Firkeel in October 1985, and a few days later at the same locality an adult male, the first to arrive in these islands.

The rufous-sided towhee is a large ground-feeding sparrow with a long rounded tail, black head and upperparts, white underparts, and rufous flanks. They usually fly close to the ground and there is much pumping of the tail. Woodland, often with heavy undergrowth, is its chief breeding season haunt in a range which encompasses much of North America from southern Canada to Mexico. Northern populations move south in autumn, with some reaching Central America for the winter.

An adult female rufous-sided towhee on Lundy on 7 June 1966 is still the only record accepted for the British Isles. One at Spurn Point from 5 September 1975 to 10 January the following year was considered to have been more likely an escape for it showed the characteristics of the western race, though as we have seen there are many instances of the unexpected.

One of the largest of the North American sparrows, the fox sparrow is a heavily streaked bird with chestnut upperparts, an orange rump and tail, a breast spot, and two fine white wing-bars. Its main haunts are coniferous thickets and scrub across much of Canada and in the north-western United States. Most winter in the south-east United States with some reaching the west coast.

There is just one record of the fox sparrow in the British Isles, a bird caught and ringed on the Copeland Islands on 3 June 1961. Why is this mid-summer record acceptable, but that of the lark sparrow not?

A shy bird, the first song sparrow on the eastern side of the Atlantic was described by its discoverer as 'like a cross between a hedge sparrow and a bunting'. Note the long roundish tail and the stout seed-eater's bill. This is a numerous bird of moist woodland margins and hedgerows over much of Canada and the northern United States, with winter quarters extending to the Gulf of Mexico.

The first song sparrow reached the British Isles on 27 April 1959 when one was discovered on Fair Isle. Here it remained until 10 May, being seen on 7 May by one of the largest gatherings of ornithologists the island has witnessed when the National Trust for Scotland's 'Island Cruise' put some 200 people ashore. There have been just four subsequent records, all at bird observatories, at Spurn on 18 May 1964, Bardsey 5 to 8 May 1970, Calf of Man from 13 May to 3 June 1971, and another on Fair Isle from 17 April to 7 May 1979. What was thought to have been the same bird was also at Sumburgh, the nearest point on Shetland Mainland, in early June.

The savannah sparrow is a heavily streaked sparrow with a notched tail and yellow lores, which spends most of its time on the ground where it runs and hops, rarely walking. As the name suggests this is a bird of agricultural country which it occupies throughout much of North America. Many move south to winter in the southern United States and Central America, with distinct passages along the east coast.

The first savannah sparrow in the British Isles was discovered on Portland Bill on 11 April 1982 where it remained until the 16th. Trapped and ringed, it was considered to be the Sable Island race, often referred to as the Ipswich sparrow. There is one further record, a bird at Fair Isle on 30 September 1987.

The lark sparrow is a large sparrow with handsome head markings of chestnut, a black chest spot, and unmarked underparts. The rounded tail is white-tipped. It occurs mainly to the west of the Mississippi, wintering in Central America.

At present the lark sparrow is only admitted to Category D of the British and Irish Lists with just a single record, one at Landguard Point from 30 June to 4 July 1981.

The white-crowned sparrow is a large, handsome sparrow with a black and white patterned head, grey breast and throat, and streaked warm-brown upperparts. It prefers hedgerows and woodland margins in a breeding range across much of northern and western Canada, with winter quarters in the southern United States.

There are two records of the white-crowned sparrow in the British Isles, both in the same week. One at Fair Isle on 15 and 16 May 1977 was quickly followed by another at Hornsea Mere on the 22nd.

Look for the well-defined white throat and the yellow lores of the white-throated sparrow which otherwise has a rather similar head pattern to the previous species. The dark bill and compact, almost short-necked posture are further identifying features. In its breeding haunts of dense undergrowth and scrub its song of 'Old Sam Peabody, Peabody, Peabody, Peabody' will soon draw attention in a range which extends from the Mackenzie to Newfoundland, and south to the north-west United States. Winter quarters reach into Mexico.

The first white-throated sparrow in the British Isles had the misfortune to be shot at noon at the lighthouse on Eilean Mor, largest of the Flannan Islands, on 18 May 1909. This bird was not accepted as a genuine immigrant until 1960, with the second in the following year, one at Needs Oar Point on 19 May. There have been 14 others since, single records in a year save for 1968 and 1987 when there were two sightings. The majority, 10, have been in spring, from early April to mid-June, the other five in autumn from mid-October to late November. Six of those recorded have been in Shetland, the others in Yorkshire, Suffolk, Sussex, Hampshire, Lancashire, Caernarvonshire, and Antrim. Several have been long-staying birds, notably those at Herringfield, Lowestoft, from 16 November 1968 to New Year's Day when it died, at Thurso for nearly four months from early May 1970, and at Duncrue Marsh from 1 December 1984 until the following May.

A slate-grey bunting, the dark-eyed junco was once appropriately known as the slate-coloured junco, for it has superb grey upperparts contrasting with white below. It breeds in coniferous clearings and along woodland edges over much of Canada, wintering throughout the United States, except the extreme south.

Dark-eyed juncos have in the past been imported regularly into Europe as cage-birds and for this reason early records were always suspected as being escapes. The first accepted was one shot at Loop Head on 30 May 1905, the next was not until 1960 at Dungeness, also in May. All but one of the subsequent 10 records have been in the spring, from late March to late May. The exception was a bird at Rotherham in early January 1977. In 1975 and again in 1977 there were two records and in 1983 three, all in south-west England. Three birds have reached Shetland, and elsewhere there are single reports from Inverness, Dorset, Cornwall, Somerset, Gloucestershire, and Caernarvon. In addition one was caught on board a ship in the North Sea about 30 miles (48 km) north-east of Cromer (Norfolk) in May 1981.

The rose-breasted grosbeak is the size of a small thrush, heavily built, with a large head and pale bill. In the adult male the upperparts are black with white on the wings, rump and tail, and white underparts with red on the breast and underwings. Females and immatures are streaked brown above with yellowish underwings. A bird of woodlands, parks and gardens across much of eastern North America from New Brunswick and Nova Scotia to the central United States, it moves south to Central America and the northern countries of South America for the winter.

A first-winter male rose-breasted grosbeak on Cape Clear on 7 October 1962 was the first for the British Isles. A further 20, all first-winter birds, have subsequently been recorded, with no fewer than five in 1983. Except for a December record (incidentally the only one from the east coast), at Leigh-on-Sea in 1975, all have been in October. In addition to the first a further six have been in Ireland, all in Cork save for one found injured near Kilmore in 1985. Other records are from South Uist, Bardsey, Skokholm, Skomer, Lundy, and eight in Scilly, of which one in 1983 was taken by a cat.

Smallest of the grosbeaks, the blue grosbeak is larger than the indigo bunting with which it might be confused. The male is a violet blue, the female brown, while both sport two rusty-brown wing-bars. A common bird of hedgerows and roadsides in the southern United States, it winters largely in Mexico and Central America.

The blue grosbeak is a regular cage-bird and for that reason the three records for the British Isles have been placed in Category D. The first was on the Out Skerries during much of August 1970, the next one at Kiltarlity in March 1972, the last was caught by a cat at Newent on 9 May 1986.

The male indigo bunting, as the name suggests, is a resplendent bird of brilliant irridescent blue plumage and not surprisingly features strongly in aviary collections. Females are plain brown, with just a hint of blue in the tail. It breeds in the eastern United States from the Canadian border to the Gulf of Mexico, and winters in Central America.

Because of possible cage-bird antecedents, records of the indigo bunting are alway viewed with grave suspicion. Although the first two were probably genuine migrants they still remain in Category D. These were birds at Fair Isle on 3 August 1964, and Walton-on-the-Naze on 8 September 1973. An immature caught and ringed on Cape Clear on 9 October 1985 is thus currently judged the first immigrant. One further occurrence was a first-year bird at Well Woods, Holkham, in late November 1988.

A glance at a painted bunting, either the multi-coloured male, a brilliant mixture of blue, red, green, yellow, and grey, or the stunning yellow-green female, is enough to confirm that this would be much sought-after as a cage-bird, and indeed it is commonly kept in captivity. It occurs in thicket country in the southern United States and parts of Central America, with some southward movement in autumn.

There are only seven records of the painted bunting for the British Isles, and all placed in Category D. The first was at Portland in 1802, the next, a male, was at Voe in May 1972, with three more also from Scotland, on Yell, Fair Isle, and Noss. The others were at Carnforth in April 1974, and St Mary's in June 1978.

The male bobolink is the only North American landbird black below and light above, having a yellow-buff nape, white in the wings and a white rump. Females and immatures are yellow-buff, well streaked and with blackish crown stripes. Note also the pointed tail in both sexes. It is rather bunting-like, a bird of open country from Nova Scotia to Saskatchewan and into the north-eastern United States. The bobolink makes the longest migration flight of any North American passerine, winter quarters being on the plains of southern Brazil, Uruguay and Argentina. In Jamaica, through which it passes on autumn migration, it is known as the 'butter-bird' on account of the large fat deposits it accumulates before commencing its southern journey.

The first bobolink in the British Isles was one on 19 September 1962 on St Agnes, with just 13 subsequent records. Only in 1986 with two were there more than one in a year. All have arrived between mid-September and mid-October. There have been just three northern records, birds on Out Skerries in 1975 and Fair Isle in 1986, when there was also one on St Kilda. The majority of the remainder, seven in all, have been on Scilly, where one actually mingled with the house sparrows in Hugh Town, St Mary's, in the autumn of 1983. The other individuals were reported from Lundy, Hook Head and Cape Clear.

The eastern meadowlark is a stocky, rather upright bird, almost the size of a song thrush. The throat and underparts are a bright yellow with a large gorget of black on the breast, and the upperparts are a mottled brown and white, with a small patch of yellow in front of the eye. It breeds over much of the eastern United States, moving south in winter.

There are four records of the eastern meadowlark from the nineteenth century, which though not accepted to the British List are well worth recalling. There were three from East Anglia; is there some significance in this? The first was in Norfolk in October 1854, the next one at Thrandeston in March 1860, and a third at South Walsham on 13 October 1876. There is also an undated occurrence at Cheltenham some time prior to 1871.

The red-winged blackbird is considerably smaller than our own native blackbird, and they are not related. The male is a handsome, irridescent black with red shoulders having a yellow band, females are a heavily streaked brown and resemble large sparrows. It is an abundant bird over much of North America, with some movement south in winter.

There are no fewer than 16 records of the red-winged blackbird in the British Isles between 1824 and 1886. But were any genuine transatlantic migrants, or were they all escaped cage-birds? Certainly this is a favourite with aviculturalists, while on several occasions birds have deliberately been released. The spread of records through the year is not helpful to the case for immigration, birds having been noted in March, May, June, July, October, and December. One in Banff in 1866 was the furthest north, while other counties visited were Northumberland, Yorkshire, Norfolk, Suffolk, Hertfordshire, Middlesex, Kent, Sussex, Hampshire, Cornwall, and Glamorgan. This latter occurrence, actually the last, on 27 October 1886 at Nash Lighthouse seems as likely as any, though we will never know. It will surely not be long before another red-winged blackbird makes it across the Atlantic and on to the British or Irish Lists without controversy and speculation.

The rusty blackbird, the size of the previous species though with a longer tail, is all black save for its white eyes. In the autumn it takes on its handsome rusty plumage, while retaining black in the wings and tail. Wooded swampy areas are its home, and here it is common in a range which extends over much of Alaska, Canada, and the extreme north-east of the United States. In winter most move to the central and south-eastern United States.

There is just one record of the rusty blackbird in the British Isles, one shot near Cardiff on 4 October 1881 immediately after unusually strong and persistent north-west winds. Although not accepted to the British List it does seem highly likely to have arrived unaided and that was the view of no less than that doyen of Welsh ornithologists, Colonel H. Morrey Salmon, who with his co-authors in their *Birds of Glamorgan* published in 1967 (centenary year of the Cardiff Naturalists' Society) gave it full and proper status.

The northern oriole, previously known as the Baltimore oriole, is a starling size bird, handsome in any plumage, being black and orange, or olive and orange, with two white wing-bars. It breeds from Alberta to Nova Scotia, and south to Texas and Georgia, with winter quarters extending from Mexico to Columbia.

The first northern oriole in the British Isles was on Lundy from 2 to 9 October 1958, though there is an earlier record, alas seemingly now forgotten, which apparently has a good claim to be in the record books, one in Shetland on 26 September 1890. Of the subsequent 16 since 1958, all but three have been in September and October. Two of the exceptions were from Pembrokeshire, a male at Hook near Haverfordwest in May 1970, and the remarkable bird which fed at a garden bird table at Roch from January until late April 1989. The other was on Bodmin Moor in May 1968. Such spring records may suggest that some like the Roch bird are capable of successfully overwintering. Pembrokeshire also boasts an autumn record, one on Skokholm, while the others have been in South Uist, Fair Isle, Beachy Head, Calf of Man, Lundy, where in addition to the first there have been two more, Porthgwarra, and Scilly, with four records. A final reminder that even the rarest of our visitors need not only occur at coastal localities, for a northern oriole, alas dead, was found near Coventry in December 1968.

Appendix 1: List of Rare Birds

List of rare birds recorded in England (including the Isle of Man), Ireland, Scotland, and Wales with the date of the first record, and totals for the British Isles, before 1958 and from 1958 to 1988. First records to June 1990 are also included.

* Recorded in this country.
** Not yet accepted to British and Irish Lists.

E=England, I=Ireland, S=Scotland, W=Wales

	First record	E	I	S	W	Before 1958	Since 1958
GAVIIDAE							
White-billed Diver	1829	*	*	*		18	109
PODICIPEDIDAE							
Pied-billed Grebe	1963	*		*	*	0	13
DIOMEIDAE							
Black-browed Albatross	1897	*	*	*	*	2	24
PROCELLARIIDAE							
Soft-plumaged Petrel	1974	*	*			0	4
Capped Petrel	1850	*				1	1
Bulwer's Petrel	1837	*	*			3	1
Little Shearwater	1883	*	*	*	*	5	70
Audubon's Shearwater**	1936	*				1	0
HYDROBATIDAE							
Wilson's Storm-Petrel	1838	*	*			4	10
White-faced Storm-Petrel	1897			*		1	0
Madeiran Storm-Petrel	1911	*	*			2	0
PHALACROCORACIDAE							
Double-crested Cormorant**	1988	*				0	1
PELECANIDAE							
White Pelican	1964	*		*	*	0	15
Dalmatian Pelican	1967	*				0	1

	First record	E	I	S	W	Before 1958	Since 1958
FREGATIDAE							
Magnificent Frigate-bird	1953			*		1	0
ARDEIDAE							
American Bittern	1804	*	*	*	*	50	8
Little Bittern	?	*	*	*	*	150	160
Night Heron	1782	*	*	*	*	165	228
Green Heron	1889	*				1	2
Squacco Heron	1775	*	*	*	*	95	25
Cattle Egret	1805	*	*	*	*	2	49
Little Egret	1826	*	*	*	*	23	447
Great White Egret	1821	*	*	*	*	10	30
CICONIIDAE							
Black Stork	1814	*	*	*	*	26	40
THRESKIORNITHIDAE							
Glossy Ibis	?	*	*	*	*	Many	51
ANATIDAE							
Lesser White-fronted Goose	1886	*	*	*	*	47	75
Red-breasted Goose	1776	*	*		*	15	24
Ruddy Shelduck	1776	*	*	*	*	Many	?
American Wigeon	1837	*	*	*	*	22	177
Baikal Teal	1906	*		*		6	4
Black Duck	1954	*	*	*	*	1	14
Blue-winged Teal	1858	*	*	*	*	19	131
Ring-necked Duck	1955	*	*	*	*	1	237
Lesser Scaup	1987	*	*			0	2
King Eider	1832	*	*	*	*	62	139
Steller's Eider	1830	*		*		5	8
Harlequin Duck	1862	*		*		7	4
Surf Scoter	1838	*	*	*	*	75	243
Bufflehead	1830	*		*		4	2
Barrow's Goldeneye	1913			*		2	1
Hooded Merganser	1830	*	*	*	*	5	1
ACCIPITRIDAE							
Black Kite	1866	*	*	*	*	5	111
Swallow-tailed Kite**	1805	*				5	0
White-tailed Eagle	?	*	*	*		Many	16
Bald Eagle	1978		*		*	0	2
Egyptian Vulture	1825	*				3	0
Griffon Vulture	1843	*	*			3	0
Pallid Harrier	1931	*		*		4	0
Red-tailed Hawk**	1860	*				1	0
Red-shouldered Hawk**	1863			*		1	0
Spotted Eagle	1845	*	*	*		12	0

	First record	E	I	S	W	Before 1958	Since 1958
FALCONIDAE							
Lesser Kestrel	1867	*	*		*	11	10
American Kestrel	1976	*		*		0	2
Red-footed Falcon	1830	*	*	*	*	100	313
Eleonora's Falcon	1977	*				0	2
Saker	1976			*		0	2
Gyrfalcon	?	*	*	*	*	Many	87
RALLIDAE							
Sora Rail	1864	*	*	*	*	5	6
Little Crake	1791	*	*	*	*	68	31
Baillon's Crake	?	*	*	*	*	Many	6
Allen's Gallinule	1902	*				1	0
American Purple Gallinule	1958	*				0	1
American Coot	1981		*			0	1
GRUIDAE							
Sandhill Crane	1905	*	*			1	1
OTIDIDAE							
Little Bustard	1751	*	*	*	*	92	13
Houbara Bustard	1847	*		*		5	1
Great Bustard	Bred	*	*	*	*	Many	21
RECURVIROSTRIDAE							
Black-winged Stilt	1684	*	*	*	*	98	138
GLAREOLIDAE							
Cream-coloured Courser	1785	*	*	*	*	32	6
Collared Pratincole	1812	*	*	*	*	30	44
Oriental Pratincole	1981	*				0	2
Black-winged Pratincole	1909	*	*	*	*	5	20
CHARADRIIDAE							
Semipalmated Plover	1978	*				0	1
Killdeer	1859	*	*	*	*	9	34
Greater Sand Plover	1978	*		*	*	0	9
Caspian Plover	1890	*		*		2	2
American Golden Plover	1882	*	*	*	*	3	129
Pacific Golden Plover	1975	*	*	*		0	8
Sociable Plover	1860	*	*	*	*	5	27
White-tailed Plover	1975	*				0	4
SCOLOPACIDAE							
Great Knot	1989			*		0	1
Semipalmated Sandpiper	1953	*	*		*	2	54
Western Sandpiper	1956	*		*		1	5
Red-necked Stint	1986	*				0	1

	First record	E	I	S	W	Before 1958	Since 1958
Long-toed Stint	1982	*				0	1
Least Sandpiper	1853	*	*	*	*	6	26
White-rumped Sandpiper	1836	*	*	*	*	24	290
Baird's Sandpiper	1903	*	*	*	*	5	137
Sharp-tailed Sandpiper	1848	*		*	*	5	15
Broad-billed Sandpiper	1836	*	*	*	*	23	111
Stilt Sandpiper	1954	*	*	*		1	20
Great Snipe	?	*	*	*	*	180	61
Short-billed Dowitcher	1862	*	*			4	1
Long-billed Dowitcher	1800	*	*	*	*	9	132
Hudsonian Godwit	1981	*				0	2
Little Whimbrel	1982	*			*	0	2
Eskimo Curlew	1852	*	*	*		8	0
Slender-billed Curlew**	1910	*				6	0
Upland Sandpiper	1851	*	*	*	*	15	26
Marsh Sandpiper	1887	*	*	*	*	12	50
Greater Yellowlegs	1906	*	*	*	*	12	17
Lesser Yellowlegs	1854	*	*	*	*	35	161
Solitary Sandpiper	1860s	*	*			6	20
Terek Sandpiper	1951	*		*		3	28
Spotted Sandpiper	1866	*	*	*	*	6	83
Grey-tailed Tattler	1981			*		0	1
Wilson's Phalarope	1954	*	*	*	*	1	219
LARIDAE							
Great Black-headed Gull	1859	*				5	0
Laughing Gull	1923	*	*	*	*	2	51
Franklin's Gull	1970	*		*		0	15
Bonaparte's Gull	1848	*	*	*	*	11	51
Slender-billed Gull	1960	*				0	5
Thayer's Gull**	1989	*	*			0	2
Ross's Gull	1847	*	*	*	*	2	49
Ivory Gull	1822	*	*	*	*	76	30
STERNIDAE							
Gull-billed Tern	?	*	*	*	*	52	183
Caspian Tern	?	*	*	*	*	30	163
Royal Tern	1954	*	*		*	1	3
Elegant Tern	1982		*			0	1
Lesser Crested Tern	1982	*			*	0	4
Forster's Tern	1980	*	*	*	*	0	16
Aleutian Tern	1979	*				0	1
Bridled Tern	1931	*	*	*	*	3	9
Sooty Tern	1852	*		*		16	10
Least Tern	1983	*				0	1
Whiskered Tern	1836	*	*	*	*	20	83
White-winged Black Tern	1841	*	*	*	*	50	506

	First record	E	I	S	W	Before 1958	Since 1958
ALCIDAE							
Brunnich's Guillemot	1906	*	*	*		2	23
Ancient Murrelet**	1990	*				0	1
PTEROCLIDIDAE							
Pallas's Sandgrouse	1859	*	*	*	*	Many	6
COLUMBIDAE							
Rufous Turtle Dove	1889	*		*		2	6
Mourning Dove**	1989	*				0	1
CUCULIDAE							
Great Spotted Cuckoo	1842	*	*	*	*	6	22
Black-billed Cuckoo	1871	*		*		4	8
Yellow-billed Cuckoo	1825	*	*	*	*	22	28
STRIGIDAE							
Scops Owl	1805	*	*	*	*	64	16
Eagle Owl	<1768	*		*		20	0
Snowy Owl	1808	*	*	*	*	Many	92
Hawk Owl	1830	*		*		8	3
Tengmalm's Owl	1812	*	*	*		49	5
CAPRIMULGIDAE							
Red-necked Nightjar	1856	*				1	0
Egyptian Nightjar	1883	*				1	1
Common Nighthawk	1927	*		*		3	10
APODIDAE							
Needle-tailed Swift	1846	*	*	*		2	5
Pallid Swift	1978	*			*	0	6
Mottled Swift**	1988	*				0	1
Alpine Swift	1829	*	*	*	*	150	267
Pacific Swift	1981	*				0	1
Little Swift	1967	*	*	*	*	0	9
Chimney Swift	1982	*				0	4
ALCEDINIDAE							
Belted Kingfisher	1908	*	*			1	4
MEROPIDAE							
Blue-cheeked Bee-eater	1921	*				2	2
Bee-eater	1668	*	*	*	*	154	282
CORACIIDAE							
Roller	1864	*	*	*	*	135	78

	First record	E	I	S	W	Before 1958	Since 1958
PICIDAE							
Yellow-shafted Flicker**	1836	*				1	0
Yellow-bellied Sapsucker	1975	*	*			0	1
TYRANNIDAE							
Eastern Phoebe**	1987	*				0	2
ALAUDIDAE							
Calandra Lark	1961	*		*		0	3
Bimaculated Lark	1962	*		*		0	3
White-winged Lark	1869	*				6	1
Black Lark**	1907	*				7	0
Short-toed Lark	1841	*	*	*	*	40	296
Lesser Short-toed Lark	1956		*			42	0
Crested Lark	<1845	*		*	*	13	5
HIRUNDINIDAE							
Tree Swallow**	1850	*				1	1
Purple Martin**	1839	*	*			2	0
Crag Martin	1988	*				0	2
Red-rumped Swallow	1906	*	*	*	*	7	167
Cliff Swallow	1983	*				0	2
MOTACILLIDAE							
Blyth's Pipit	1882	*				1	1
Olive-backed Pipit	1948	*	*	*	*	1	68
Pechora Pipit	1925	*		*		13	17
Red-throated Pipit	1854	*	*	*	*	30	181
American Pipit	1910	*	*	*		3	2
Citrine Wagtail	1954	*	*	*		2	44
BOMBYCILLIDAE							
Cedar Waxwing**	1985		*			0	1
MIMIDAE							
Brown Thrasher	1967	*				0	1
Gray Catbird	1986	*	*			0	2
PRUNELLIDAE							
Alpine Accentor	1817	*		*	*	29	6
TURDIDAE							
Rufous Bush Robin	1854	*	*			6	5
Thrush Nightingale	1845	*		*	*	3	78
Siberian Rubythroat	1975			*		0	1
Red-flanked Bluetail	1903	*		*		3	7
White-throated Robin	1983	*				0	1

	First record	E	I	S	W	Before 1958	Since 1958
Daurian Redstart**	1988			*		0	1
Moussier's Redstart	1988				*	0	1
Isabelline Wheatear	1887	*		*		1	4
Pied Wheatear	1909	*	*	*	*	3	14
Black-eared Wheatear	1878	*	*	*	*	15	30
Desert Wheatear	1880	*		*		11	17
White-crowned Black Wheatear	1982	*				0	1
Black Wheatear	1912	*	*	*		4	0
Rock Thrush	1843	*	*	*	*	6	16
Blue Rock Thrush	1966	*		*	*	0	4
White's Thrush	1828	*	*	*		29	11
Siberian Thrush	1954	*	*	*		1	4
Varied Thrush	1982	*				0	1
Wood Thrush**	1987	*				0	1
Hermit Thrush	1975	*		*		0	3
Swainson's Thrush	1956	*	*	*	*	1	12
Grey-cheeked Thrush	1953	*	*	*	*	1	32
Veery	1970	*				0	2
Eye-browed Thrush	1964	*		*		0	11
Dusky Thrush	1905	*		*	*	1	7
Black-throated Thrush	1868	*		*		3	14
American Robin	1876	*	*	*		11	19
SYLVIIDAE							
Fan-tailed Warbler	1962	*	*			0	4
Pallas's Grasshopper Warbler	1908	*	*	*		3	9
Lanceolated Warbler	1908	*		*		9	36
River Warbler	1961	*		*	*	0	10
Moustached Warbler	1946	*				5	2
Paddyfield Warbler	1925	*	*	*		2	14
Blyth's Reed Warbler	1910	*	*	*		9	6
Great Reed Warbler	1847	*	*	*	*	23	126
Thick-billed Warbler	1955			*		1	1
Olivaceous Warbler	1951	*	*	*	*	2	12
Booted Warbler	1936	*		*		1	26
Marmora's Warbler	1982	*				0	1
Spectacled Warbler**	1979		*			0	1
Subalpine Warbler	1894	*	*	*	*	12	211
Sardinian Warbler	1955	*		*	*	1	17
Ruppell's Warbler	1977	*		*		0	2
Desert Warbler	1970	*				0	5
Orphean Warbler	1848	*		*		2	3
Green Warbler	1984	*				0	1
Two-barred Greenish Warbler**	1987	*				0	1
Greenish Warbler	1896	*	*	*	*	13	166

	First record	E	I	S	W	Before 1958	Since 1958
Arctic Warbler	1902	*	*	*	*	19	140
Pallas's Warbler	1896	*	*	*	*	3	469
Radde's Warbler	1898	*	*	*	*	1	82
Dusky Warbler	1913	*	*	*	*	1	69
Bonelli's Warbler	1948	*	*	*	*	3	98
Golden-crowned Kinglet**	1897	*				1	0
Ruby-crowned Kinglet**	1852	*		*		3	0
MUSCICAPIDAE							
Brown Flycatcher**	1909	*				1	0
Collared Flycatcher	1947	*		*	*	2	14
CITTIDAE							
Red-breasted Nuthatch	1989	*				0	1
TICHODROMADIDAE							
Wallcreeper	1792	*				6	4
CERTHIIDAE							
Short-toed Treecreeper	1969	*				0	7
REMIZIDAE							
Penduline Tit	1966	*			*	0	24
LANIIDAE							
Brown Shrike	1985			*		0	1
Isabelline Shrike	1950	*		*	*	1	26
Lesser Grey Shrike	1842	*	*	*	*	32	97
Woodchat Shrike	?	*	*	*	*	101	437
Masked Shrike**	1905	*				1	0
CORVIDAE							
Nutcracker	1753	*		*	*	45	358
STURNIDAE							
Rose-coloured Starling	1743	*	*	*	*	160	179
Daurian Starling	1985			*		0	1
PASSERIDAE							
Spanish Sparrow	1966	*				0	3
Rock Sparrow	1981	*				0	1
Snowfinch**	1905	*				6	0
VIREONIDAE							
Red-eyed Vireo	1951	*	*	*	*	1	54
Philadelphia Vireo	1985	*	*			0	2

	First record	E	I	S	W	Before 1958	Since 1958
FRINGILLIDAE							
Citril Finch	1904	*				1	0
Arctic Redpoll	?	*		*		30	126
Two-barred Crossbill	1802	*	*	*	*	40	29
Parrot Crossbill	1818	*		*		10	221
Trumpeter Finch	1971	*		*		0	6
Pallas's Rosefinch**	1988			*		0	1
Pine Grosbeak	<1831	*		*		8	2
Evening Grosbeak	1969			*		0	2
American Goldfinch**	1894		*			1	0
PARULIDAE							
Black and White Warbler	1936	*	*	*	*	1	10
Golden-winged Warbler**	1989	*				0	1
Tennessee Warbler	1975			*		0	3
Northern Parula	1966	*	*			0	11
Yellow Warbler	1964				*	0	1
Chestnut-sided Warbler	1985			*		0	1
Cape May Warbler	1977			*		0	1
Magnolia Warbler	1981	*				0	1
Yellow-rumped Warbler	1955	*	*	*		1	16
Blackburnian Warbler	1961			*	*	0	2
Palm Warbler	1976	*				0	1
Blackpoll Warbler	1968	*	*	*	*	0	25
American Redstart	1967	*	*			0	7
Ovenbird	1969	*	*	*		0	4
Northern Waterthrush	1958	*	*			0	5
Yellowthroat	1954	*		*		1	2
Wilson's Warbler	1985	*				0	1
Hooded Warbler	1970	*				0	1
THRAUPIDAE							
Summer Tanager	1957				*	1	0
Scarlet Tanager	1963	*	*			0	7
EMBERIZIDAE							
Rufous-sided Towhee	1966	*				0	1
Fox Sparrow	1961		*			0	1
Song Sparrow	1959	*		*	*	0	5
Savannah Sparrow	1984	*		*		0	2
Lark Sparrow	1981	*				0	1
White-crowned Sparrow	1977	*		*		0	2
White-throated Sparrow	1909	*	*	*	*	1	15
Dark-eyed Junco	1905	*	*	*	*	1	11
Pine Bunting	1911	*		*		2	14
Rock Bunting	1902	*			*	4	2
Cretzschmar's Bunting	1967			*		0	2

	First record	E	I	S	W	Before 1958	Since 1958
Yellow-browed Bunting	1975	*		*		0	2
Rustic Bunting	1867	*	*	*	*	34	181
Little Bunting	1864	*	*	*	*	93	367
Chestnut Bunting	1974			*	*	0	4
Yellow-breasted Bunting	1905	*	*	*	*	10	131
Pallas's Reed Bunting	1976			*		0	2
Red-headed Bunting	1931	*	*	*	*	?	?
Black-headed Bunting	1868	*	*	*	*	9	73
Rose-breasted Grosbeak	1962	*	*	*	*	0	21
Blue Grosbeak	1970	*		*		0	3
Indigo Bunting	1964	*	*	*		0	4
Painted Bunting	1802	*		*		1	6
ICTERIDAE							
Bobolink	1962	*	*	*		0	14
Eastern Meadowlark**	1854	*				3	0
Red-winged Blackbird**	1824	*			*	?	0
Rusty Blackbird**	1881				*	1	0
Northern Oriole	1958	*	*	*	*	0	17

Appendix 2: Locations in the British Isles

Locations in the British Isles mentioned in the text, with grid references (post-1974 counties in brackets).

Abberton Reservoir	Essex	TL 9818
Aber	Caernarvonshire (Gwynedd)	SH 6473
Aberlady Bay	East Lothian (Lothian)	NT 4581
Abersoch	Caernarvonshire (Gwynedd)	SH 3128
Aberthaw	Glamorgan (S. Glamorgan)	ST 0366
Achill Island	Mayo	F 6505
Acton Lake	Armagh	J 0540
Adswood Tip	Manchester (Greater Manchester)	SJ 8888
Ainsdale	Lancashire (Merseyside)	SD 2911
Aldeburgh	Suffolk	TM 4656
Alderburn & Rush Green	Buckinghamshire	TQ 0285
Alloa	Clackmannan (Central)	NS 8893
Allonby	Cumberland (Cumbria)	NY 0843
Alnwick	Northumberland	NU 1813
Altrincham	Cheshire	SD 7787
Amesbury	Wiltshire	SU 1544
Appledore	Kent	TQ 9529
Arlington Reservoir	Sussex (E. Sussex)	TQ 5407
Audenshaw Reservoirs	Cheshire (Greater Manchester)	SJ 9196
Auskerry	Orkney	HY 6716
Axmouth	Devon	SY 2591
Ballinester	Kerry	Q 3705
Ballyajora	Isle of Man	SG 4790
Ballyconneely	Galway	L 6344
Ballycotton	Cork	W 9964
Ballymacoda	Cork	X 0772
Ballynaclesh	Wexford	S 8008
Ballyteigue Bay	Wexford	S 9406
Ballyvaughan	Clare	M 2308
Balta Sound	Shetland	HP 6208
Baltimore	Cork	W 0526
Bamburgh	Northumberland	NU 1835
Bann Estuary	Londonderry	C 7936
Bardsey Island	Caernarvonshire (Gwynedd)	SH 1121

Barmston	Yorkshire (Humberside)	TA 1659
Barn Elms Reservoir	Surrey (Greater London)	TQ 2276
Barnes Common	Surrey (Greater London)	TQ 2276
Bass Rock	East Lothian (Lothian)	NT 6087
Beachy Head	Sussex (E. Sussex)	TV 5995
Bearah Tor	Cornwall	SX 2574
Beauly Firth	Inverness (Highland)	NH 6147
Beccles	Suffolk	TM 4289
Belfast	Antrim	J 3575
Belfast Lough	Antrim	J 3985
Belmullet	Mayo	F 7032
Bembridge Pools	Isle of Wight	SZ 6387
Bempton Cliffs	Yorkshire (Humberside)	TA 2073
Benbecula	Outer Hebrides (W. Isles)	NF 8052
Benderg Bay	Down	J 6043
Bexhill-on-Sea	Sussex (E. Sussex)	TQ 7407
Birsay	Orkney	HY 2427
Blackpill	Glamorgan (W. Glamorgan)	SS 6290
Blackrock	Dublin	O 2229
Blackrock Lighthouse	Mayo	F 4815
Blacktoft Sands	Yorkshire (Humberside)	SE 8423
Blagdon Lake	Somerset	ST 5159
Blakeney Point	Norfolk	TG 0046
Blandford	Dorset	ST 8806
Bleasdale Fells	Lancashire	SD 6049
Blennerville	Kerry	Q 8112
Blythburgh	Suffolk	TM 4575
Bodmin Moor	Cornwall	SX 1877
Boulmer	Northumberland	NU 2614
Bournemouth	Hampshire	SZ 0990
Bracknell	Berkshire	SU 8769
Bray	Wicklow	O 2718
Brent Reservoir	Middlesex (Greater London)	TQ 2187
Bressay	Shetland	HU 5040
Breydon Water	Norfolk	TG 5007
Bridges of Ross	Clare	Q 7250
Bridlington	Yorkshire (Humberside)	TA 1867
Brighton	Sussex (E. Sussex)	TQ 3003
Brill	Buckinghamshire	SP 6513
Brimpton	Berkshire	SU 5564
Brimpton Gravel Pits	Berkshire	SU 5763
Brinsop Court	Herefordshire (Hereford & Worcestershire)	SO 4445
Bromley-by-Bow	London (Greater London)	TQ 3686
Brownstown Head	Waterford	X 6197
Bryher	Isles of Scilly	SV 8714
Bude	Cornwall	SS 2006
Budleigh Salterton	Devon	SY 0681
Bulcote	Nottinghamshire	SK 6444
Bull Rock	Cork	V 4039

Bury	Lancashire	SD 8010
Caerlaverock	Dumfries (Dumfries & Galloway)	NY 0565
Cahore Point	Wexford	T 2247
Caister	Norfolk	TG 5212
Caldey Island	Pembrokeshire (Dyfed)	SS 1396
Calf of Man	Isle of Man	SC 1565
Cambridge Sewage Farm	Cambridgeshire	TL 4759
Cannock Chase Reservoir	Staffordshire	SJ 9915
Cape Clear	Cork	V 9419
Cardiff	Glamorgan (S. Glamorgan)	ST 1776
Carnforth	Lancashire	SD 4970
Carrick	Orkney (Eday)	HY 5638
Castle Rising	Norfolk	TF 6624
Castlederg	Tyrone	H 2685
Castlefreke	Cork	V 6645
Castlegregory	Kerry	Q 6213
Cefn Sidan	Carmarthenshire (Dyfed)	SN 3505
Cemlyn	Anglesey (Gwynedd)	SH 3393
Charing	Kent	TQ 9549
Charlton's Pool	Durham (Cleveland)	NZ 4623
Chasewater	Staffordshire (W. Midlands)	SK 0308
Cheltenham	Gloucestershire	SO 9521
Cherry Hinton	Cambridgeshire	SP 4856
Chew Valley Lake	Somerset (Avon)	ST 5659
Chichester Gravel Pits	Sussex	SU 8703
Chingford	Essex (Greater London)	TQ 3994
Chiswick Eyot	Middlesex (Greater London)	TQ 2377
Christchurch	Hampshire	SZ 1791
Church Norton	Sussex (W. Sussex)	SZ 8695
Claggain Bay, Islay	Argyll (Strathclyde)	NR 4653
Cleveleys	Lancashire	SD 3143
Cley	Norfolk	TG 0444
Clogher Head	Louth	O 1784
Cobh Harbour	Cork	W 8065
Colchester	Essex	TM 0024
Colne Bridge	Yorkshire (W. Yorkshire)	SE 1720
Colonsay	Argyll (Strathclyde)	NR 3794
Compton Downs	Berkshire	SU 5080
Copeland Islands	Down	J 5983
Coquet Island	Northumberland	NU 2904
Corbet Lough	Down	J 1744
Cot Valley	Cornwall	SW 3630
Coventry	Warwickshire	SP 3379
Crom	Fermanagh	H 3624
Cromer	Norfolk	TG 2242
Crumbles	Sussex (E. Sussex)	TQ 6402
Cuckmere Haven	Sussex (E. Sussex)	TV 5197
Culbin Sands	Moray (Grampian)	NH 9962
Cymyran Bay	Anglesey (Gwynedd)	SH 2974

Dale Fort	Pembrokeshire (Dyfed)	SM 8205
Damerham	Hampshire	SU 1015
Dawlish Point	Devon	SX 9879
Derrymore Island	Kerry	Q 2022
Devonport	Devon	SX 4454
Dinas Head	Pembrokeshire (Dyfed)	SN 0041
Ditchford Gravel Pits	Northamptonshire	SP 8362
Doncaster	Yorkshire (S. Yorkshire)	SE 5703
Donna Nook	Lincolnshire	TF 4399
Dorchester	Dorset	SY 6990
Draycote Water	Warwickshire	SP 4569
Dryslwyn	Carmarthenshire (Dyfed)	SN 5520
Dudgeon Lightship	Norfolk	TF 9785
Dummer	Hampshire	SU 5845
Duncrue Marsh	Antrim	J 1086
Dundrum Bay	Down	J 4535
Dungeness	Kent	TR 0916
Dunrossness	Shetland	HU 3815
Dunwich	Suffolk	TM 4770
Durlston Head	Dorset	SZ 0377
Durness	Sutherland (Highland)	NC 4067
Dursey Island	Cork	V 4740
Dyfi Estuary	Cardiganshire (Dyfed)	SN 6596
Easington	Yorkshire (Humberside)	TA 3919
Eastbourne	Sussex (E. Sussex)	TV 6199
Ecclesbourne Glen	Sussex (E. Sussex)	TQ 8410
Eddleston	Peebles (Borders)	NT 2447
Egypt Bay	Kent	TQ 7779
Elmley	Kent	TQ 9467
Embleton	Northumberland	NU 2423
Epping Forest	Essex	TQ 4298
Eskdale	Cumberland (Cumbria)	SD 1799
Evie	Orkney	HY 3921
Exeter	Devon	SX 9191
Exmouth	Devon	SX 9980
Eyebrook Reservoir	Leicestershire	SP 8595
Fair Isle	Shetland	HZ 2172
Fairburn Ings	Yorkshire (W. Yorkshire)	SE 4727
Fairview	Dublin	O 2031
Falmouth	Cornwall	SW 8132
Fambridge	Essex	TL 7818
Fan Pool	Montgomery (Powys)	SN 9387
Farlington Marshes	Hampshire	SU 6804
Farne Islands	Northumberland	NU 2337
Faversham	Kent	TR 0161
Felixstowe	Suffolk	TM 3034
Fenham Flats	Northumberland	NU 1139
Fetlar	Shetland	HU 6292

Fforyd Bay	Caernarvonshire (Gwynedd)	SH 4459
Filey	Yorkshire (N. Yorkshire)	TA 1280
Filey Brigg	Yorkshire (N. Yorkshire)	TA 1381
Firkeel	Cork	V 5341
Firth	Shetland	HU 4473
Fishburn	Durham	NZ 3632
Fishguard	Pembrokeshire (Dyfed)	SM 9537
Flamborough Head	Yorkshire (Humberside)	TA 2570
Flannan Islands, Lewis	Outer Hebrides (W. Isles)	NA 7241
Fleckney	Leicestershire	SP 6593
Fordwich	Kent	TR 1859
Formby	Lancashire (Merseyside)	SD 2707
Forvie	Aberdeen (Grampian)	NK 0226
Foula	Shetland	HT 9638
Foulness	Essex	TR 0495
Foxcote Reservoir	Buckinghamshire	SP 7235
Fraisthorpe	Yorkshire (Humberside)	TA 1561
Frampton-on-Severn	Gloucestershire	ST 7407
Frinton-on-Sea	Essex	TM 2419
Frodsham	Cheshire	SJ 5078
Gadloch	Lanark (Strathclyde)	NS 6571
Gairsay	Orkney	HY 4422
Galley Head	Cork	W 3431
Galway City	Galway	M 3025
Gann Estuary	Pembrokeshire (Dyfed)	SM 8106
Garrison	Fermanagh	G 9452
Gibraltar Point	Lincolnshire	TF 5657
Girdleness	Kincardine (Grampian)	NJ 9705
Gladhouse	Midlothian (Lothian)	NT 2953
Glaisdale	Yorkshire (N. Yorkshire)	NZ 7603
Glastonbury	Somerset	ST 5039
Great Horkesley	Essex	TL 9730
Great Saltee	Wexford	X 9597
Great Yarmouth	Norfolk	TG 5307
Greencastle Point	Down	J 2512
Gronant	Flint (Clwyd)	SJ 0884
Grutness	Shetland	HU 4009
Gugh	Isles of Scilly	SV 8908
Guisborough	Yorkshire (N. Yorkshire)	NZ 6116
Gunthorpe	Nottinghamshire	SK 6844
Gurnard's Head	Cornwall	SW 4338
Haddon	Huntingdon (Cambridgeshire)	TL 1392
Hadleigh Marsh	Essex	TQ 8085
Hamilton	Lanark (Strathclyde)	NS 7225
Hanningfield Reservoir	Essex	TQ 7398
Hartlepool	Durham (Cleveland)	NZ 5232
Hartsholme	Lincolnshire	SK 9469
Harty	Kent	TR 0268

Haslemere	Sussex (W. Sussex)	SU 9032
Helmsley	Yorkshire (N. Yorkshire)	SE 6184
Helvick Head	Waterford	X 3188
Hemingford Gray	Cambridgeshire	TL 2970
Hermaness	Shetland	HP 6018
Herringfleet	Suffolk	TM 4897
Hickling	Norfolk	TG 4121
Highnam	Gloucestershire	SO 7919
Hillfield Park Reservoir	Hertfordshire	TL 3314
Hillsborough Park Lake	Down	J 4074
Holkham	Norfolk	TF 8944
Holkham Meals	Norfolk	TF 8945
Holland-on-Sea	Essex	TM 2016
Holm	Orkney	HY 6331
Holme	Norfolk	TF 7043
Holy Island	Northumberland	NU 1242
Holyhead	Anglesey (Gwynedd)	SH 2482
Hook Head	Wexford	X 7397
Hopton	Suffolk	TG 5300
Hornsea Mere	Yorkshire (Humberside)	TA 1947
Hove	Sussex (E. Sussex)	TQ 2804
Howden Reservoir	Yorkshire (S. Yorkshire)	SK 1793
Hoy	Orkney	HY 2202
Hunstanton	Norfolk	TF 6741
Hutton Cranswick	Yorkshire (Humberside)	TA 0252
Inner Farne	Northumberland	NU 2135
Inner Marsh Farm	Flint (Clwyd)	SJ 3270
Irvine	Ayrshire (Strathclyde)	NS 3038
Islay	Argyll (Strathclyde)	NR 3262
Isle of May	Fife	NT 6599
Kendal	Westmorland (Cumbria)	SD 5192
Kenfig Pool	Glamorgan (Mid Glamorgan)	SS 7981
Kenmore Wood	Argyll (Strathclyde)	NN 3207
Kessingland	Suffolk	TM 5386
Killaloe	Tipperary	R 7072
Killead	Antrim	J 1579
Killingworth	Northumberland (Tyne & Wear)	NZ 2871
Kilmalcolm	Renfrewshire (Strathclyde)	NS 3569
Kilnsea	Yorkshire (Humberside)	TA 4115
Kiltarlity	Inverness-shire (Highland)	NH 5041
Kilve	Somerset	ST 1443
King's Lynn	Norfolk	TF 6220
Kingsbridge	Devon	SX 7343
Kingstown	Dublin	O 2528
Kingussie	Inverness-shire (Highland)	NH 7500
Kirkwall	Orkney	HY 4410
Kirton-in-Lindsey	Lincolnshire	SK 9398
Knockadoon Head	Cork	X 0970

Landguard Point	Suffolk	TM 2831
Land's End	Cornwall	SW 3425
Langass, N. Uist	Outer Hebrides (W. Isles)	NF 8464
Langey Point	Sussex (E. Sussex)	TQ 6401
Langton Herring	Dorset	SY 6182
Larkfield	Kent	TQ 6140
Larne	Antrim	D 4003
Larne Lough	Antrim	D 4300
Lavernock Point	Glamorgan (S. Glamorgan)	ST 1868
Lecarrow	Sligo	G 7132
Leckhampton	Gloucestershire	SO 9518
Leigh-on-Sea	Essex	TQ 8385
Lerwick	Shetland	HU 4741
Limerick	Limerick	R 5858
Linton	Cambridgeshire	TL 5547
Littlehampton	Sussex (W. Sussex)	TQ 0201
Lizard Peninsula	Cornwall	SW 6911
Llangennith Moors	Glamorgan (W. Glamorgan)	SS4191
Llantwit Major	Glamorgan (S. Glamorgan)	SS 9668
Llanwrst	Denbigh (Clwyd)	SH 7961
Llyn Alaw	Anglesey (Gwynedd)	SH 3986
Llyn Coron	Anglesey (Gwynedd)	SH 3769
Loch Brow	Shetland	HU 3815
Loch Carra	Mayo	M 1870
Loch Corrib	Galway	M 1545
Loch Druidibeg, S. Uist	Outer Hebrides (W. Isles)	NF 7937
Loch Funshinagh	Roscommon	M 9752
Loch Hallan, S. Uist	Outer Hebrides (W. Isles)	NF 7322
Loch Insh	Inverness-shire (Highland)	NH 8304
Loch Leven	Kinross (Tayside)	NO 1401
Loch Lomond	Dunbarton (Strathclyde)	NS 3598
Loch na Liana Moire, S. Uist	Outer Hebrides (W. Isles)	NF 7324
Loch of Kinnordy	Angus (Tayside)	NO 3654
Loch of Strathbeg	Aberdeen (Grampian)	NK 0758
Loch Rannoch	Perth (Tayside)	NN 5857
Loch Ranza, Arran	Bute (Strathclyde)	NR 9350
Loch Spynie	Moray (Grampian)	NJ 2366
Lodmoor	Dorset	SY 6882
Longford's Lake	Gloucestershire	ST 8698
Loop Head	Clare	Q 6846
Lossiemouth	Moray (Grampian)	NJ 2370
Low Hauxley	Northumberland	NU 2802
Lundy Island	Devon	SS 1345
Lurgan	Antrim	J 0858
Lyme	Dorset	SY 3492
Magor Nature Reserve	Monmouthshire (Gwent)	ST 4385
Mahee Island	Down	J 5464
Malahide	Dublin	O 2446
Malin Beg	Donegal	G 4980

Maltraeth Pool	Anglesey (Gwynedd)	SH 4068
Marazion	Cornwall	SW 5130
Market Deeping	Lincolnshire	TF 1410
Marston	Lincolnshire	SK 8943
Mells	Somerset	ST 7249
Menai Straits	Anglesey (Gwynedd)	SH 4763
Meols	Cheshire (Merseyside)	SJ 2389
Mickledon Clough	Yorkshire (S. Yorkshire)	SK 1998
Middleton-on-Sea	Sussex (W. Sussex)	SZ 9899
Midrips	Sussex (E. Sussex)	TR 0018
Milford	Hampshire	SZ 2891
Milford Haven	Pembrokeshire (Dyfed)	SM 9005
Minfford	Caernarvonshire (Gwynedd)	SH 6038
Minsmere	Suffolk	TM 4766
Minster	Kent	TQ 9473
Misson	Nottinghamshire	SK 6894
Moel-y-cest	Caernarvonshire (Gwynedd)	SH 5538
Moneygold	Sligo	G 6552
Moreton	Cheshire (Merseyside)	SJ 2589
Morfa Harlech	Merioneth (Gwynedd)	SH 5633
Mount's Bay	Cornwall	SW 5129
Mull	Argyll (Strathclyde)	NM 5233
Mullinavat	Kilkenny	S 5624
Mumbles	Glamorgan (W. Glamorgan)	SS 6387
Musselburgh	Midlothian (Lothian)	NT 3472
Nanquidno	Cornwall	SW 3629
Nare Head	Cornwall	SW 9137
Nash Lighthouse	Glamorgan (S. Glamorgan)	SS 9168
Navan	Meath	N 8667
Needs Oar Point	Hampshire	SZ 4297
Nene Washes	Cambridgeshire	TL 2799
Ness, Lewis	Outer Hebrides (W. Isles)	NB 5463
Nethybridge	Inverness-shire (Highland)	NJ 0020
New Grounds, Slimbridge	Gloucestershire	SO 7305
Newburgh	Aberdeen (Grampian)	NJ 9925
Newbury	Berkshire	SU 4667
Newcastle	Wicklow	O 3004
Newcastle-upon-Tyne	Northumberland (Tyne & Wear)	NZ 2563
Newent	Gloucestershire	SO 7126
Newton St Cyr's	Devon	SX 8797
Newtown	Isle of Wight	SZ 4290
Nimmo's Pier	Galway	M 3025
Nith Estuary	Dumfries (Dumfries & Galloway)	NX 9966
Nithsdale	Dumfries (Dumfries & Galloway)	NX 9383
North Bull	Dublin	O 2537
North Coates	Lincolnshire	TA 3703
North Denes	Norfolk	TG 5210
North Rona	Outer Hebrides (W. Isles)	HW 8132
North Ronaldsay	Orkney	HY 7654

North Slob	Wexford	T 0925
Northallerton	Yorkshire (N. Yorkshire)	SE 3794
Noss	Shetland	HU 5539
Old Hall Marshes	Essex	TL 9712
Old Head of Kinsale	Cork	W 6339
Omey	Galway	L 5756
Oundle	Northamptonshire	TL 0487
Out Skerries	Shetland	HU 6771
Packington	Warwickshire	SP 2283
Pagham	Sussex (W. Sussex)	SZ 8797
Paignton	Devon	SX 8960
Paisley	Renfrew (Strathclyde)	NS 4763
Papa Westray	Orkney	HY 4952
Patrington	Yorkshire (Humberside)	TA 3122
Paull	Yorkshire (Humberside)	TA 1626
Peldon	Essex	TL 9916
Pelwell	Shropshire	SJ 6733
Penmaenpool	Merioneth (Gwynedd)	SH 6918
Penally	Pembrokeshire (Dyfed)	SS 1299
Penrice	Cornwall	SX 0249
Pentland Skerries	Orkney	ND 4678
Perry Oaks Sewage Farm	Middlesex (Greater London)	TQ 0375
Peterborough	Cambridgeshire	TL 1999
Peterhead	Aberdeen (Grampian)	NK 1346
Pett Level	Sussex (E. Sussex)	TQ 9015
Plym Estuary	Devon	SX 5055
Plymouth	Devon	SX 4854
Polperro	Cornwall	SX 2150
Poole Harbour	Dorset	SZ 0089
Porthgwarra	Cornwall	SW 3721
Porthscatho	Cornwall	SW 8735
Portland	Dorset	SY 6768
Portnahaven, Islay	Argyll (Strathclyde)	NR 1652
Portnoo	Donegal	G 6999
Potteric Carr	Yorkshire (S. Yorkshire)	SE 5907
Prawle Point	Devon	SX 7735
Prior's Park	Northumberland (Tyne & Wear)	NZ 1099
Puddletown	Dorset	SY 7595
Quendale	Shetland	HU 3712
Rainham	Essex	TL 5283
Rainworth	Nottinghamshire	SK 5858
Rame Head	Cornwall	SX 4148
Ramsgate	Kent	TR 3864
Raven Point	Wexford	T 1223
Ravenglass	Cumberland (Cumbria)	SD 0695
Red Rocks	Cheshire (Merseyside)	SJ 2088

Redcar	Yorkshire (Cleveland)	NZ 6124
Rendall	Orkney	HY 4221
Rhum	Inverness (Highland)	NM 3794
River Bunree	Mayo	F 8122
River Colne	Essex	TM 0520
River Debden	Suffolk	TM 2747
River Don	Aberdeen (Grampian)	NK 9409
River Lagan	Antrim	J 2062
River Mersey	Lancashire	SJ 4080
River Neath	Glamorgan (W. Glamorgan)	SS 7292
Roch	Pembrokeshire (Dyfed)	SM 8721
Rockabill Lighthouse	Dublin	O 3263
Roe Estuary	Londonderry	C 6529
Rogerstown	Dublin	O 2658
Romney Marsh	Kent	TR 0627
Ronas Hill	Shetland	HU 3083
Rosyth	Fife	NT 1183
Rotherham	Yorkshire (S. Yorkshire)	SK 4293
Rottingdean	Sussex (E. Sussex)	TQ 3602
Royal Portbury Dock	Somerset (Avon)	ST 4776
Roydon	Essex	TL 4109
Ruan Lanihorne	Cornwall	SW 8941
Rutland Water	Leicestershire	SK 9106
Rye	Sussex (E. Sussex)	TQ 9220
Sabden	Lancashire	SD 7737
St Agnes	Scilly	SV 8808
St Alban's Head	Dorset	SY 9575
St Andrews	Fife	NO 5016
St Bride's Wentlooge	Monmouth (Gwent)	ST 2982
St Catherine's	Isle of Wight	SZ 4975
St Catherine's Hill	Surrey	SU 8957
St David's	Pembrokeshire (Dyfed)	SM 7525
St Fergus	Aberdeen (Grampian)	NK 0951
St Ives	Cornwall	SW 5140
St Just	Cornwall	SW 3631
St Kilda	Outer Hebrides (W. Isles)	NA 0900
St Margaret's Bay	Kent	TR 3744
St Mary's	Scilly	SV 9111
St Michael's-on-Wyre	Lancashire	SD 4641
Saltholme Pool	Durham (Cleveland)	NZ 5222
Sand Bay	Somerset	ST 3264
Sanday	Orkney	HY 6841
Sandbach	Cheshire	SJ 7560
Sandside	Orkney	HY 5906
Sandwich Bay	Kent	TR 3660
Sandwick	Orkney	ND 4389
Scalby Mills	Yorkshire (N. Yorkshire)	TA 0190
Scaling Dam	Yorkshire (Cleveland)	NZ 7412
Scalloway	Shetland	HU 4039

Scarborough	Yorkshire (N. Yorkshire)	TA 0488
Scatness	Shetland	HU 3809
Seahouses	Northumberland	NU 2232
Seaton Burn	Northumberland	NZ 3376
Severn Beach	Gloucestershire (Avon)	ST 5385
Shankill	Dublin	O 1535
Shannon Estuary	Kerry	R 3556
Shaw Gill	Yorkshire	SD 9242
Shefford	Bedfordshire	TL 1538
Sheringham	Norfolk	TG 1643
Shirley	Warwickshire (W. Midlands)	SP 1078
Shoreham	Kent	TQ 5162
Shotton	Flint (Clwyd)	SJ 2971
Shewsbury	Shropshire	SJ 4912
Sidlesham Ferry	Sussex (W. Sussex)	SZ 8596
Sizewell	Suffolk	TM 4762
Skaw, Whalsay	Shetland	HU 5966
Skegness	Lincolnshire	TF 5763
Skelligs	Kerry	V 2561
Sker Point	Glamorgan (Mid Glamorgan)	SS 7879
Skerryvore Lighthouse	Argyll (Strathclyde)	NL 8427
Skewjack	Cornwall	SW 3624
Skye	Inverness (Highland)	NG 4725
Sladebridge	Cornwall	SX 0171
Slains	Aberdeen (Grampian)	NK 0530
Slapton Ley	Devon	SX 8242
Slyne Head	Galway	L 5141
Soulseat	Wigtown (Dumfries & Galloway)	NX 1058
Southend	Argyll (Strathclyde)	NR 6908
South Creake	Norfolk	TF 8536
South Gare	Yorkshire (Cleveland)	NZ 5528
South Ronaldsay	Orkney	ND 4590
South Shields	Durham (Tyne & Wear)	NZ 3767
South Walney	Lancashire (Cumbria)	SD 2261
South Walsham	Norfolk	TG 3613
Spey Bay	Banff	NJ 3565
Stackpole	Pembrokeshire (Dyfed)	SR 9895
Staines Reservoir	Surrey	TQ 0573
Stakkaberg, Fetlar	Shetland	HU 6192
Stanlake	Oxfordshire	SU 8075
Start	Devon	SX 8237
Staveley	Derbyshire	SK 4575
Steart Island	Somerset	ST 2948
Stithians Reservoir	Cornwall	SW 7135
Stodmarsh	Kent	TR 2261
Stone Bridge	Middlesex (Greater London)	TQ 2083
Stone Creek	Yorkshire (Humberside)	TA 2319
Stromness	Orkney	HY 2509
Stronsay	Orkney	HY 6624
Strumble Head	Pembrokeshire (Dyfed)	SM 8941

Studland	Dorset	SZ 0382
Sudbourne	Suffolk	TM 4453
Sule Skerry	Orkney	HX 6224
Sumburgh	Shetland	HU 4009
Sutton Broad	Norfolk	TG 3723
Sutton Strawless	Norfolk	TQ 3924
Swaffham Heath	Norfolk	TF 7907
Swona	Orkney	ND 3884
Swords	Dublin	O 1747
Tacumshin	Wexford	T 0505
Tadcaster	Yorkshire (N. Yorkshire)	SE 4843
Tanfield	Yorkshire (N. Yorkshire)	SE 2778
Tavistock	Devon	SX 4874
Telscombe	Sussex (E. Sussex)	TQ 4003
Terrington	Norfolk	TF 5423
Tetney	Lincolnshire	TA 3101
Thetford Warren	Norfolk	TL 9090
Thrandeston	Suffolk	TM 1176
Thurso	Caithness (Highland)	ND 1168
Tincleton	Dorset	SY 7791
Tiree	Argyll (Strathclyde)	NL 9640
Titchwell	Norfolk	TF 7544
Three Cliffs	Glamorgan (W. Glamorgan)	SS 5387
Toe Head	Cork	W 1526
Tophill Low Reservoir	Yorkshire	NZ 0642
Tory Island	Donegal	B 8547
Totton	Hampshire	SU 3613
Tresco	Isles of Scilly	SV 8914
Tring Reservoirs	Hertfordshire	SP 9012
Trinity College	Dublin	O 1535
Truro	Cornwall	SW 8244
Tuam	Galway	M 4352
Tunstall	Yorkshire (Humberside)	TA 3031
Tuskar Rock	Wexford	T 2207
Tutbury	Staffordshire	SK 2128
Tyninghame	East Lothian (Lothian)	NT 6079
Unst	Shetland	HP 6316
Upton Warren	Worcestershire	SO 9367
Uyeasound	Shetland (Unst)	HP 5900
Valencia Island	Kerry	V 3877
Virginia Water	Surrey	SU 9867
Virkie Pool	Shetland	HU 3911
Voe	Shetland	HU 4063
Vorran Island	Outer Hebrides (W. Isles)	NF 7234
Walberswick	Suffolk	TM 4974
Walney Island	Lancashire (Cumbria)	SD 1767

Walthamstow	Essex	TQ 3688
Walton-on-the-Naze	Essex	TM 2521
Wandsworth Common	Middlesex (Greater London)	TQ 2773
Warden Point	Kent	TR 0272
Warwick	Warwickshire	SP 2865
Weaverham	Cheshire	SJ 6274
Wells	Norfolk	TF 9244
Wembury	Devon	SX 5148
West Loch Bee	Outer Hebrides (W. Isles)	NF 7743
West Sedgemoor	Somerset	ST 3623
Westleton	Suffolk	TM 4469
Wetherby	Yorkshire (S. Yorkshire)	SE 4048
Weymouth	Dorset	SY 6879
Whale Firth	Shetland	HU 4693
Whalsay	Shetland	HU 5461
Wharmton Clough	Lancashire	SD 9607
Whitby	Yorkshire (N. Yorkshire)	NZ 9011
Widdrington	Northumberland	NZ 2595
Widewall	Orkney	ND 4390
Wigan	Lancashire (Greater Manchester)	SD 5606
Willen Lake	Buckinghamshire	SP 8839
Winchelsea	Sussex (E. Sussex)	TQ 9017
Winchester College	Hampshire	SU 4828
Winterton	Norfolk	TG 4919
Woodbridge	Suffolk	TM 2749
Woodchurch	Kent	TQ 9434
Worth Matravers	Dorset	TQ 9434
Wycliffe	Yorkshire	NZ 1114
Yantlet Creek	Kent	TQ 8578
Yare Valley	Norfolk	TG 3306
Yarmouth	Norfolk	TG 5307
Yarmouth Denes	Norfolk	TG 5304
Yatton	Somerset	ST 4265
Yell	Shetland	HU 5085
Ynyslas	Cardiganshire (Dyfed)	SN 6295
Youghal	Cork	X 1077
Ythan Estuary	Aberdeen (Grampian)	NK 0025

Appendix 3: Further Reading

Not a complete bibliography, but suggestions for further reading to aid the pursuit of rare birds, past and in the future, in the British Isles.

Bannerman, D. A. *The Birds of the British Isles* Volumes I to XII (Oliver and Boyd, 1953 to 1963)
It is appropriate that this classic should commence this short bibliography, having been described as 'a work on British birds in the grand manner, the like of which one had hardly expected to see again'.

Birding World (Sub-titled *The magazine of the bird information service*)
A monthly journal with the emphasis on rarer British and Western Palearctic birds with a high degree of topical interest. Includes descriptions of recent rarities, identification articles, bird-finding notes and other essential information for the watcher interested in rare birds whether in the field or from the armchair. Subscription information from Stonerunner, Coast Road, Cley-next-the-Sea, Holt, Norfolk, NR25 7RZ.

British Birds
Published monthly since 1907, it contains in most issues articles about rare birds, often detailed accounts of first occurrences, and frequent papers on identification topics. The annual report on rare birds cannot afford to be missed. Subscription information from Fountains, Park Lane, Blunham, Bedford, MK44 3NJ.

British Ornithologists' Union *The Status of Birds in Britain and Ireland* (Blackwell, 1971)

Bruun, B., Delin, H., and Svensson, L. *Birds of Britain and Europe* (Hamlyn, 1986)

Chandler, R. J. *The Macmillan Field Guide to North Atlantic Shorebirds* (Macmillan, 1989)

Cramp, S. and Simmons, K. E. L. *The Birds of the Western Palearctic* Volumes I to V, with Volumes VI & VII in preparation (OUP, 1977 and subsequently)
Expensive, but an absolute must, it will remain the standard work well into the next century.

Dymond, J. N., Fraser, P. A., and Gantlett, S. J. M. *Rare Birds in Britain and Ireland* (Poyser, 1989)

Grant, P. J. *Gulls: a guide to identification* (Poyser, 1982)

Hancock, J., and Kushlan, J. *The Herons Handbook* (Croom Helm, 1984)

Harrison, C. *An Atlas of the Birds of the Western Palearctic* (Collins, 1982)

Harrison, P. *Seabirds* (Christopher Helm, 1983)
First of a series of outstanding handbooks.

Hayman, P., Marchant, J., and Prater, A. *Shorebirds* (Christopher Helm, 1986)

Heinzel, H., Fitter, R., and Parslow, J. *The Birds of Britain and Europe* (Collins, 1972)

Hollom, P. A. D. *The Handbook of Rarer British Birds* (Witherby, 1977)

Hollom, P. A. D., Porter, R. F., Christensen, S., and Willis, I. *Birds of the Middle East and North Africa* (Poyser, 1988)

Hutchinson, C. *Birds in Ireland* (Poyser, 1989)
This and those on Scotland and Wales referred to later are essential reference works.

King, B., Woodcock, M., and Dickinson, E. C. *A Field Guide to the Birds of South-east Asia* (Collins, 1975)

Lovegrove, R. and Williams, G. *Birds in Wales* (Poyser, in preparation)

Madge, S., and Burn, H. *Wildfowl* (Christopher Helm, 1988)

Mearns, B., and Mearns, R. *Biographies for Birdwatchers* (Academic Press, 1988)
Bedtime reading about those who discovered and named or had named after them the Western Palearctic birds.

National Geographic Society *A Field Guide to the Birds of North America* (NGS, 1983)

Pemberton, J. *The Birdwatcher's Yearbook* (Buckingham Press)
An indispensable handbook published annually.

Porter, R. F., Willis, I.W., Christensen, S., and Nielsen, B. P. *Flight Identification of European Raptors* (Poyser, 1972)

Saunders, D. *Where to Watch Birds in Wales* (Christopher Helm, 1987)
One of a series of guides to the places to watch birds in the British Isles, and

which need to be on every bookshelf, or in the car when setting off to look for rare birds at some of the localities mentioned in the text of the present volume, and many more besides.

Sharrock, J. T. R. *Scarce Migrant Birds in Britain and Ireland* (Poyser, 1974)

Sharrock, J. T. R. and Sharrock, E. M. *Rare Birds in Britain and Ireland* (Poyser, 1976)

Sharrock, J. T. R. (ed) *Birds New to Britain and Ireland* (Poyser, 1982)

Thom, V. M. *Birds in Scotland* (Poyser, 1986)

Turner, A., and Rose, C. *A Handbook to the Swallows and Martins of the World* (Christopher Helm, 1989)

Index of Rare Species with Scientific Names

Note: Page numbers in *italics* signify illustrations; those in **bold** denote the main references.

Index of Other Birds with Scientific Names